GW00702175

ART AND DESIRE

ACT AND DESIRE.

Art and Desire

A Study in the Aesthetics of Fiction

Brian Rosebury

Senior Lecturer in English
Lancashire Polytechnic

St. Martin's Press   New York

First published in the United States of America in 1988

Printed in Hong Kong

ISBN 0-312-02062-7

Library of Congress Cataloging-in-Publication Data
Rosebury, Brian.
Art and desire.
Bibliography: p.
Includes index.
1. Fiction — Esthetics. 2. Brontë, Emily, 1818–1848.
Wuthering Heights. I Title.
PN3335.R67   1988   801'.953   88–6566
ISBN 0-312-02062-7

For my parents,
Alwyn and Hilda Rosebury

Contents

Acknowledgements

Every sentence one writes is indebted to others, whether or not one remembers or acknowledges the fact. A pre-eminent debt in this instance is owed to Michael Irwin of the University of Kent, for his sympathetic, witty and searching supervision of the PhD thesis which provided the nucleus of the book; David Ellis of Kent and Miriam Allott of Birkbeck College also commented helpfully at that stage. Latterly, and especially in writing the *Appendix*, 'The Justification of Criticism', I have benefited from the ideas of my colleagues and students at Lancashire Polytechnic, in particular from the contributions of George Campbell, Linda Donaghie, Michael Hayes and Daniel Lamont to a symposium on critical theory; and from conversation on philosophical and political issues with Terry Hopton. I am most grateful to all the above, and happy to acquit them of responsibility for my opinions or my lapses of sense and style. I am grateful also to Mrs Doreen Huntley who typed the manuscript.

I would like to offer the warmest thanks to my family and friends for sustaining my morale with their encouragement and affection over the ten years in which the book was written and the even longer period of its gestation. The most profound debt is to the dedicatees; among many others, I hope I may be forgiven for mentioning especially Barbara and John Cain; Claire Mayers; David Harrison; Jane Darcy and Kevin O'Sullivan; Peter Weedon and Libby White; and Janice Wardle.

I am grateful to the following for permission to quote copyright material: Methuen & Co. Ltd for *Linguistics and the Novel* by Roger Fowler; the estate of F. R. Leavis and Chatto & Windus Ltd for *Dickens the Novelist* by F. R. and Q. D. Leavis; Routledge & Kegan Paul Plc for *Language of Fiction* by David Lodge; and Routledge & Kegan Paul Plc and Harcourt Brace Jovanovich Inc for *Principles of Literary Criticism* by I. A. Richards.

Preface

The subject of this book is the nature of fiction, and the form of criticism appropriate to it. Its central proposition, or hypothesis, is a single idea: that the nature and function of the arts, including literature as a particular but not exceptional case, and fiction as a particular but not exceptional subdivision of literature, is simultaneously to quicken and order desire. But this idea had a dual origin, and has multiple implications. It arose, on the one hand, from two intuitions, confirmed by repeated introspection: first, that though art is emotionally stimulating, it is not in its direct effect emotionally satisfying or consoling; and second, that though desire (stimulation without satisfaction) is painful, one would rather not be without it – that desire appears to have a psychological value of an important and characteristic kind. If these intuitions were correct, the second, it seemed to me, might help to solve the problem evidently posed by the first: the problem of why we should value so highly an experience which does not satisfy.

The other, and apparently far distant, source of this central idea lay in a discontent, recurrently provoked by particular works and increasingly calling out for theoretical formulation, with certain common beliefs about literature; and especially with those which ascribe to literature, or demand of it, the fulfilment of a number of functions which are also those of other forms of discourse, such as the revelation of truth about the world, or the imparting of moral guidance. Such expectations of literature, and the sententious air assumed by at least some critics who uphold them, struck me as misplaced and productive of analytical error. But to controvert them need not, I hoped, entail the relegation of literature to a trivial or contemptible status, as an entertainment, an aesthetic toy, a game with language, or a psychotherapeutic drug. Their falsity could be expressed, and the real human importance of literature asserted, by a theory founded upon the two intuitions described above: a theory which would maintain that literature, though its imaginative materials potentially include all human experience which can be verbally articulated, is concerned essentially with the desirable and the undesirable, not, except instrumentally, with the actual, the probable or the possible; that the truths it reveals are, and can only be, truths about the reader's feelings revealed to himself. Literature, on this theory, would be classified as a special form of discourse, related, certainly, in its medium, language, to other forms of discourse, but more closely related in its purpose, the quickening and ordering of desire, to the other, non-linguistic arts. Much of what follows might indeed be described as an attempt to transfer literature, in our conventional disposition of the arts and sciences, from the company of other types of language-discourse to the company of, for example, painting and music; the transfer requiring to be justified both positively, by the vindication for literature of the central thesis about the nature of art, and negatively, by demonstrations of the inadequacy of critical techniques which blur the essential distinction of purpose between literature and other forms of discourse.

That the contribution of this book to general aesthetic theory is in intention a positive one, while its contributions to questions of critical practice are to be primarily negative, a matter of excluding errors rather than instituting techniques, accords, I believe, with a common-sense view of the likely usefulness of any further contribution to literary theory. It seems improbable, to put it mildly, that a 'correct' method of criticism remains to be discovered, at least if this is conceived as a kind of trick which the critical community is waiting for someone to hit upon. The present work does not pretend to offer any such monotechnic innovation. On the other hand, it seems an entirely plausible supposition that a great deal of criticism is bedevilled by theoretical misconceptions about the nature of literature and in consequence about fundamental critical principles. To exorcise some of these misconceptions would in itself be a worthwhile activity. It seems plausible, too, that a number of these disabling misconceptions might have in common their neglect of, or incompatibility with, a single theoretical point. Thus in propounding and defending that theoretical point, one might hope at the same time, and as part of the same process, to confront and refute the related misconceptions. And there is a further methodological justification for this procedure which has particular force in the case of the present work. My central proposition, as I remarked in the first paragraph, has multiple implications. Whatever practical value it may have will only become plain when these implications have been explored, and the principal objections it invites have been clearly stated and clearly answered. The content of a general idea only properly emerges when we have distinguished what it entails from what it does not entail; and a useful way of determining this is to expose it to the criticism which would charge it with having unacceptable consequences. Thus the confrontation and refutation of relevant misconceptions, salutary in itself, should serve at the same time to refine and clarify the central proposition.

The structure of the book reflects this quasi-Popperian mode of argument. In Chapter 1 I briefly state the central proposition, and the reasoning which is its immediate origin, and attempt to anticipate the objections which might be levelled against it, grouping these under four necessarily schematic, but I hope serviceable, headings. The next four chapters elaborate, and respond to, these four types of objection. Chapters 2 and 3 consider objections from the standpoints of historical and moral realism: critical positions which (dogmatically conceived) I take to blur the distinction between literature and other kinds of discourse. Chapter 4 concerns itself with possible objections from those critical positions, rooted in stylistics or in the tradition of New Criticism, which (in my view) make fallacious methodological inferences from the truism that the medium of literature is language. Chapter 5 defends my view against the objections commonly levelled at theories of literature which refer to affects, and suggests that unlike other affective theories it provides a basis for good (that is, disciplined, pertinent and flexible) critical practice. Finally, at the beginning of the sixth and final chapter, I recapitulate the central argument in an expanded form. A speculative *Appendix* explores some of its implications for the ethical and political justification of literary criticism and for the teaching of literature.

At all stages in the argument I have felt an obligation to relate theoretical principles extensively and intensively to the analysis of actual literary works. Accordingly, each of Chapters 2 to 5 incorporates discussion of the work of a critic or critics whose theory and practice contradict my main thesis in respects closely related to the general theme of the chapter. In Chapters 2, 3, and 4 I look at analyses of specific works of fiction, and seek to demonstrate that methodological errors on the part of the critics in question entail distortions in analysis. Chapter 5 is a rather different case, in that its general theme is the practicability of criticism within the theoretical guidelines I propose: and in this instance the corresponding practical analysis is given a chapter (6) to itself. Here an extended consideration of a single work, *Wuthering Heights*, is presented in four discrete parts answering to the themes of Chapters 1 to 4: so that it would be possible (were any reader so minded) to review individual strands of argument by moving directly from Chapter 1 to section (1) of the analysis, and so on.

This interweaving of theoretical argument and related practical analysis gives the work a hybrid quality, for which I make no apology but for which the reader should be prepared. One effect of it is a certain loss of sustained logical rigour by comparison with an unequivocally philosophical work such as John M. Ellis's *The Theory of Literary Criticism: A Logical Analysis*,[1] a powerful and convincing book which fully justifies its subtitle but which quite properly says little, and demonstrates nothing, about the details of critical practice. Practical literary analysis, however disciplined, inevitably involves some appeal to intuitive rather than logical judgement: it entails the argumentative risk of saying, or implying, 'This is so, don't you feel?' But I hope that there will be compensating gains, at least for a reader primarily interested in literary criticism, who may welcome a rigorously argued critical theory but will look for practical demonstration as well. Empirical proof (or falsifiability by experiment, in strict Popperian fashion) is not, of course, in question: my main thesis is not of the kind which could be proved or falsified by a particular novel or poem, since it is ultimately a proposition not about the observable properties of literary objects – though, as Chapter 5 will make clear, these observable properties are to remain firmly at the centre of analytical attention – but about the characteristic *use* to which our minds put literary objects: the nature of our responses to them as conditioned by the conventions through which we regard them. Nevertheless, any general idea of this kind, if it is to carry conviction for a practising critic, must be seen to be compatible with our considered judgements in specific cases: either it must be refined until it is in harmony with our intuitive judgements; or it must be so persuasive that we are induced, on reflection, to refine our intuitive judgements into considered judgements which accord with the general theory. Both processes move, or aspire, towards a 'reflective equilibrium' (in John Rawls' phrase[2]) in which general theory and particular judgements are perceived to be consonant. Given the enormous multiplicity of literary works, it is inconceivable that this state should be finally attained, and it will certainly not be finally attained through a reading of this book. But a perceived consonance, in a series of cases, between (refined) general proposition and (refined) particular judgements justifies at least a strong presumption that the general proposition is worth taking away and testing against other cases. The purpose of this book, and in particular of its combination of theory and practice, is therefore to induce in the reader that degree of provisional assent to the main thesis which will dispose him to scrutinise, and if appropriate consider the option of re-formulating, his particular judgements in the light of it.

The references above to Popper and Rawls, and indeed the general direction of the argument, will have alerted the reader to the fact that the theoretical traditions to which the present work is indebted are not those which have dominated literary-critical debate over the last couple of decades. Nor is the work a critique of those traditions (structuralism, post-structuralism, deconstruction), except incidentally and tangentially, in parts of Chapter 4 and of the *Appendix*: such controversy would require a substantial volume to itself. Essentially *Art and Desire* is an attempt to open, or rather to re-open, and articulate in a fresh form and in a new context, theoretical issues of a quite different kind. But this preference for exploring one set of issues rather than another has, naturally, a basic premise or deep theory underlying it (and it is this point of theory which forms the theme of such transitory contacts as the work makes with the post-structuralist debate). This basic premise is that literature is not a product of language, but a language-game, in Wittgenstein's phrase, played by human beings, who are members of societies, for reasons which can be interpreted and according to rules, or conventions, which distinguish this game from all others played through language. Novels, plays and poems are not, on this view, 'texts', but works; literature is a humane activity practised by sentient beings, writers and readers, and the question of its function can be addressed (as certain questions of moral and political theory can be addressed) by reference to the common experiences and intuitions of the participants, refined, clarified and structured by the processes of rational discourse.

Structuralist and post-structuralist writing is often disparaged for its dependence on 'jargon' – a feeble objection in itself, since it can reasonably be replied that distinctive ideas require distinctive linguistic expression, and that this is often more economically achieved by means of a newly-minted term or a special usage than by an elaborate locution in familiar idiom. A related but more significant reservation about recent developments in 'theory' is that, however great their noetic fertility, they do not have much to do with the kind of enquiry about literature which practising writers or non-specialist readers might, one supposes, naturally make: inquiry which would extend beyond such limited and adjunctive activities as 'interpretation' and 'evaluation' to explore the primary and inclusive aesthetic question of the relationship, or set of relationships, between artistic composition and reader experience. In attempting to initiate an answer to precisely that question, the present work will, I hope, retain sufficient idiomatic breadth to be readable (or better still, actually find readers) outside the community dedicated to 'literary theory' as it has come to be defined.

Brian Rosebury

1

Art and Desire

I would like to introduce my argument with an illustration from a non-literary art – or more exactly, with an anecdote, whose source I have been unable to discover. It is said that Mozart could be roused from bed in the morning by the playing of a discord on a piano in an adjoining room. Unable to tolerate an unresolved dissonance, the composer would be obliged to get up, go to the piano, and play the concord required to resolve it. This story may be false or exaggerated, but it is psychologically plausible: it credits Mozart with an occupationally intensified form of a sensitivity which all of us, except the tone-deaf, possess, and upon which the intelligibility of tonal music depends. A literary analogy to Mozart's compulsion might be the distress which impels literate people to correct errors of spelling and grammar on public posters, or – better, since here the educative motive is absent – in official letters and circulars.

On second thoughts, however, this analogy is not quite satisfactory. A dissonance in music is not, after all, a 'mistake' to be corrected, but an essential part of a simple musical structure, requiring a second part to complete it. A better analogy would be the completion of a fragmented *haiku*, or Fr Geoffrey Bliss's rounding-off of unfinished couplets in Hopkins' 'The Woodlark':

> And after that off the bough
> (Hover-float to the hedge brow.)
>
> Through the velvety wind V-winged
> (Where shake shadow is sun's eye ringed)[1]

and so on.

Against this new comparison two objections might be raised. It might be urged that while a *haiku* or couplet is already a literary *invention*, a couple of chords are merely the pre-existent material of composition, analogous to the sculptor's stone. And this distinction would be reinforced by a second: a discord, it would be said, calls for a single particular resolution, whereas an incomplete poem can be completed in an almost infinite number of different ways. But I think the analogy can survive these objections. To answer the second point first, a dissonance can, in fact, introduce any number of different harmonic sequels: that Mozart chose the shortest and most obvious, instead of improvising a 'Dissonance' sonata, may be put down to the exigencies of the situation. If it is true that harmonic tensions point forward more decisively, so to speak, to their possible resolutions than, say, the octaves of sonnets to their sestets, the difference is one of degree, arising from the more promiscuous interrelations open to verbal material: there remains in both cases a forward impulse, an anticipation of something more, and something necessary, to come, which serves a structural purpose. And the answer to the second point supplies the answer to the first. Where there is a choice to be made between alternative continuations, there is, *ipso facto*, composition going on, if of a rudimentary kind. Had Mozart gone so far as to pronounce the result of his action 'a composition', one would have had, certainly, to take the lowest view of its merits, but would have had no logical reason to dissent from the description: not, at any rate, with the hindsight of a tolerant age which has accepted four minutes thirty-three seconds of instrumental silence, and twelve hundred blows on a cast-iron frying pan (works by John Cage and La Monte Young) as 'compositions'. On the same ecumenical principle, a banal and timeworn *verbal* pattern, such as

No
Parking

must, if offered as a poem, be accepted as such, and no doubt would be.

To approach the question from another direction, the harmonic relationships in the most complex musical work are in the last resort as 'pre-existent' as the simple relationship in a two-chord progression: the latter is just too obvious, too easily discovered, to excite attention in isolation. Similarly, verbal inventions are in a sense 'pre-existent' as relationships possible within the conventions and vocabulary of a particular language: as with harmonic patterns, whether one speaks of *inventing* or of *discovering* them depends on whether one has the activity of the artist or the passivity of the material primarily in mind.

Thus when the essential differences of scope and material have been admitted, one may point to an important affinity between literature and music, the presence of a forward impulse arising from aroused expectations: an affinity which after all simply derives from the fact that both are art-forms moving in time, requiring for their effectiveness that what appears at points A and B shall engender an interest in what is going to happen at points B and C respectively.

II

Now let us look more closely at these 'forward impulses'. In the case of music, the unrest which (allegedly) impelled Mozart to resolve the dissonance can be taken as a paradigm of at any rate an aspect of the listener's experience of tonal music. The satisactory closure of a tonal work (whether a brief hymn-tune or an hour-long symphony) depends upon a return to the home key – or, in certain cases, to a key significantly related to that which the work establishes at the beginning: in other words upon the resolution of tonal tensions set up during the course of the work. Pause on the penultimate note of a simple melody, and you will experience a kind of dissatisfaction: your mind's ear will probably insist upon the final note. The nature of the psychic unrest engendered by tonal tensions is not easily analysed;[2] but it is safe to say that levels of response deeper than the intellectual or perceptual are brought into play: no-one, for example, would sit through four hours of *Tristan and Isolde* merely in order to follow through the endless harmonic ambiguities and satisfy himself that they were intelligibly resolved.

Once we look at an extended work rather than an abstracted fragment, further structural relations – relations of internal symmetry, of continuity and development in the thematic 'argument', of congruity and contrast and tone-colour, rhythm and dynamics – assert themselves as prerequisites for satisfaction. (In non-tonal music these tend to assume a proportionately greater importance, as tonal tensions are excluded.) These too have, loosely speaking, an emotional as well as a perceptual burden. The completeness of Beethoven's fifth symphony is a completeness of developed argument, and the fulfilment of a tonal process; yet it is also (and I apologise for a necessarily feeble verbalisation) a spiritual completeness: if the scherzo and the finale were to be lost we should feel deprived of a dramatic climax, of an intelligible emotional fulfilment, as we are (though it is slightly heretical to say so) in the case of Schubert's unfinished eighth. The physicality of music, which appeals directly to the sense of hearing, and in its rhythms, its foundation in regular yet not quite mechanical time-intervals, approximately imitates bodily processes such as respiration and the beating of the pulse, makes it particularly easy to appreciate the interdependence between perceptual and emotional elements in the listening experience, for to a considerable extent it is the physical sensation which mediates between them. We are all familiar with the physical symptoms (such as breathlessness, or the impulse to dance or imitate conducting) sympathetically set up by rhythmically vigorous music, and with the altered states of mind which come in their train. The trance-state induced by ritual music among primitive peoples is an epitome of this psychosomatic effect. The mental quietude brought about by calm music is also conditional upon a mediating physical response, as anyone may discover by trying to listen receptively to the first movement of the 'Moonlight' sonata while vigorously ironing shirts or dusting furniture.

Once again literature, as an art-form moving in time, offers a number of resemblances to music. Its internal tensions, like those of music, have obviously an emotional as well as a perceptual content. Our concern to see verbal structures through to their completion arises from more than a mere grammarian's tidy-mindedness; characteristically these structures embody matter which (for whatever reason) assumes an importance for our feelings: the dubieties we wish to have settled are emotional tensions, mild or intense, as well as cognitive uncertainties. Literature, again like music, has extended structures of symmetry and 'argument' which exert a dynamic effect. Devices such as rhyme- and metre-schemes, sonnet- and ode-forms, and certain basic and recurrent plot-patterns in drama and fiction (analogous, perhaps, to sonata-form or fugue), establish, once the reader has grasped that they are in operation, expectations which draw his interest on. These devices would commonly be classed as structures of 'form'; but, of course, in any particular case structures of 'content' would be presumed to accompany them:

conventionally, for example, octave and sestet in a sonnet are related not only by a regular proportion of 8 : 6, but by a fitting (in both senses of the word) deployment of subject matter. Indeed, the demarcation between form and content, which is sometimes supposed to differentiate literature from music, is of questionable definition and importance. Even an elementary 'story', which compels the reader's attention by virtue of its content, by making him wonder what will happen next, can nevertheless hardly be conceived without any formal dynamic at all, as a series of utterly disconnected happenings. (In fact many unsophisticated tales make particularly obvious use of a formally structured arousal of expectations: consider the fairy-tales which announce themselves as being about the adventures of three brothers, or the jokes which begin, 'There was an Englishman, a Scotsman and an Irishman'.) The most episodic of stories contains, if nothing more, a repeated pulsation between suspense and disclosure which draws the reader forward with, as it were, a series of jerks. Every 'and then...' is a structural forward impulse, though of a kind which, unless reinforced by longer-term expectations, is likely to yield diminishing returns. Parts of the *Odyssey* have this character to some extent, modified however (and this is an important advance by comparison with a truly episodic narrative such as the *Epic of Gilgamesh*) by the continual pull of expectation which Odysseus's urge to reach Ithaca, rendered important for the reader by revulsion from the Suitors and sympathetic engagement with Telemachus's quest for his father, exerts over the long progress of the books which chart his journey. Once a basic story is treated with any literary sophistication, and apprehended by minds attuned to the appropriate format or *genre*, it tends to develop more complex dynamic structures, speeding or slowing its progress at certain stages, strengthening certain crises: as with the devices of *reversal* and *recognition* detected by Aristotle in Greek tragedy, which through the audience's unconscious absorption of dramatic norms, and perhaps by reason of some intrinsic psycho-logical validity, reinforce with an effect of inevitability the fundamentally hopeless anxiety which the direction of events induces. Here 'form' and 'content' are as much a unity as in the return to the home key which signals the positive conclusion of a symphonic finale.

A further dissimilarity between the two art-forms is more problematical, however. In the case of music, its physical impact,

whether tending to provoke or to inhibit physical activity, has
been cited as combining, or mediating between, the perceptual
and emotional, the object and the affect. With literature this
trump-card cannot be so confidently played. The physical appeal
of literature is smaller, or at least less direct (though, of course, the
rhythms of verse and prose are intimately connected with and
dependent upon the process of breathing). And literature appears
to possess a quality which, except metaphorically, is absent from
music: meaning. To a common-sense view it seems obvious that
what above all interests us in literature, what engages our
attention from the beginning of a work to the end, is the unfolding
of its meaning, not any forward pull exerted by 'tensions',
'expectations' and other such reductive generalities. Both these
points derive from the fact that the fabric of literature consists not
of self-sufficient sense-impressions but of abstract symbols (those
of language) which must undergo interpretation by the intellect if
literature, rather than the aesthetics of calligraphy or the merely
phonetic beauty of patterned speech, is to be in question. In
apprehending a word we begin with a physical event (the sense-
impression of the symbol on the page or sound in the ear) and end
with a psychical event; moreover, in at least a number of cases,
such as those in which the word evokes the image of an object, the
psychical event should perhaps itself be divided into two successive stages, the conception of the image, and the emotional
response to it. A similar situation arises with music only on the
rare occasions when part of the musical material has a symbolic
significance which requires interpretation – as with the use of
'God Save the King' and a French marching song in Beethoven's
'Battle Symphony'.

This characteristic of literature – the presence in language of a
referential as well as an emotive potential – raises problems which
will have to be discussed at some length in a later chapter.[3] For the
moment it must suffice to point out that even a written work of the
most unquestionably referential meaning – a tract on economics,
for example – contains end-directed structures: arguments which
we would not wish to judge, or feel capable of judging, until we
had reached their ends; accumulations of evidence a partial
reading of which would be insufficient to enforce (or decisively
fail to enforce) the proposed conclusion – for if it were sufficient
there would be no point in continuing the accumulation – and so
on. Such a work may not engage our most passionate emotions,

but if it is competent and if we have the requisite interest to give, it does draw us onward by inducing at least those minimal affects, such as curiosity and the desire to see a process of reasoning completed, which are necessary to motivate any intellectual inquiry at all. The problem is not, therefore, that referential meaning is incompatible with end-directed affect-inducing structures: on the contrary, referential meanings may provoke affects, even intense ones. It is rather that referential meaning is generally supposed to perform other tasks (such as conveying information or understanding) to which affects may be merely secondary. To sustain my analogy with music, and the observations associated with it, therefore, I must show that in the case of the written works we call 'literature' it is these other uses of the referential which are merely secondary or subservient to that of inducing affects. But this is to anticipate much that is extensively treated later.

III

I have argued that literature and music, the art-forms moving in time, achieve dynamic coherence and continuity by means of end-directed structures: from the perceiver's point of view, by creating and resolving tensions, by arousing and satisfying curiosity and expectation. On the face of it, then, one would expect the experience of art – the reading of a novel, say – to be followed by a feeling of vacancy; the tensions introduced into the mind by the work having been evacuated therefrom by their resolutions, the aroused curiosity having been satisfied. According to this view, a novel once read to the end becomes, as far as the reader's state of mind is concerned, as if it had never been: all that has been given, emotionally, has been taken away (unless the novelist leaves some loose end untied, some structural tension unresolved, in which case the reader presumably retains a certain frustration); and only a memory of having, as a matter of fact, been through the experience, remains to be docketed by the mind. It is hardly necessary to point out the inadequacy of this picture. For one thing, it provides no motive for taking an interest in these arts – for why should one consent to have one's peace of mind disturbed merely to have it undisturbed later, with no lasting effect? And I think that the view that the experience of literature or music terminates in a condition of emotional vacancy is manifestly at

odds with common observation, whether external (of the demeanour of a concert audience for example), or introspective.

An alternative hypothesis would see the resolution of tensions
in literature or music as a kind of therapy for the reader or listener,
procuring a discharge of psychic frustrations already present in
the conscious or subconscious mind, and resulting not in a return
to a neutral condition but in a state of contentment and repletion.
The obvious parallel would be with the parabola of sexual desire
and satisfaction. The work would be conceived as luring forth
wishes or appetites from the perceiver's psyche, implicating them,
so to speak, in the structural tensions of the work, raising them to
a certain pitch of exasperation, and then gratifying them by means
of the resolution. Thus the story of *Little Red Riding Hood* (as
usually told) would draw out a wish of the reader's – roughly, the
wish that little girls should escape being eaten by wolves (one
more naturally thinks of the reader's emotion here as anxiety, but
an anxiety is only the obverse of a wish) – intensify it by means of
tensions (suspense, withheld information), and finally gratify it at
the dénouement, bringing about a happy feeling of contentment
in the reader. Of course, this is a crude example, and the kinds of
desire aroused and gratified by, say, *Pride and Prejudice*, would be
conceded to be more delicate and various, and more difficult to
isolate in analysis.

This hypothesis is an improvement on the first in that it
provides the reader or listener with a motive, and acknowledges,
what is common experience, that the reading or listening process
is influenced by what one brings to it from one's thoughts and
feelings, and in turn influences one's thoughts and feelings after
the work is over. But it has two weaknesses. Firstly, and most
obviously, this picture of straightforward gratification does not
seem universally applicable: it does not, for example, fit the
earlier, Perrault version of *Little Red Riding Hood*, in which the child
is eaten by the wolf, unless enjoyment of this version (and for that
matter all tragedy from Sophocles downwards) is to be attributed
to sado-masochism. Secondly, and crucially for my argument, this
hypothesis no more accords with experience than the first. Art
never produces a happy feeling of contentment *tout court*: the
satisfaction derived from it is always accompanied by a degree of
unrest.

This may look like a contentious or hyperbolic statement. To some
extent my defence of it must rest upon a further appeal to common

experience, or rather, to introspection. I shall assert, somewhat bluntly, that our feelings immediately after the experience of a work of art which has made an impression on us include an element of excitation or yearning, an unfulfilledness of emotion which cannot exactly be called pleasurable yet seems the inescapable corollary of our approval and satisfaction; and that when the work has made a great impression, this unrest can reach a quite painful intensity, much more akin to sexual desire, or to being in love, than to any kind of gratification. (Once again I am conscious of the hit-or-miss quality of such verbalisations, and must plead for a suspension of judgement if these do not strike home.) The reader may, of course, reject this assertion out of hand. It can, however, claim at least some external support. In the first place, it gains plausibility from the fact that laughter and tears are often among our responses to works which we find effective: for both of these are physiological reflexes designed to release uncontrollable psychosomatic tensions; and if experiencing the work itself fully released such tensions, we should not need to have recourse to them. It is true that laughter and tears sometimes occur during the act of reading or listening, rather than at the end of it; but this is not universally so – and I shall be suggesting later, in any case, that the unrest felt at the end of a work is at least latent throughout, is indeed a necessary accompaniment of all aesthetic experience. (Conversely, the *relative* satisfaction produced by the resolution of tensions during the course of a work, or at its end, does not affect the proposition that the *absolute* effect of the work as a whole is to provoke rather than appease dissatisfaction.) The unrest stimulated by works of art also accounts for the phenomena of enthusiasm and admiration, in so far as they exceed mere approving judgement: the behaviour pattern in which the reader, listener or spectator cannot contain himself, but must discharge his excitement – either physically, by vocalising, stamping his feet, or striking the palms of his hands together (a social ritual often, no doubt, but one which would not gratify the performers if it did not imitate a genuine display of overflowing excitement), or intellectually and socially, by recommending the work to friends, writing fan-letters, and so on. If art-works produced contentment and repletion, the natural response would be not enthusiasm but gratitude, a quite different emotion which tends to be expressed very discreetly if at all. (Compare the cries and gestures which greet the arrival of a new course on the dinner-table with the almost perfunctory murmurs which follow its consumption.)

This assertion, that unrest is among the residues of an experience of an art-work, may appear to contradict much of what I have
already said. In the first two sections of this chapter I argued that
end-directed structures in literature and music progress from
tensions (which induce unrest in the perceiver) to resolutions
(which must, correspondingly, induce rest). The story of Mozart's
compulsion to resolve a dissonance was offered as a simple image
of this process. How, then, if a work is structurally sound and
leaves no loose ends, can there remain unrest in the perceiver's
mind after it has finished?

The answer, I believe, is that there is unrest after the work has
finished because there was unrest before it began. The perceiver
brings his own wishes and anxieties to the work (even if it is the
work itself which draws them to the surface of his mind) and they
are returned to him at the end whether he likes it or not, and
whether the work in its own terms meets or denies them.

Let me return to my simple example, the story of Red Riding
Hood. According to this third, my own, hypothesis, the reader's
latent protective anxiety towards little girls menaced by wolves (a
specialisation, of course, of the more general desire for the
deliverance of himself and others from malice and danger) is
brought to consciousness by the story and intensified by its
tensions; it consents, as it were, to be implicated in the end-
directed structure of the work and does not, while engagement in
the work continues, address itself to reality. But when the work
comes to an end, the relation to reality suppressed during the
reading springs into view; and the desire brought to a final
resolution within the work – whether by decisive disappointment
as in the earlier version of the story, or by gratification as in the
later – becomes again a desire seeking gratification in reality, an
unrest. Robbed of its objective correlative, the matter of the work,
it vibrates momentarily in the void, like the after-echo in London's
Albert Hall, until the mind readjusts itself to other concerns.

A qualification or two needs adding at once to this account.
Firstly, it may be objected that the decisive disappointment of a
desire within the imaginary world of a story might often quell
rather than quicken it. Though the Perrault *Red Riding Hood* may
still leave us wishing that little girls might be delivered from
wolves, one can imagine a different case – for example, a story in
which an agreeable life of crime ends with the criminal being hung,

drawn and quartered – in which a desire initially quickened might be very firmly repudiated by the reader's feelings at the end. But this is simply to say that a second, contrary, desire (roughly, an aversion to the notion of being hung, drawn and quartered) has been brought into significant relation to the first, and has come to predominate. Indeed, though I have been speaking for brevity's sake of this or that desire, as of independent entities, I shall be suggesting that every unit of language in a literary work stimulates a certain kind and degree of desire, and that the total affectual product of the experience of a work is a desire-complex with its own internal tensions. This explains why the tragic and trium-phant versions of *Little Red Riding Hood* do in fact differ in their final emotional impact: in both the protective anxiety is quickened, but in the Perrault it is predominantly compounded with affects of revulsion against the sanguinary wolf, while in the later version it is predominantly compounded with affects of admiration towards the woodcutter.

For simplicity's sake, too, I have been over-schematic in suggesting that the suppression of the relation to reality is lifted all at once when the work ends. It is much more plausible to suppose that an underlying awareness of this relation and the fact of its suppression is a permanent element in the aesthetic experience. If, indeed, we lost at any point our awareness of the distinction between the imaginary world of the art-work and the world of reality, we should fall into a condition not only psychologically perilous but plainly unfitted to the experiencing of art, since we should take feigned actions for real ones (like the celebrated theatre-goer shouting abuse at 'Iago'), and be disorientated by those necessary conventions, such as the elision of time-intervals in drama, which differentiate fictional sequences of events from real ones. Thus, while the progress of a work is likely to include passages of comparatively high tension and anxiety (the scherzo of the fifth symphony, the wolf in grandmother's nightcap), and passages of comparative relief and resolution (the opening of the finale, the arrival of the woodcutter), the awareness that the experience being presented by the work is hypothetical and not actual must at some level persist throughout, and with it the emotional unfulfilledness that arises from the gap between the idea and the reality. We experience, that is to say, two types of unrest in connection with the work: on the one hand, an unrest which the work itself induces (through suspense, dissonance or whatever)

and finally resolves in one way or another, engendering a degree
of comparative pleasure or at least relief; and, pre-dating and post-
dating the first type, an unrest arising from the intrinsically
hypothetical and unsatisfying nature of the materials of art, their
property of arousing our desires without offering anything to
gratify them. The first serves to stimulate our desires to a high level
of definition; the second ensures that the aesthetic experience
cannot appease them (except in the local sense, already alluded to,
in which one desire can be 'appeased' by being overridden by an
opposed and stronger one).

As in the case of an earlier, rejected, hypothesis, the question
which imperiously demands to be answered is why we should
value a process which, if my account is correct, disturbs us so
much and apparently offers us so little. The answer is that during
our experience of the work two changes have occurred (changes
not, perhaps, finally distinguishable from each other) in our state
of mind. Firstly, desires which were only latent, or feebly charged,
have become fully conscious; a sum of desire, or rather a complex
of interacting – contending, or mutually reinforcing – desires,
presents itself to the mind with an unusual lucidity. And secondly,
this sum or complex of desire has become associated with a
structure of tensions in the work, and these tensions have been
progressively resolved, the structure disclosed as complete, intelligible: the work as an aesthetic object thus constitutes a model, a
paradigm, of psychological governance over the quickened desire.

These changes explain why our high valuation of art can survive
the characteristic unrest which it engenders. In the first place art
produces lucid, concentrated desire out of the somewhat indistinct
and fitful discontents which normally comprise our hour-by-hour
mental life. Quickened desire is, of course, a form of pain, since it
is synonymous with an acutely felt absence of satisfaction. But it is
a spiritually indispensable and illuminating pain: desire is to lack
of desire as life is to death, and though we feel pleasure when our
desires are satisfied, we also consider it a test of our well-being
(physical or psychological) that they should renew themselves. In
the second place, and as a kind of compensation for what is
painful in this sharp excitation, the aesthetic wholenesses of art,
its realised structures, offer a paradigm of control over desire, a
promise, in Freudian terminology, of the possible dominion of the
ego over the id. Consequently it does not matter that some art
presents stimuli to anxiety rather than to positive desires, or

engages desire whose fulfilment it repudiates at the last. If we enjoyed art because it gratified our wishes, the tragic or pessimistic in art would be intolerable (except, again, to sado-masochists who *wish* for defeat – which concedes my point). But we do not enjoy art for that reason: if we did, we could not even enjoy the harmonious resolution of comedy or the classical symphony for long, since our pleasure at the gratification of our wishes in the work would instantly give way to resentment and a feeling of futility at the recognition that we were no nearer gratification in reality. We enjoy art, I suggest, because it produces quickened desire, which makes life seem worth contending with, and because it holds up a vision of mastery over the chronic disorder of our feelings, irrespective of whether it represents our wishes as being, in its insulated world, satisfied or denied. These alternatives (and the range of possibilities in between them) are of great, but secondary, importance: neither of them is a *condition* of our enjoyment, or high valuation, of art.

IV

My central argument, then, rests on the claim that art offers us not, as may be supposed, emotional satisfaction, but rather emotional dissatisfaction: the quickening of desire. In this aspect, it stands close to the view attributable to Plato,[4] that art produces an overflow of emotion; and opposed to the view attributable to Aristotle,[5] of art as catharsis – or the view of Joyce's Stephen Dedalus, that true art does not have a 'kinetic' effect upon the emotions of the observer, but rather induces an aesthetic stasis.[6] But it suggests also that art compensates for its quickening effect by presenting paradigms of *governance* over desire; and in this aspect the main thesis might be taken as a re-phrasing, if a somewhat drastic one, of the Aristotlean and Joycean views.

In the last section of this chapter I will anticipate as well as I can the many forceful objections which may be raised against what has been said so far, and which, indeed, require to be answered if my argument is to be clear and to lose some of its narrow and reductive appearance. Here I will add a few immediate points of clarification which structural exigencies have excluded from the preceding pages.

If the effect of a work upon our desires falls short of the effect of reality, so that the perceiver whose desire has been engaged is left with a surplus of energy which cannot find an outlet, it is for the obvious reason that the materials of literature and music – and here the visual arts may be added – can never offer to desire the satisfaction which reality can (sometimes) provide. Psychoanalytical theory, which might seem pertinent here, has contrived to overlook, or at least to articulate imperfectly, this almost self-evident feature of aesthetic experience: Freud's reverent admiration for the arts leads him to dwell on the temporary and sublimative fantasy-satisfactions they provide, and to pass relatively lightly over the crucial residue of dissatisfaction that these must entail.[7] (As for Lacan's claim that the instability of the signifying order of language is a determinant of our mental system, creating 'desire' – in the Lacanian sense which distinguishes it from 'need' – it is not to our present purpose, despite its faint verbal resemblance to my present point.[8] Lacan is addressing the linguistic mismatch between signifier and signified; I am addressing the experiential shortfall between imagining and having.) A word, a phrase, a sentence prompts our attention towards – makes us 'intend', in philosophical idiom – what it designates – an object, an action, a state, a quality – yet does not enable us to arrive there – and indeed, so long as we occupy ourselves with the word, we will never do so. (What it designates may or may not actually exist; in either case it is unattainable during the aesthetic experience.) This felt insufficiency of the conception in comparison with the actual object, action, state or quality can itself be considered as a kind of dissatisfaction (or, in my deliberately wide sense, desire); if the object, action or whatever is agreeable to the reader, this dissatisfaction will assume the character of what is more conventionally called desire, while if it is disagreeable, a negative desire (an anxiety or aversion) will be produced. The targets, so to speak, of desire are therefore as numerous as the conceptions that literature can engender; the totality of desire quickened and ordered by a given work is correlative to the totality of interrelated conceptions, and cannot be correlated (except in a necessarily and admittedly simplifying process of critical analysis) with broadly defined 'desires' (ambition, lust, fear, gregariousness, or whatever). On the contrary: by 'desire' should be understood not merely general and nameable drives, but all the delicacies of attraction and aversion possible to the human mind in its intercourse with the world. Still less should the desire-complex evoked in the reader be confused with the imaginary desires attributed to the characters, though these will, like any other conceptions, contribute to the desire-complex, and sympathetic engagement with character-aspirations is a common mode of emotional response. In the last resort, as Nabokov pungently if unphilosophically puts it, 'the good, the admirable reader identifies himself not with the boy or the girl in the book, but with the mind that conceived and composed that book.... Of all the characters that a great artist creates, his readers are the best'.[9] The desire-complex is (ideally) a response to the entire work, to its most delicate as well as to its most sweeping brush-strokes. To speak of a literary work as quickening desire is not, then, as may be feared, to offer a simplistic view of its substance, or indeed to say anything about its substance; it is to assign our experience of that substance – every part of it – to the mode of desire. It is, of course, in practice possible for us to respond to what we read with anaesthetic neutrality – naturally some commitment of will and attention by the reader is necessary for any aesthetic experience, and the *sine qua non* of composition is the capture, retention and intensification of that attention – but I venture to doubt whether, given the linear nature of language, even the definite article can in principle be acquitted of tending to stir up psychic unrest: an inconsequent 'the' (at the foot of the page, let us imagine it) promotes in the English reader a conditioned expectation of some continuation drawn from the universe of nameable objects and states, and this expectation is a minimal desire. All words which do not in themselves engender conceptions (of objects, actions, states or whatever) have this effect of signalling continuations, which (like the effect of the unresolved dissonance) keeps alive and uninterrupted the reader's dynamic involvement as his eye and mind pass rapidly over the word: articles, conjunctions and prepositions (at least those such as 'with', which lack the spatial reference which might be said itself to engender a conception) are the most obvious examples. Once minimal desires are aroused, and once these have begun, in response to a local structuring within the work, to interconnect, to reinforce and subtilise one another, the aesthetic experience is under way.

The disparity, touched upon above, between the operations of literature and music may be re-invoked at this point. Literature, it may be said, tantalises us by engendering conceptions of objects or actions; but music does not deal in such conceptions; its influence upon our feelings is different in kind, in that when, for example, it makes us joyful, it does not present us with *reasons* for being joyful, as the return of Hermione in *The Winter's Tale* can plainly be called a *reason* for being joyful. This observation is correct, and locates a fundamental dissimilarity between the two arts; but the point should not be overstated. Though music does not identify, or even incontestably suggest, objects or actions (leaving aside exceptional cases such as the unmistakable flock of sheep in Strauss's *Don Quixote*), it could, I think, properly be said to suggest *states* through psychosomatic mediation: a physical (aural) agitation implying, or rather psychosomatically inducing, within the controlled aesthetic situation, agitation of mind, and so on. It is possible, too, that – as with communication by means of speech – music has developed a language, or set of languages, with conventional emotional equivalences which have been unconsciously absorbed to a greater or lesser degree by their users and auditors.[10]

Finally, it may be worth pointing out that the difference between the art-forms which move in time and those (most of the visual arts) which do not by no means precludes the applicability to the latter of the reasons I have advanced for our high valuation of art. The materials of the visual arts have the same property as those of literature and music, namely that they stimulate a psychic unrest which would normally seek satisfaction in reality,[11] implicate it in their structures, and send it away in a more lucid and concentrated condition. The mind and eye observing a painting or sculpture, and *a fortiori* a building, pass incessantly between the (incomplete) part and the (complete) whole, and this process may be compared to the progressive creation and resolution of tensions in literature and music. Accordingly, the visual arts too have a time-dimension, though one in which the sequence of perceptions is on the whole not dictated by the creator but left to the instinct and judgement of the perceiver. (This, incidentally, is true also of at least one work of literature, B. S. Johnson's *The Unfortunates*,[12] and more or less true of certain musical works, such as Cage's piano concerto, in which the performers are instructed to play the sections, or even the notes, in any order they wish.)

V

Although the arguments advanced above are intended to be applicable to literature in general, and indeed trespass upon the other arts, the chapters which follow will be largely concerned with fiction and fiction criticism. One trivial reason for this is that it was the criticism of fiction, as currently practised, which first provoked my interest in this area of theory. A second, and slightly better, reason is that, given the limited space at my disposal, I have to restrict my scope in one way or another. But my main justification, to revert to the Popperian principle cited in the *Preface*, is that fiction offers probably the severest test of my hypothesis. All art-forms present certain common problems for the view I have put forward: problems concerned with the feasibility, or methodological propriety, of discussing affects, for example. But fiction also presents, more strongly even than poetry or drama, special problems resulting from its representational and narrative properties, its close resemblance to informational and persuasive discourse: for these qualities have given rise to the suppositions that fiction (putting it crudely) *reveals truths, argues cases,* or *points morals.* If works of fiction, in common with other art-works, are structured so as to quicken desire, these purposes must have at best a subsidiary priority; and there is a natural reluctance to accord them this inferior status. Analysis referring to emotional impact on the perceiver is consequently even more firmly in the doghouse in the case of fiction than in the case of the other art-forms; it is generally held that fiction of real worth does something much more austere and creditable than, for instance, quicken the heart's desire. A typical view is expressed by Anthony Storr (who, as a psychologist, might be expected to be rather sympathetic to criticism which gives prominence to affects, but here purports to refute Freud's view of art as wish-fulfilling fantasy):

An Ian Fleming or a romantic lady novelist are indeed using phantasy to enable us to escape from reality, and we need not necessarily despise their efforts at providing us with what may be a useful safety-valve. In so far as such literary efforts serve a 'therapeutic' or healing function, they may be compared to abreaction: the provision of an opportunity to 'blow off steam'; to rid the psyche of impulses which cannot find expression in ordinary life, as well as compensating for the disappointments of reality. But the great novelists are not concerned with escape. George Eliot, Tolstoy and Proust, to take but three examples, are concerned to depict life as it is lived, and to make some sense out of it. Their imaginations are used, as Freud's was, to penetrate below surface appearances to reach a deeper and richer truth.[13]

I shall be trying to suggest that arguments of this kind, plausible though they are – and admirable in their intention of celebrating what is dignified, rational and humane in literature – are nevertheless fundamentally misconceived.

The possible objections against the description of the aesthetic experience (and in particular the experience of fiction) offered in the present chapter can be grouped under four general headings: objections from historical realism, objections from moral realism, objections from the point of view of stylistics or language analysis, and objections on grounds of methodological impracticability or impropriety. There may be serious problems which I have overlooked; I shall at any rate try to state the objections I have been able to anticipate as forcefully as I can. Among 'objections', incidentally, I have counted not only logical or empirical objections, but also some general prejudices or anxieties which amount to saying 'If this is true, we don't like it'.

The first group of objections will lead us into the philosophical quagmire surrounding the notion of 'realism'. If, as I have argued, the nature and function of literature (considered from the point of view of its effect upon the reader) is to quicken desire, that is, to work upon something which is *already present* in the reader's psyche, what, it might be asked, becomes of literature as a means of conveying knowledge or understanding? Can we seriously conceive of literature merely as a manipulator and intensifier of our existing feelings? Is it not, on the contrary, capable of conveying into our understandings, and depositing in our memories, insights which we did not possess before – into thoughts, passions and motives quite unlike our own, into unfamiliar life-styles, into social and cultural changes, into remote historical periods, into the shapes and qualities of the physical world? Even where we might possibly grant (as, say, in the case of *Jane Eyre*) that the main effect of a work may be to quicken desire – to engender a state of mind characterised by unfulfilled and aspiring emotion – does not such a work at least incidentally convey much information about the primary world of reality – in this case, about various aspects of early nineteenth-century English society at a certain level: the forms of religious persuasion, the theory and practice of education, the status of governesses, and so on? And may not these revelations constitute the principal interest of the book for a certain type of reader, who ought not to be ruled out of court for that reason? Again, has it not often been demonstrably the author's *intention* to teach a lesson or lessons about the real social world, as with *Hard Times* or *Nicholas Nickleby*, or the novels of H. G. Wells; to conduct a kind of political analysis, as with Koestler's *Darkness at Noon*, or Morris's *News from Nowhere*; or to project a philosopy of life, as with *Jude the Obscure* or *The Brothers Karamazov*? And if so, how can a critic be justified in setting aside these conscious purposes and declaring that nonetheless the work does no more than quicken desire? Why do we applaud the close social observation of George Eliot or Gissing, or the close psychological observation of Stendhal or Proust, and approve, as a matter of course, of plausibility and consistency in the presentation of society and character, unless the communication of an accurate vision of reality is among the central purposes of literature?

A second series of objections concerns the moral status of literature. If the central affective characteristic of literature is the quickening of desire, what literary genres could be more representative, a sceptic might protest, than pornography and the 'romantic novel'? These might indeed be reckoned the most successful of all forms of literature, since to stimulate longings of various kinds is their undoubted *raison d'être* and their undoubted effect. Yet we retain a powerful intuition that the value of much of the greatest literature – *King Lear*, say, or the *Divine Comedy* – lies at least partly in its taking a decidedly bracing attitude towards our unregenerate desires, and appealing rather to our moral sensibility and our willingness to confront imaginatively the least alluring features of our nature and our experience. Such intuitions about value, if they are not to be argued away, must somehow be reconciled with any affective theory of literature. A further reflection may raise even deeper misgivings. If we assert that literature quickens desire, we are bound to concede that some literature may quicken cruel, destructive and anti-social desire; and this concession may be feared to lead (as a somewhat similar line of argument, already mentioned, in Plato's *Republic* leads) to a depreciation of the social value of literature, even to a vindication of censorship.

The third main group of objections concerns the linguistic medium of literature. The (admittedly simplified) comments in earlier sections on *Little Red Riding Hood* and the *Odyssey* concerned themselves primarily with a feature of 'content': the sequence of incidents in a story. But 'content', it may be urged, inheres in or is derived from the language of the text, and it is with this that critical analysis should begin. Conventionally, too, we distinguish 'content' from 'style' – the emergence of literary stylistics within linguistics has tended to reinforce this convention – and register distinctive responses to the latter. These responses are certainly affects corresponding to something in the substance of the work; but how, if at all, can they be said to resemble the affects of attraction and repulsion induced by conceptions of objects, or the affects of hope, sympathy, terror and so on induced by the large-scale devices of 'story', which have been characterised above as affects of desire? Close analysis and evaluation raise further problems. How can a theory that literature quickens and orders desire generate, or find a place for, analysis of the linguistic surface sufficiently detailed to account for the distinctive effective-ness of (say) the style of a Henry James novel? Isn't the offered aesthetic, in short, appropriate only to what John Crowe Ransom calls 'gross and overall effects'[14] – effects which are really of secondary and merely instrumental importance to the expression of sensibility through style? Or alternatively, if we protest that style and content are ultimately inseparable, does it not remain true that, since linguistic details are prior to the conceptions they give rise to, the critical act should primarily concern itself with language analysis, at a level of specificity which would largely preclude general observations about affectual response?

The fourth and final group of objections questions the critical usefulness, even the critical propriety, of discussing the effect of a literary work upon a presumed or actual reader. Is this not (it may be asked) psycho-analysis – or worse, autobiography – rather than literary criticism? Doesn't this kind of critical method divert the critic into a *cul de sac* in which analysis of the *subject* (the reader's, or *this* reader's experiences in reading, with their inevitable under-lying biases of temperament and personal history) is substituted for analysis of the *object*, the work itself? Indeed, given the wide variations among readers' emotional responses to works of literature, is a criticism that refers to affects even possible without arbitrariness and partiality? This practical objection may well seem the most damaging of all.

Though in some cases I intend to meet these criticisms head-on, and to argue that they arise from misapprehensions about the nature of literature, most of them express perfectly understandable doubts about the implications of the arguments I have put forward. In Berkeley's words, however, I would describe these arguments, in their present untested state, as

> passages that, taken by themselves, are very liable (nor could it be remedied) to gross misinterpretation, and to be charged with the most absurd consequences, which, nevertheless, upon an entire perusal will appear not to follow from them.[15]

In the remaining five chapters I hope to show that the bare propositions of this first chapter are in fact consistent in theory and in practice with a thorough and appreciative critical account of the literary text; and are far from precluding an understanding of its moral value, or its relations to its author, its readers, and its social and historical context.

2

Objections from Historical Realism

In Chapter 1 I argued that literature, in common with the other arts, simultaneously quickens and orders desire. The central question of the present chapter (which will attempt to answer the first class of objections outlined at the end of Chapter 1) is whether a theory of this kind, which locates the essential function of literature in the evocation and efformation of dispositions already present in the reader's psyche, rather than in the transmission to him of new knowledge or new understanding of the exterior world, entails a false account of the relation between literature and reality. I have remarked that this discussion will involve us in the problematics of 'realism'; but this term has a variety of senses, and not all of them conflict with my theory. I naturally do not, for example, deny that some works of literature are more attentively mimetic of the real universe than some others. When we read an opening which runs

> The Mole had been working very hard all the morning, spring-cleaning his little home. First with brooms, then with dusters; then on ladders and steps and chairs, with a brush and a pail of whitewash . . . [1]

we anticipate fictional representations which, if offered as representations of the primary world of reality, we would dismiss without hesitation as lies or absurdities. When, on the other hand, we read an opening which runs

> Two mountain chains traverse the republic roughly from north to south, forming between them a number of valleys and plateaux. Overlooking one of these valleys, which is dominated by two volcanoes, lies, six thousand feet above sea-level, the

town of Quauhnahuac. It is situated well south of the Tropic of Cancer...²

we can reasonably infer that the secondary, fictional world we are being introduced to will be represented in terms closely similar to those we use to describe the primary world; many statements in a novel of this kind will be indistinguishable, except by their context, from statements offered as true report. Only the withholding of a name for the republic in the first sentence – which would be slightly puzzling in a travelogue, and serves as an immediate signal to the reader that *the republic of this novel*, and not the closely associated but conceptually distinct *republic of Mexico*, is to be the preoccupation of his thought and imagination – betrays the fictional source of this quotation. A third kind of relation between the representations of fiction and representations of reality may be exemplified by the well-known opening sentence of *Anna Karenin*.

All happy families are alike but an unhappy family is unhappy after its own fashion.³

Where the previous extract imitates testimony, the recording of fact, this sentence imitates interpretation; just as the former might be transplanted into a geography of Central America, Tolstoy's sentence might be reproduced as an aphorism in conversation, or as an observation in a deplorably crude work of social psychology (though – a suggestive point – we do not complain of its crudity in the novel). It is mimetic, but what it imitates is a typicality, a recurrent pattern of primary experience, not the specific details of a singular event or state. These three types of opening correspond, in miniature, to three common types of fiction: the fantasy, which acknowledges no consistent mimetic obligation (and under which heading for brevity's sake we will include fairy-tale, science fiction, dream literature, and literature depicting gods or supernatural powers); the highly naturalistic, near-autobiographical or near-documentary fiction, which is closely mimetic of some specific primary condition or event; and the classic 'realist' fiction, which is not necessarily concerned to satisfy detailed requirements of mimetic exactitude, but is felt to preserve a general plausibility, perhaps to achieve an unusual degree of understanding, in its exemplary representations of human behaviour and society. Needless to say, there are countless gradations in this spectrum of mimetic precision, and many works defy simple classification: *Ulysses*, for example, which touches extremes of fantasy and naturalism without being resolved into either.

The fact that literary works often simulate description of, and narrative about, the primary world poses no difficulty for my argument as long as such narrative and description is indeed understood as 'simulation' through and through: as representation of the real world feigned for a particular purpose, namely the quickening of certain kinds of desire. From this assumption one could go on to observe, for example, that fantasy gains access to desires which naturalism cannot (the desire, say, to communicate with the dead, or live in a world without politics or electric trains); while naturalism works upon desires closely bound up with the particularities of an immediate human and social situation, the more potently by virtue of the swift recognition we return to its prosaic and (if we are close ourselves to its period and social context) familiar materials. The degree of approximation to reality, in other words, depends upon the psychic dispositions to which an appeal is being addressed; and the function of such approximation is to promote conceptions in the reader's mind which have the power to activate certain desires or desire-complexes. Close approximation to reality is not, then, on this view, an obligation or even necessarily a virtue; it is simply one technical option among others, appropriate to certain evocative purposes.

If, on the other hand, what I have been begging the question by calling 'simulated' description, and 'imitation' of testimony or interpretation, can in some useful sense be considered as description, testimony or interpretation proper (direct or through a transparent substitution of fictional exemplars for primary realities), so that the reader of a novel can meaningfully be said to have had his knowledge or understanding of the primary world supplemented or deepened by it, then a pointed objection to my theory immediately presents itself. The function it attributes to literature now has to compete with another. The two functions – the quickening of desire, that is, the stimulation of pre-existent dispositions, and the communication of fresh knowledge, fresh understanding of the primary world – are not logically incompatible, but they are quite disparate and may be presumed to demand different compositional principles and priorities. Illumination of the inner world of feeling is one thing, illumination of the outer world of objects, states and events another. And if a work of literature really transmits to the reader new data which he can legitimately permit to alter or augment his view of exterior reality, then we may well feel that the justice or accuracy of the picture it presents must be a major test, perhaps the major test, of its quality. For revealing the truth is, at least arguably, and on some views incontestably, a more important enterprise than quickening desire – or indeed purging our emotions, providing entertainment, being beautiful for beauty's sake, or performing most of the other functions with which works of art have been credited. A particularly ardent and influential partisan of the view that literature reveals truths, and is of little account unless it reveals important truths, has been Georg Lukács, who in the following passage gives it forthright expression.

Great literature of all ages, from Homer to the present day, has, in the final analysis, 'contented itself' with showing how a given social condition, a state of development, a developmental tendency, has intrinsically influenced the course of human existence, human development, the dehumanisation and alienation of man from himself. Since artistically this is inconceivable without a portrayal of the concrete social forces at work, there results a picture of social existence, based on this point of view, which is more lucid than that which social existence itself is able to invoke directly. For this reason, not unimportant effects can, under certain circumstances, originate in the social *praxis* of human beings though this is often not apparent on the surface. The bias of true art is distinguishable from the tendencies of ephemeral literature by the fact that in meeting the challenge of its time, the former is able to concentrate on the whole complex, on the true essence of social phenomena and not be obliged to provide specific solutions to mere day-to-day problems.[4]

This is, of course, criticial 'realism' of a particular kind, and not merely in the narrow sense that Lukács employs the terms of marxist historical analysis. It is notable that, despite his refusal to burden literature with the *minutiae* of day to day social problems, Lukács reserves the title of 'genuine literature' for work which is precisely mimetic of singular historical developments; though it is broad social phenomena, not ephemeral and localised historical details, which are to be 'shown', nevertheless the 'showing' is to be literal and accurate – to represent the 'concrete social forces' as they really are or were. The question of abstract or extra-historical 'truths', such as the opening sentence of *Anna Karenin* may be held to expound, does not arise, since to Lukács as a marxist and a historicist human experience does not contain such truths but is always shaped by and contingent upon historical forces. Lukács, in other words, can be classified as a historical realist; whereas F. R. and Q. D. Leavis, whose work will be treated in the next chapter, are primarily moral or normative realists who, though they pay some attention to the portrayal of historical phenomena in novels, are mainly concerned to find in literature support for ethical norms which are ultimately independent of the historical occasion. And to Lukács the depiction of historical reality is the essential purpose of literature; its value lies precisely in its instructiveness about the real world, its 'picture of social existence ... more lucid than that which social existence itself is able to invoke directly'. Great literature offers an account of the external, social world informed by an exceptional truthfulness of perspective; and from this account, this truthfulness, it is proper that 'effects in the social *praxis* of human beings' may follow. The difference between greater and lesser literature lies in the breadth and completeness with which the former reveals to us a given social condition or development. As for what I have called 'fantasy', the class of fictions whose representations are not confined to the demonstrably real, it can scarcely enter into this reckoning at all, unless by distilling a social meaning from it – a procedure of this kind legitimises Lukács' exaltation of Homer – it can be shown to be about the primary world after all.

Historical realism is, of course, especially congenial to a marxist reader, since it provides a historically dynamic and progressive role for ('genuine') literature; but as a half-formulated assumption about the nature and purpose of literature it can be found across a wide ideological spectrum, in the form of a more or less conscious prejudice in favour of literature which shows an instructive concern with social actualities, a somewhat defensive attitude towards works which appear to aim at elegance of form or style, or to explore matters of private behaviour or sensibility (one need only think of the energy which Jane Austen's admirers have expended in excusing her from the charge of neglecting the great public events and social changes of her time), and a readiness to credit novels and plays with powers of secular revelation: to believe, for instance, that *Hard Times* exposed to a shamed or horrified public the evils of Utilitarianism or the squalor of northern mill-towns in the 1840s. Convictions and prejudices of this kind rest, I believe, partly on a logical confusion and partly on a blurred perception of the ways in which literature actually influences our attitude towards society and the exterior world in general. For an instance of the first, I turn to another extract from Lukács, in which the supposed salutary influence of a specific author is celebrated. This is a rather earlier (but, unlike some of Lukács' very early work, unrepudiated) passage, from *Studies in European Realism*, constructed in 1948 out of essays written some ten years previously.

> Gorki's 'human comedy' is not only an immortal picture of a world that is no more, but a powerful weapon in the struggle against its surviving, harmful remnants. Not for nothing have Lenin and Stalin carried on an incessant struggle against the petty-bourgeois world surrounding the working class. This petty-bourgeois influence took a variety of forms in the great country of Socialism. But the brutal violence of the kulaks and the refined 'culture' of the wreckers had their roots in the same soil of Asiatic capitalism, the merciless exposure of which constituted the greater part of Gorki's life-work. Even today, when a Socialist society has become a reality, it would be a mistake to think that we have nothing further to learn from Gorki. Stalin's warning about the need to overcome the residue of capitalism in the being and consciousness of men reminds us how up-to-date this aspect of Gorki's life-work still is.[5]

I quote this passage not in order to draw attention to its (as they now appear) lamentable political inferences from Gorki's work (though these are certainly a melancholy warning against a belligerent confidence in the 'reality' of one's favourite 'realism'; as Montaigne remarks, it is setting a very high value on one's own judgements to burn a man to death on the strength of them), but to point out that they are not really inferences at all, and cannot be. If anything is clear from this extract, it is that Lukács has begun with convictions about the actual social and political events, and *from* those convictions has drawn an inference *about* Gorki's work, namely that its fictional representations correspond with the truth. Had Gorki portrayed Asiatic capitalism as a fountainhead of loyalty to the Revolution, we can be sure that Lukács would have rejected it as a libel and a deception; he would not, in other words, have drawn a different inference *from* it, but have drawn a different inference *about* it, namely that its fictional representations did not correspond with the truth. This in itself is entirely natural and inevitable, since in assessing the elements of 'realism' in a fiction one has only one's own conception of 'reality' to work from; but it does not square with the claim, or implication, that the fiction can be the agent in forming convictions, that it can be 'learned from'. To labour the point: one cannot distinguish between a true and a false picture, in fiction, of the 'concrete social forces', unless one already knows, or thinks one knows, what the concrete social forces are. Therefore the fiction cannot be the source of the knowledge; the most it can do is attach to a pre-existent belief – based (one hopes) on evidence and reasoning – that *p* is the case, a fictional representation of *p*'s being the case. Lukács' assertion that 'it would be a mistake to think that we have nothing further to learn from Gorki' can hardly be accepted, therefore, unless it is understood as referring to that emotional reinforcement of an existing conviction which a fictional representation of it as being correct does undoubtedly provide. But this is a very different matter from 'learning' in its ordinary meaning of having one's knowledge or understanding increased. We cannot 'learn' from a teacher whom we appoint to the job on condition that he teaches us things we believe we know already. (Yet the fallacy is an alluring one and we shall encounter it again.[6])

At this point it may be objected that the experiences of readers of fiction are a matter for empirical observation, not for logic, and that – whether or not this logically *ought* to be the case – a great deal of human knowledge is actually diffused through the medium of fiction, and many social evils, for example, have as a matter of fact been brought to the attention of an otherwise ignorant and indifferent public by works of fiction. But this contention blurs, I suggest, three distinct though closely con-nected processes: the direction of public attention towards a particular issue, the disclosure of facts relevant to it, and the arousal of public agitation concerning it. Sociological research, journalism, the reports of public Commissions, and word of mouth can in various circumstances accomplish all three: fiction, I submit, can accomplish only the first and third, and not even those for any length of time (except in the most extraordinary cases of mass delusion – Orson Welles's 1938 radio dramatisation of *The War of the Worlds* might be instanced) – unless the second service is performed by some other medium of discourse. Several considerations point to this conclusion. In the first place, much of the apparent impact of a fiction on the beliefs of its readers about the primary world is actually the impact of attendant publicity. Every student reading *Nicholas Nickleby* knows that in Dotheboys Hall Dickens created a fictional exemplar of a type of educational establishment which flourished in Yorkshire in the 1830s and 40s: he knows this not from the novel, but immediately from the editorial introduction to his text, and obliquely from a storehouse of received knowledge about nineteenth-century society and its evils which has acquired almost the status of folk-belief – just as he derives from the same sources the conviction (which again could not be inferred from the novel in isolation) that in the Cheerybles Dickens did *not* create exemplars of nineteenth-century capitalists. (Ironically enough, Dickens insisted in his preface that the Cheerybles were drawn from living people whereas Squeers was not.) Every viewer of the first performance of Jeremy Sandford's once-celebrated television play *Cathy Come Home* in 1966 was aware that broadly similar inhumanities (in provision for the homeless) were actually being endured; those who had not read the publicity material may be presumed to have recognised in the play a style of documentary naturalism then fashionable, from which it might reasonably – though not, of course, conclusively – have been inferred that the events represented resembled real ones. But the knowledge that a fiction is 'based upon' reality is a knowledge *about* the fiction, not a knowledge of which the fiction is the source.

In the second place, in any work of realist or naturalist fiction, narrative and description which would be valid if offered as an account of the primary world are intermingled with, and structurally inseparable from, narrative and description of a 'purely' fictional kind – that is, concerned with the doings of characters who, however socially or psychologically typical, are nonetheless required to experience individual and contingent lives of their own. In the Austerlitz and Borodino episodes of *War and Peace*, for example, the novelist's wish, or obligation, to preserve and elaborate the characterisation of Prince Andrei, Pierre, Boris and other *dramatis personae* entails a selectiveness of viewpoint, a pointing of mood, a calculated sequence of incident, which cannot but impair the translatability of these chapters into primary

historical accounts. A simple instance is the removal of Prince
Andrei by injury before he can take an active part at Borodino,
which ensures that the quite different physical and metaphysical
qualities of Pierre will be the lens through which the reader
perceives the close action of the battle. This problem is particularly
obvious in the case of historical fiction, where specialised knowledge may be required to distinguish between the 'primarily' true
and the 'primarily' false. While readers may very loosely be said to
learn about Puritan New England from Hawthorne, or about
Imperial Rome from Robert Graves, it is clear that this learning is
only helpful to a reader who has sufficient historical sense to
distinguish the probably authentic from the probably romantic;
that it cannot be relied upon; that it is likely to be so partial in scope
as to be quite worthless as a general picture of the society in
question (economic factors in particular tending to get left out); and
that it can have no value retold to a second person without external
corroboration. (It would hardly be proper, for example, to advance
in argument a piece of evidence for which one had no other
authority than a historical novel.) In the case of contemporary
social realism, we are more strongly tempted to assume that we
can tell at a glance the substance of truth from the merely fictional
elaboration or distortion, but this temptation probably testifies to
the strength of our prejudices rather than the precision of our
knowledge and judgement; it is salutary to read contemporary
notices of nineteenth-century fiction and to observe, for instance,
London reviewers greeting *Wuthering Heights* as a kind of sociological study of West Riding manners and morals.[7]

In the third place (though essentially all three points are versions
of the same point, the limitations of the fictional convention), the
liberty of the author of fiction is plainly incompatible with the rules
of evidence. Had Dickens wished to write a *Nicholas Nickleby*
portraying Yorkshire Schools as institutions of exceptional learning
and humanity, it would have been within his powers to do so. That
is the ineradicable difference between disclosure and invention;
disclosure (unless it is really deception) can disclose only what is
behind the curtain, x; invention is at liberty to create x or *not-x* or
any transformation thereof without transgressing its terms of
reference. And we do not ordinarily accept as authoritative the
statements of a man who is occupationally accustomed to affirming
the unreal with impunity. However much Dickens's public may
have had its attention concentrated by *Nicholas Nickleby* on the state

of elementary education (and it seems that Dickens's was only a doubtfully significant influence on a long and fitful process of reform[8]), however painfully the depiction of Dotheboys Hall may have stirred its emotions, we may assume that at least the brighter readers were more or less clear about the need for corroborative evidence. Or are we to suppose that if no proof had been forthcoming that institutions of the kind represented did actually exist, government and people would nevertheless have pressed ahead with reform on the authority of Charles Dickens's third novel?

Of course, it may be objected that all statements whatever, whether in the context of a novel, of a tract, or of a political speech, require corroboration before we are justified in believing them. This is perfectly true, though it points in the direction of treating information as fiction (until proved otherwise), not that of treating fiction as information. But if we accept that in the last resort we must look to written testimony for the nearest approach to decisive proof of matters outside our sensory experience, then it is natural to examine the relative reliability of different forms of discourse; and such examination suggests that fiction occupies a quite special position. It is symptomatic, for one thing, that before accepting the primary truth of a statement in a novel we would expect corroboration from a different *kind* of discourse; to confirm the truth of my first quotation in this chapter, for instance, we would probably look to a monograph on the habits of the mole, and would hardly be convinced by finding that in another novel a mole was represented as behaving in a similar way. If, on the other hand, we now doubted the truth of a statement in the monograph, we would be likely to seek confirmation in another and perhaps more authoritative monograph, not in a quite different form of discourse – and certainly not in a work of fiction. This strongly suggests that we regard fiction as requiring corroboration (for this purpose) not only in the way that all discourse does, but in a way peculiar to itself. But the matter goes deeper than this. On casual reflection one may tend to feel that a statement (the linguistic construction containing a subject and a main verb), is, after all, a statement – meaning an assertion that such-and-such is truly the case; and that the burden of proof is on those who would attribute to the statements made by fiction an exceptional, non-assertive quality; so that while some fictional statements (for example, the opening sentence of *The Wind in the Willows*) can, no doubt, be shown to be expressions of imaginative play or daydreaming, the rest (such as the opening sentence of *Anna Karenin*) retain their status as assertions like any other. But this view of the nature of statements will not bear scrutiny. Language itself has no built-in propensity to tell, or even claim to be telling, the truth. It can as easily formulate a falsehood or absurdity ('square moon', 'man with two heads') as a reality ('round moon', 'man with one head'), and is, if one may put it this way, indifferent to the question of whether or not its formulations are true or offered as true. Only by the evolution of numerous specialised rules and conventions – the rules of logic, the conventions governing the presentation of evidence in a court of law or doctoral thesis, perhaps above all the obloquy which conventionally descends upon a person who in certain types of statement in certain types of discourse is seen to have knowingly or negligently perpetrated an untruth – can a particular form of discourse be made into a medium through which reliable information can be communicated from one person to another; and such a medium is then naturally employed for statements which are assertions that such-and-such is truly the case. But one may deliver statements for other reasons. If I utter the statement, 'There are fairies at the bottom of my garden', in one tone, I will be understood to assert that such is truly the case, while if I utter it in other tones, or sing it, I will be understood to be making an inane joke, or impersonating a lunatic or Dame Clara Butt: the tone gives the determining convention. Accordingly, one can imagine a mode of discourse for which the restrictive conventions required for truth-telling have not evolved, or have been suspended; for which, perhaps, quite opposite conventions, such as the permissibility of stating that which is untruthful but nevertheless interesting, or the desirability of producing an aesthetically pleasing object or engaging the emotions of a reader – preoccupations which could only be deplored as a dangerous distraction in a truth-telling mode of discourse – are in force. In such a mode of discourse, the linguistic event that we call a 'statement' would not have acquired the specialised contextual meaning of 'an assertion that such-and-such is truly the case': and such a mode is fiction. Fiction – let us say 'imaginative literature' so as not to appear to exclude the fictive elements in poetry and drama – is, in fact, the only mode[9] in which a square moon or a two-headed man might be stated to exist without a breach of convention, an offence against the purpose of the mode, being normally assumed to have occurred. It is the closest, perhaps (if one may venture a somewhat Freudian speculation[10]), to the intrinsic irresponsibility of language, which human society has sought to subjugate in order to create media for truth-telling, and its existence is no threat to these last as long as its functions are not confused with theirs.

(The effectiveness of our underlying sense of discourse-conventions can be illustrated by the following example. A book is published under the title *The Diaries of Ronald Reagan: A Novel*, having the form of a series of diary entries representing the observations and reflections of one 'Ronald Reagan', a politician. Mr Mikhail Gorbachev writes to the publishers protesting that one of the 'entries' misquotes a remark of his. A year later, the actual diaries of Ronald Reagan are published under the title *The Diaries of Ronald Reagan: Reflections of a Lifetime*, and prove by chance to have exactly the same text as the novel of the previous year. Mr Gorbachev despatches the carbon copy of his earlier letter. Would any literary critic deny that in the first case Mr Gorbachev would be committing an absurd and elementary critical solecism; or that in the second case he would be perfectly within his rights? Thus the conventional distinction between fiction and other modes can be of decisive importance *even when the textual substance is the same.*)

Admittedly, one cannot logically refute the critic who at this point goes to the length of insisting that fiction is indeed governed by restrictive conventions which make for a (humanly speaking) truth-telling mode of discourse – though one might ask what the point of imaginative literature can be if it is to duplicate the functions of other modes. But the rules and conventions which define a type of discourse and distinguish it from other types are, like all definitions, a matter of general acceptance and agreement. There is no sanction behind them. No-one can be prevented from reading fiction as a true report, as the child Edmund Gosse did with *Tom Cringle's Log*,[11] or from reading government White Papers as fiction (which is not the same as reading them with the conventions of a truth-telling discourse in mind, and coming to the conclusion that they are untruthful); one can only point to the custom in these matters, and observe that fiction characteristically makes unreliable report, and most White Papers dull fiction.

A couple of further objections perhaps require some attention. Firstly, it may be suggested that I have been unduly literal-minded in discussing fiction as if it were composed of atomic 'statements';

that the truth of a great novel is not literal and detailed, but
'essential' truth, as Q. D. Leavis says of a scene in Dickens which
contains a legal implausibility[12] – a truthfulness of world-view not
to be resolved into propositions. One reply to this might be that if
imaginative literature does contain truth of this kind, critics had
better leave it well alone, since the inevitable effect of the
interpretative commentary is precisely to render it down into
propositional form. But the argument rests on a confusion
anyway. The larger meanings of an extended work, which cannot
be articulated as atomic statements, arise out of, and are
dependent upon, the smaller meanings which can. I have done
my best to establish that a statement in the context of a work of
fiction, even though it might as it happens stand equally
appropriately in a textbook or a Reuters report, is debarred by the
fictional convention from being properly an assertion that such-
and-such is truly the case. If this is correct, then the same must be
true of any super-articulate consequence generated by the sum of
such statements. A cause from which truth-telling is absent cannot
produce an effect in which truth-telling is present – unless we are
to believe that simulated details (simulated not in the sense that
perjured evidence is simulated, but within a convention which
makes no pretence that they are other than simulated) can uphold
a conclusion which is primarily true, and *offered as true*: which
would be like an advertising circular frankly admitting that the
claims made for its product were pure invention, but nevertheless
urging the reader to buy the product on the strength of just those
claims. This basically simply point is obscured by the fact that the
literal details in a fiction tend to be matters of information (is
Quauhnahuac south of the Tropic of Cancer?) while the super-
articulate consequences, or 'essential truths' tend to be matters of
opinion (what does the degeneration of an exiled drunken
Englishman reveal about the human condition? – or something
like that) – and where an opinion is simulated our eagerness to
agree with its 'essential truth' often inclines us to forget that it is a
representation of, or an implication about, a secondary, invented
world, not the primary one. (When we do agree, that is; when we
disagree we usually manage to remember that we are reading a
story, and that the conclusion or implication is contingent upon a
lot of details which the author has made up.) Even so, I think it
would be true to say – though I can only appeal to common
experience on this point – that most sensitive readers instinctively

grasp, as an underlying convention of fiction, that the 'opinions' as well as the 'information' presented in a novel are of a secondary, non-assertive kind. This was the point of my parenthetical remark above that we do not complain of the simplistic nature of the observation which opens *Anna Karenin*. Whether or not the observation would be true if it were considered as a description of the primary world, it is certainly true as a description of the secondary world of *Anna Karenin*, because the text says that it is true, and the text is co-terminous with our apprehension of the secondary world. (If the text contradicts itself, we have a self-contradictory secondary world.) Our reaction, I submit, is not normally,[13] 'Is this so? Yes or no?' – a reaction which would be sure to lead us through a train of thought terminating in complicatedly qualified assent or dissent, or in elaborately suspended judgement, and effectively divert our attention from the novel; our reaction if we are to continue to read must be closer to the following: 'This statement raises interesting expectations about the world we are about to enter, and we will look forward to its elaboration'. We string along, in other words, because for all its dogmatic form we appreciate that we are no more being challenged to give primary assent to this statement than to the next,

Everything had gone wrong in the Oblonsky household.

As descriptions of the secondary world of the novel the two statements differ only in their degree of generality.

Secondly, it may be objected that many authors – D. H. Lawrence is an outstanding example – have demonstrably, and in no uncertain terms, set out with the intention of prosecuting a view of the real world. In a sense this consideration can simply be dismissed as irrelevant. No 'intention' to do something can affect the question of whether or not that thing is possible. It is important to realise, though, that my argument does not in fact very significantly abridge the legitimate motives and purposes of the author, and certainly does not imply that an author who believes his work to be morally or politically committed is the victim of a delusion. It concedes that an author may intend to produce, and succeed in producing, an emotional, and perhaps in consequence even a practical, effect upon his readers by the nature of the imaginary world he represents; indeed in hypothesising a 'quickening of desire' as the central quality of the literary affect, it directs attention towards the possibility of such an influence. That a fictional representation of *p*'s being the case can sometimes stir public feeling in a way in which a scrupulously authenticated demonstration that *p* truly is the case cannot is a matter of human psychology, and it is quite understandable that an author who feels strongly about a particular issue should wish to use the emotional potency of his work to influence public feeling about it. My argument merely maintains that if an author intended to transmit through his fiction new knowledge or understanding of the primary world, and thereby to compel in the reader primary belief that such-and-such is the case (in the sense that a cogent argument or a scientific demonstration may properly be said to compel belief), or imagined that he had actually done so, he would have misconstrued the nature of his contribution, which *qua* novelist is not and cannot be to public knowledge, only to public feeling. An author may or may not believe that what his work affirms about its secondary world is also true of the primary one but it would surely be unreasonable of him to expect that its primary truth should be publicly accepted *on the strength of* his fictional representation, in view of the fact that he might just as easily (except from the point of view of motivation) have composed a fiction representing the opposite.

Finally, in this section, let me offer some conjectural explanations of the obscurity which has gathered around the relation between literature and reality. There are, I think, three probable motives behind the reluctance of the partisans of realism (a class which includes virtually all of us, including the present writer, on occasion) to shed the delusion that literature can transmit knowledge or understanding of the primary world. In the first place, the very quickening of desire accomplished by a fiction with which we are fully engaged may be suspected of impairing the power, or rather the willingness, to distinguish invention from disclosure. We have a natural tendency to approximate what we believe to be true to what we desire; or more subtly, to seek objective correlatives for our sympathies and antipathies in the primary world, which nevertheless contains endless complexities which irritate and defy them, as when a politician whom we have grown pleasantly used to despising suddenly annoys us by performing an admirable act. The fact that the world of a fiction which has strongly engaged our sympathies appears more emotionally lucid than the messy, frustrating primary world, and the fact, too, perhaps, that in reflecting upon an event depicted in an imaginary world we can be more confident of responding 'appropriately' than when we encounter such an event in the heat of an actual moment, may be translated into a conviction that the invention embodies a 'higher' reality which is regrettably obscured by primary experience; the truth being, on the contrary, that the invention lacks the elusiveness and intractability of reality, and for that precise reason is better able to secure a firm hold on our feelings. An example of this delusion at work over a long period is the conversion, indignantly traced by Raymond Williams in *The Country and the City*,[14] of a literary wish-vision of an English rural past into a matter of literal or semi-literal, belief – a belief expressed in its most generalised form in a sentence Williams quotes from G. Ewart Evans' *The Pattern under the Plough*:

A way of life that has come down to us from the days of Virgil has suddenly ended.[15]

But while Williams is no doubt right to protest against this formula, and to perceive that the pastoral visions (for no two versions are precisely the same) are invidious *if they are believed to be real*, he falls into the same error himself by ransacking imaginative literature, as well as primary sources such as diaries, letters, pamphlets and descriptive accounts, and with little apparent recognition of the conventional differences between them, for support for his own view of English rural history, accepting passages from Crabbe or Edward Thomas which conform to it as 'observation' or 'actual response', and dismissing others which do not (with obvious bitterness that they should be so interlaced with the former) as 'rhetoric' or 'theatre'. The bitterness, and the quixotic regret that such phenomena as 'country-based fantasy, from Barrie and Kenneth Grahame through J. C. Powys and T. H. White and now to Tolkien' should have 'scribbled over and hidden from sight'[16] the reality disclosed in such works as Fred Kitchen's autobiography *Brother to the Ox*, would be rendered unnecessary by the reflection that what readers usually seek in 'country-based literature' is an enlivening of that part of their appetite for happiness which seeks satisfaction in the natural world (wild or ordered); and that no harm is done by their being so enlivened by a conventionally fictionalised 'England' provided that they find room in their minds for the knowledge (easily derivable from other sources) that the historically real England is and was quite different.

In the second place, the realist who ascribes a truth-telling function to imaginative literature may suppose that he is exalting it by doing so – or rather, perhaps, defending it against the suspicion of dilettante isolation from the social and political realities which are the proper study of mankind. One can sympathise with this view if it is believed that the alternative to literature as information or revelation is literature as mere entertainment (and one of the purposes of my argument is to suggest that that is not the alternative); but essentially it expresses a prejudice against the nature of imaginative literature itself – namely, that it is imaginative. If this lowers the status of literature, then let it be lowered; literary critics are probably occupationally inclined to exaggerate it anyway; and it is better to have a modest status which can be upheld than a lofty one which cannot. But in any case, not everyone will accept that a direct concern with the socio-political dimension is the main or the only test of the value of a form of discourse; and it is possible that, by illuminating a reader's desires to himself, literature may, though in a less immediately didactic way than a historical realist would have us believe, do something to influence his behaviour towards other persons and towards his community. If the purpose of politics and of social organisation is to serve human happiness – that is, to satisfy desires – a lively and continuing awareness of the elusiveness and multifariousness of the forms of happiness (and of misery) would seem to be an asset to those who pursue that purpose.[17]

Thirdly, and least creditably, reading literature as disclosure is a temptingly easy way of becoming an expert (or rather acquiring a serviceable 'viewpoint') on society and history; much easier, for example, than weighing ambiguous evidence, scrutinising semi-illegible documents and trying to assess their trustworthiness, undergoing training in the interpretation of statistics, absorbing and criticising the work of prolific predecessors, and so forth. John Gross points out the danger of this abuse of literature:

> In *Theory of Literature* Wellek and Warren quote from a German historian, Kohn-Bramstedt, to the effect that 'only a person who has a knowledge of a society from other sources than purely literary ones is able to find out if, and how far, certain social types and their behaviour are reproduced in the novel'. This might seem too obvious to need saying, to anyone who hadn't seen what actually goes on, to anyone who hadn't, for example,

come across students praising *Hard Times* for the deadly accuracy of its satire on Utilitarianism, a subject on which it turned out most of their ideas derived from – *Hard Times*.[18]

I do not want to say that no-one except a trained historian or social scientist is entitled to have an opinion about the past or the social present – though I would, I think, have a fair case if 'commit to print as scholarship' were substituted for 'have'. But the kind of circularity Gross observes is a perpetual risk – or invitation – to the historical-realist critic who lacks the professional historian's well-informed modesty about the knowableness of the past but possesses the literary critic's flair for assimilating a complex text to a less complex thesis. The result, commonly offered as a mutual enrichment of historical and literary sophistication, is often questionable (at best) from the point of view of both disciplines. Section III below will attempt to show the distorting effect of a historical-realist procedure in Lukács' writings on Tolstoy.

II

I have argued, then, for the rejection of 'realism' with the emphasis on the 'real-': the critical theory which ascribes a truth-telling function to imaginative literature. But, as I implied at the beginning of the chapter, this is not to deny the validity, as a critical classification, of 'realism' with the emphasis on the '-ism': a sub-convention of fiction in which the description and narration are deliberately and consistently imitative of reality. With the denial that fiction can be a truth-telling mode of discourse, however, the *raison d'être* of realistic writing might seem to have disappeared. If imaginative literature does not transmit information about the primary world, what (it may be asked) can be the point of the close mimesis of reality which is undoubtedly characteristic of some fictions?

I have already suggested one answer: that fictions which are mimetic of the primary world and fictions which are not mimetic address themselves, to a large extent, to different kinds of desire, call forth responses from different parts of the psyche. By reason of the limitations of subject-matter which characterise it, realism cannot appeal directly to certain imaginative aspirations and terrors. Realists cannot send their characters travelling through time, for example. On the other hand, the great strength of realism as a sub-convention, and one which goes a long way to justify the expectation that the reading public will continue to look on its works with favour, is that a secondary world closely mimetic of the primary one tends to enjoy a more rapid access to the reader's sympathies. The desires we most immediately recognise and acknowledge to ourselves are naturally those whose correlative objects are continually present in our experience: the anxieties set in motion by the conceptions 'war', 'adultery' or 'unemployment', and their elaborations, are, if not more intense than those aroused by 'vampire' or 'Martian invasion', at any rate more often to be found in the foreground of our awareness, and consequently more readily available for quickening; there are some readers, indeed, for whom a work which does not restrict itself to concerns of primary possibility can have little or no interest.

(For other readers, though, the contrary instinct may be just as strong; to feel that their emotional engagement with the typical problems of contemporary social life is already sufficiently intense, and to look to literature for a redressing of what is felt as a disproportionate development of certain psychological preoccupations. Before dismissing all such as feckless escapists, we should reflect that a particularly-constituted society or culture may not exhaust every possibility of human feeling; that unreal things, such as reunion with the dead, nameless menaces in the dark, and instantly seducible women, may be just as regular and persistent objects of longing and fear as the most routine and practical concerns – of which they are often, indeed, intensified versions; and that the very impossibility of attaining a state of being in this world may make the desire for that state psychically highly significant and influential, as in the case of the aspirations of religion. The correspondence of a fiction to the realities of the world, and its correspondence to the realities of human desire and aversion, are different and often contradictory things; once we affirm that it is the latter which is principally in question, the distinction between a realist centrality of concern and the esoteric fancies of romance, fairy-tale, dream and myth becomes a matter for categorisation rather than for value-judgement.)

A second advantage of realism is its ability to summon ideas and images into the reader's mind by allusion rather than extended description. To be able to refer to a railway platform, say, or a suburban villa, in reasonable expectation of evoking a conception of some complexity, represents a considerable economy of words and consequently a certain tautening of structure. How heavily, for example, the nostalgic evocativeness of the following passage depends upon a shared familiarity of cultural detail and tonality between author and reader: a familiarity which the author of a fantasy or a science-fiction story (not rooted in the present) would be obliged to create painstakingly and *ab ovo* by his own efforts.

All through that year the kinemas showed scenes from the Exhibition on Gaumont Graphic or Pathé Pictorial (for the cowboys much largo to express wide open spaces, but for the little geisha girls the piano sounded a touching staccato). Audiences caught quick jerky glimpses of huge cartwheel hats wreathed in ostrich feathers, of trains dragging in the dust, of bowlers and toppers and peaked cloth caps and little round caps set with their tassels on the back of thickly brilliantined heads, of parasols and button boots, of sailor suits and knickerbockers, of pearly waistcoats and choker scarves, of bad teeth and no teeth, of princess petticoats, squirrel skin, sable and beaver, neapolitan ices (Oh, oh Antonio) and of hot potatoes for the muff, each in its season of a sari or two, of the kaffir chief's headdress, of a guardsman's busby, and of a little toque of violets worn on a Great Personage's head (Viking daughter from over the sea so splendidly null in half mourning), of the Big Wheel, the Water Shoot, the Balloon, the Haunted House, and of diabolos everywhere, of Kaiser Bill moustaches, and, above all, of even more imperial moustaches curled like a buffalo's horns, Buffalo Bill himself. Was it S. F. the showman and not the great Colonel at all? Who could tell? And true to say, who cared? It was ideal for the children. With their broad-brimmed hats, their fringed breeches, their lassoes and their whips. In the Wilds of West Kensington the West was now long established.[19]

This passage from Angus Wilson's *No Laughing Matter* exploits the rapidity of recognition afforded by realism at the level of highly specific cultural-historical detail (and perhaps with only passing effectiveness – will it be long, one wonders, before even the middle-class English reader has to look up 'toppers' and 'brilliantined' in a dictionary, and misses entirely the social and cultural resonances of 'West Kensington'?); but the ready comprehensibility of a realistic context can equally serve to expedite our responses

to important developments in plot and character. One thinks of
the many nineteenth-century novels which turn upon a largely
assumed appreciation of the implications of certain contemporary
social customs and expectations: the marriage contract, the laws of
inheritance, the ethics and metaphysics of established religion;
focusing, generally, upon the extreme predicaments which most
powerfully provide desire and fear – the temptations and anxieties
of adultery, the sudden acquisition, or loss, of great wealth, crises
of religious faith. Even at a certain historical distance, we grasp
readily enough the anguish of Bulstrode's entrapment by his
progressive improbities, or Theobald Pontifex's subjection to his
father's purse-strings, because though we may not have been in
precisely these situations ourselves, their underlying causes and
their implications remain intelligible in a society which still takes
law, private property and the 'nuclear' family for granted, and
guide us smoothly towards a perception of the psychological core
of the invented situation. The presentation of moral predicaments
or emotional problems is not, of course, the exclusive province of
social realism, but it is a reasonable assumption that a complex
dilemma will present itself to us most lucidly, all other things
being equal, in a physical and social context which is either
immediately familiar or fairly quickly assimilated to our general
knowledge. The lower the tax levied on the reader's imaginative
energy by the externals of setting and circumstance, the greater
the energy available for responding to the essentials of character
and plot. It is a question of Occam's Razor: not to multiply
difficulties without obtaining compensatory advantages. Accordingly, while the departure from primary plausibility in a story by
Poe, Kafka or the brothers Grimm may be justified by the access it
gains to desire which is not evocable by the materials of realism, a
failure of consistent and plausible mimesis in a realist work is a
blemish because, in a literary sub-convention in which immediacy
of recognition serves vitality of response, it interposes a superfluous perplexity between the reader and the emotional substance
of the work.

The distinction employed a moment ago between 'essentials'
and 'externals', between material which embodies the emotional
substance of a work and material which facilitates the reader's
imaginative concentration on that substance, needs a good deal of
qualification. It certainly does not simply correspond to the
distinction between the human and the non-human, for very often

the latter carries something, or much, of the emotional burden of a story. The physique of the House of Usher, though 'external' to Roderick Usher's personality, rivals or perhaps surpasses it in evoking apprehension and dread; while even in realistic or naturalistic works, inanimate things – the trains in Zola's *La Bête Humaine*, for example – can exert the evocativeness of symbolic suggestion. Indeed, if, as I have argued, the simplest linguistic material, down to the definite article, has a propensity to promote psychic unrest, no fraction of a work can, strictly speaking, be considered as in itself emotively inert, as entirely subordinated to the task of facilitating comprehension of more highly charged material. Nevertheless, in a literary structure as complex as a novel, there are bound to be crises, points of concentrated tension, in comparison to which other parts are, relatively speaking, of a subordinate, facilitating importance. Stendhal's description of 'Verrières' at the beginning of *Le Rouge et Le Noir* may be appetising and absorbing in itself, but it remains true that it is mainly there to provide a social and geographical background for the adventures of Julien Sorel. How much meaning can be given to this distinction between the mainly functional and the emotionally 'essential' varies, of course, from work to work. (One could hypothesise a (perhaps) ideal novel in which the distinction would be quite meaningless, every part supporting every other part in perfect balance and symmetry.) For relatively clear instances one might point to those opening lines in Shakespeare scenes which let the audience know, as economically as possible, as much of the supposed location and situation as it needs to appreciate what follows:

Before Angiers well met, brave Austria.[20]

Though there are tiny emotive stimuli in this line from *King John* – most obviously in 'well met' and 'brave' – which must be regarded as making some, however slight, contribution to the total experience of the work, there is no getting away from the fact that it is primarily there to identify the setting and the speakers, to remove as quickly as possible any uncertainty about the circumstances which might impair apprehension of the dialogue and action.[21] The opening of Malcolm Lowry's *Under the Volcano*, quoted above, serves a similar purpose. But this laconic directness is untypical of either fiction or drama. More commonly an effort is made to combine the specification of scene and situation with more immediately exciting material: compare the crude line from *King John*, for example, with the arresting eavesdropping effect at the beginning of *Antony and Cleopatra*:

> Nay, but this dotage of our general's
> O'erflows the measure: those his goodly eyes
> That o'er the files and musters of the war
> Have glow'd like plated Mars, now bend, now turn
> The office and devotion of their view
> Upon a tawny front.[22]

The first two paragraphs of *Jane Eyre*, quoted below, not only fix the approximate age and situation of the narrator with admirable brevity, but introduce, in miniature, some of the most emotionally charged material of the novel: Jane's sense of isolation, and tendency to self-abasement; the brooding, minatory weather (looking forward to Jane's water-colours, the storm that follows Rochester's proposal, and much else); and the physical privation ('nipped fingers and toes' anticipating Lowood).

> There was no possibility of taking a walk that day. We had been wandering, indeed, in the leafless shrubbery an hour in the morning; but since dinner (Mrs. Reed, when there was not company, dined early) the cold winter wind had brought with it clouds so sombre, and a rain so penetrating, that further outdoor exercise was now out of the question.
>
> I was glad of it; I never liked long walks, especially on chilly afternoons: dreadful to me was the coming home in the raw twilight, with nipped fingers and toes, and a heart saddened by the chidings of Bessie, the nurse, and humbled by the consciousness of my physical inferiority to Eliza, John, and Georgina Reed.[23]

Nevertheless, though it is in the novelist's interests to disguise the fact, especially in the very earliest pages when a reader whose desires are only flickeringly engaged is liable to put the book away, the comparatively low-intensity facilitating material in a novel tends (since it must precede what it facilitates) to be distributed towards the beginning rather than the end; a tendency endorsed by the well-known compositional principle that a major character should not be introduced after about the half-way point. This may in part explain why (as David Lodge notes in *Language of Fiction*,[24] though he attributes it to a different cause) the opening chapters of a novel are on the whole more slowly read than the later. (And perhaps more slowly written, as I have heard Angus Wilson affirm of his own novels.)

Both the justifications so far advanced for realistic mimesis of the primary world – the immediacy of response attainable through the representation of familiar objects and types of experience, and the relative lucidity with which an emotionally-charged situation, condition or event is appreciated when its underlying or ambient circumstances interpose no problems of comprehension – refer largely to the disturbing, tension-inducing aspect of the experience of literature: the arousing and quickening of desire. A third justification refers correspondingly to the resolving, compensatory aspect, in which (I have suggested)[25] after a complex of desire has become implicated in a nexus of tensions in the work, the progressive resolution of those tensions in an aesthetically coherent structure provides a paradigm of psychological governance over the quickened desire. (Actually, as this formulation itself implies, the distinction between the two aspects, though sometimes analytically convenient, is at least partly artificial: to render a body of material lucid, and therefore effective in promoting affects, and to render it structurally coherent, and therefore a paradigm of governance, are closely related enterprises.) In the novel, as in most painting, and as in other forms of literature (though perhaps to a greater extent than in most, in view of the comparative freedom of fiction from strictly formal structures such as the verbal patternings of poetry or the dramatic patterns conditioned by theatrical feasibility), the content or representation – what is represented as happening and existing, being thought and felt – is a major constituent element in the total structure. The shape of the novel is, most obviously, the shape of the story. Structural cohesion accordingly entails cohesion in the representation, and this in turn calls, among other things, for an impression of basic internal consistency which, in such matters as physical laws and social possibilities, is most easily procured by adherence to primary plausibility. By preserving the illusion of identity with the primary world, the author maintains a presumption of internal consistency in his imagined world which can only be destroyed by a significant lapse in realist simulation. If one of the characters in *Middlemarch* happened to be able to fly, and the novel was otherwise the same, we would be likely to allege an impairment of its structural unity; from the affective point of view, we would not know what to do with the desires or anxieties stimulated by this perplexing detail, which would appear to belong to a quite different zone of feeling from those engaged by the rest of the novel's material, and would thus elude the governance of a coherent structure. For the restoration of structural completeness and intelligibility, we should require either the deletion of the non-realistic detail, or the development of an alternative and self-consistent natural history for the secondary world of the novel – something like that of *Peter Pan*, perhaps – to replace that taken over from the primary world; and from this would follow a decided shift in the psychological concerns to which the work addressed itself.[26] Maintaining primary plausibility is not, of course, any guarantee of overall structural cohesion; the most scrupulous mimesis of the primary world can only provide the appearance of a self-consistent background, and if the foreground of a specific narrative is incoherent, the work will be incoherent. Equally clearly, a work which is not realistic can have the internal laws of its imaginary world so thoroughly developed that the reader comes to accept them as the natural background to the action, and is no more perplexed (that is, jerked into an area of response to which the rest of the work seems immaterial) by the appearance of a cyclops or a Morlock than the reader of *Middlemarch* would be by the appearance of a solicitor. But, again, the advantage of realism is that of economy: it is easier, less expensive in time and words, to assume the primary world's substratum of laws and possibilities than to invent an alternative substratum; which is not to deny that an alternative substratum may make a potent appeal to our desires.

III

The fictional works of Tolstoy, and especially his two longest novels, are by general consent among the central texts of 'realism', however that term is interpreted; and they have attracted close and approving attention from both historical and moral realists. The complexity and seemingly effortless directness of their mimesis of the social world, the lively interest with which they invest their representations of common, even commonplace, human experiences, and what is felt to be a sensitive openness, a freedom from melodramatic typing in their characterisation, are matters of almost universal agreement. Our present question is whether we are to take this close mimesis of reality as an end, and seek to analyse it more precisely, to distil the essence of what Tolstoy has to show us or tell us about reality, or whether, in accordance with the view put forward in section II above, we are to take it as a means of access to the reader's feelings, and ask what ends it serves in the evocation and concentration of desire. To a considerable extent the two kinds of interpretation may run parallel. When F. R. Leavis says that *Anna Karenin* 'compels us to recognise'[27] how far from simple is the moral entanglement between the individual and society, we may know exactly what he is looking at, but still scrupulously dissent from the word 'compel', reflecting that only knowledge of the primary world can possibly compel 'recognition' (which in this context clearly carries the sense of 'conviction') and insisting that what *Anna Karenin* more precisely does is to set forth an imaginary world of moral dilemmas and choices by which our sympathies are variously engaged.

Lukács, whose work on Tolstoy extends from *The Theory of the Novel*[28] (1914–5, decisively repudiated later) through *The Historical Novel*[29] (1936–7) to an extended treatment in *Studies in European Realism* (1948), sees in him (in Lenin's words) 'the mirror of the Russian Revolution'; more precisely, the portrayer of the internal contradictions of Russian society in the period between the emancipations of the serfs and the 1905 revolution, of the 'inexorable division between the "two nations" in Russia, the peasants and the landowners'.[30] Tolstoy's illusions about the possibility of reconciling social conflicts through an ethical or religious reformation do not, Lukács explains, prevent him from 'depicting social reality in a comprehensive, correct and objective way', because the illusions themselves arise out of the essence of the historical situation.

Only illusions motivated by the social movement depicted, i.e. illusions – often tragic illusions – which are historically necessary, do not prevent the author from depicting social reality with objective truth.

Such were the illusions of Balzac, of Shakespeare, and such too, in the final count, were Tolstoy's illusions. Lenin said: 'The contradictions in Tolstoy's views ... are a true mirror of those contradictory circumstances in which the historical activity of the peasantry in our revolution took place'.

All Tolstoy's illusions and reactionary Utopias – from Henry George's world-liberating theory to the theory of non-resistance of evil, were all without exception rooted in the specific position of the Russian peasantry. Recognition of their historical necessity does not of course make them less Utopian or less reactionary. But the effect of the historical necessity of these illusions is that, far from hampering Tolstoy's realism, they actually contribute to its greatness, depth and feeling, although naturally in a very contradictory fashion.[31]

Lukács never explains where historically *un*necessary illusions come from; indeed the notion is an odd one to be used, or implied, by a Marxist who presumably holds that ideas, ethical, political, or religious, are the product of history, or 'social movements'. But it is important for him to provide a privileged, non-pernicious status for Tolstoy's 'illusions', since he wishes to assert, as a historical realist must, that the essential meaning and value of Tolstoy's work lies in its depiction of social realities, and its adaptation of fictional technique to that end.

The true artistic totality of a literary work depends on the completeness of the picture it presents of the essential social factors that determine the world depicted. Hence it can be based only on the author's own intensive experience of the social process. Only such experience can uncover the essential social factors and make the artistic presentation centre round them freely and naturally. The hallmark of the great realist masterpiece is precisely that its intensive totality of *essential* social factors does not require, does not even tolerate, a meticulously accurate or pedantically encyclopaedic inclusion of all the threads making up the social tangle; in such a masterpiece the most essential social factors can find total expression in the apparently accidental conjunction of a few human destinies.[32]

And a contrast is drawn with the kind of writer who, instead of depicting reality in its essentials (that is, with the social determinants accurately placed), merely reproduces certain 'superficial visible traits' of the social world; or alternatively, orders his material according to a 'system originating in his own mind and nowhere else';[33] this is the downward path which begins, roughly, with *Madame Bovary* and ends in the nihilistic solipsism of Becket.[34]

It has already been pointed out that interpretation and evaluation on this basis depend upon firm pre-conceptions of what the social determinants are – pre-conceptions which therefore cannot be derived from literature itself. Indeed, Lukácsian analysis proceeds by broad strides in which we are only likely to follow him if we are willing to accept further fundamental and contentious assumptions: about the socio-historical determination of literary possibilities, about the priority of the social over the psychological, in life and in literature, about the relative greatness of particular writers. Thus, the evolution of bourgeois society after 1848 (first assumption) is supposed to explain the alienation of writers from the social process during that period (second assumption), and this in turn to account for the absence of a great realism (third assumption) except in the special case of Tolstoy. All this may be true, but Lukács does little more than assert it. The analysis of specific texts is as sweeping and as arbitrary. Defending *Le Rouge et le Noir*, for example, against Zola's charge that Julien and Mathilde and their relationship are extraordinary and artificial, Lukács explains that these 'above-average' characters are necessary to Stendhal in order to 'bring in his criticism of the hypocrisy, duplicity and baseness of the restoration period, and show up the infamously greedy and mean capitalist essence of its feudal-romantic ideology. Only by creating the figure of Mathilde, in whom the romantic ideology of reaction grows into a genuine passion, even though in heroically exaggerated form, could Stendhal raise the plot and the concrete situations to a level at which the contrast between these ideologies and their social basis on the one hand, and the plebeian Jacobinism of the Napoleon-admirer Julien Sorel on the other, could be fully developed'.[35] But this doesn't answer Zola's point: why, one might still ask, does Mathilde's passion have to be 'in heroically exaggerated form' for Stendhal's purpose to be achieved? If the purpose is indeed to show social phenomena manifested through personal behaviour, surely an unexaggerated (and therefore more realistically representative) example would illustrate the point as convincingly, or more so? But, again, what is most striking is the length of Lukács' interpretative leap, from a complex of characterisation and plot to a simple, if abstruse, historical perception; and a great deal seems to be left behind. Certainly there is social satire in *Le Rouge et le Noir*; and one expects satire, an emotive, not an informative, kind of discourse, to represent extreme cases in order to incite in the reader vigorous rejection of what it satirises. But the vicissitudes of the Julien-Mathilde relationship also embody a concern, more premonitory of Proust than of Balzac, with the psychological origins and effects of sexual love. Mathilde's passion is surely not *wholly* rooted in 'the romantic ideology of reaction'. And it is with respect to this extra-historical erotic element that the reader may sense (though I myself do not) a degree of contrivance and overkill.

Likewise, in his treatment of Tolstoy Lukács frequently elides important details and significant, even central, contrasts of feeling in order to sustain his association of the 'artistic totality' of the works with the depiction of the 'essential social factors' as his own historical retrospect identifies them. Two examples will illustrate this. The first is a comment on *Anna Karenin* from *The Historical Novel*; Lukács is discussing the uses of the 'parallel plot' in fiction and drama.

> If there is a parallel plot in tragedy, it complements and underlines the main collision. Think of the already mentioned parallel between the fates of Lear and Gloster [*sic*]. In the novel it is quite different. Tolstoy, for example, has several plots to parallel the tragic fate of Anna Karenina. The pairs Kitty-Levin, Darya-Oblonsky are only the big central complements to Anna and Vronsky; there are other, more episodic, parallel plots beside. In both cases the plots complement and illuminate one another, but in quite different directions. In *Lear* the fate of Gloster underlines the tragic necessity of what happens to the principal hero. In *Anna Karenina* the parallel plots stress that the heroine's fate, while typical and necessary, is yet an extremely individual one. Obviously her fate reveals the inner contradictions of bourgeois marriage in the most powerful terms. But what is also shown is first, that these contradictions do not always necessarily take this particular path, thus that they may have an altogether different content and form, and, secondly, that similar kinds of conflict will only lead to Anna's tragic fate in very specific and individual conditions.[36]

Despite its characteristically problem-fudging verbal formulas (is the 'tragic necessity' of Lear's fate a necessity in terms of the dramatic structure of the play, or a revealed historical necessity? does 'shown' really bridge the conceptual gap, as it is meant to, between 'represented in the novel' and 'revealed to be actually the case'? how 'extremely individual' can something be before it ceases to be 'typical and necessary'? how 'altogether different' can the 'content and form' of a contradiction be before it ceases to be that contradiction and becomes something else?), the passage is convincing enough in its general contrast between plays and novels, and in its observation that the depiction of non-fatal marital difficulties disarms any suspicion that Anna's fate is being offered as an inevitable consequence of 'bourgeois' marriage. But, read carefully, it clearly implies that not only the Dolly-Oblonsky marriage but also the Kitty-Levin one 'reveals the inner contradictions of bourgeois marriage', if not, perhaps, in the most powerful terms; and this is a placing of emphasis so eccentric as to amount to falsification. Lukács paints out, so to speak, probably the most pervasive and striking contrast in the novel, the almost too evident opposition and juxtaposition of the plummetting marital and sexual career of Anna, and the irregularly rising one of Levin. If one did not know the novel, one would never gather from Lukács' treatment, which both here and in *Studies in European Realism* is almost entirely concerned with the extraction of social and historical problems, that the Levin-Kitty relationship is charged with positive feeling, or indeed that, because of the prominence of this affirmative element, the work as a whole is as much a comedy (in the wider sense) as a tragedy. It is not simply that Levin is a sympathetic personality with a capacity for enjoyment, a more expansive character than the conscience-stricken landowner of Lukács, 'moving from crisis to crisis in trying to convince himself that his existence as landowner is justified and that he has the right to exploit his peasants'.[37] It is a question of the structural unity of the work; for if Anna's fall is the vertical axis of the novel, Levin's progress is the horizontal. Through the portrayal of Levin's developing thoughts, experiences and relationships, a repeated comedic pattern, a kind of minor-major shift, is enacted on every scale from the most detailed to the most general, and becomes a characteristic emotional progression in the work, a complement and counterbalance to the long downward progression of the 'Anna' material. The pattern is enacted, obviously enough, in Levin's two proposals: the first unsuccessful, the second (its delicate anxiety intensified for the reader as for the participants by the recollection of the first) successful – and followed by a quite exceptional phenomenon in fiction, three chapters devoted almost entirely to the representation of happiness (*IV*, 14–16). It is enacted in small incidents, mirroring the impulsive fluctuations of Levin's consciousness, before and during the wedding. Levin painfully questions whether Kitty can really love him; she reassures him (*V*, 2). Levin is delayed in his hotel room, and arrives at the church late and in confusion; the confusion 'suddenly vanishes' as he glances at his bride during the service (*V*, 3–4). It is enacted in the episodes of jealousy and reconciliation (*VI*, 7; *VI*, 14; *VII* 11), and supremely in the childbirth scene, which is perhaps worth quoting. Out of context it can seem faintly embarrassing; in the due sequence of the novel, upheld structurally by the pervasiveness of the emotional progression of which it is an instance, and vindicated by our acquaintance with the possibilities of feeling in Levin's personality, its directness is entirely supportable.

'It will soon be over now,' said the doctor. And the doctor's face was so grave as he said it that Levin thought he meant that it would soon be over with Kitty and she was dying.

Beside himself, he rushed into the bedroom again. The first thing he saw was the midwife's face looking more frowning and stern than ever. Kitty's face was not there. In its place was something fearful – fearful in its strained distortion and the sounds that issued from it. He let his head drop on to the wooden rail of the bed, feeling that his heart was breaking. The terrible screams followed each other quickly until they ceased. Levin could not believe his ears, but there was no doubt about it: the screaming had ceased, and he heard a soft stir, a bustle, and the sound of hurried breathing, and her voice, faltering, vibrant, tender, and blissful as she whispered, 'It's over!'

He lifted his head. With her arms feeble stretched out on the counterpane, she lay gazing silently at him, looking extraordinarily lovely and serene, trying unsuccessfully to smile.

And suddenly Levin felt himself transported in a flash from the mysterious, awful, far-away world in which he had been living for the last twenty-two hours back to his old everyday world, glorified now with such luminous happiness that he could not bear it. The taut strings snapped, and the sobs and tears of joy which he had never foreseen rose within him with such force that they shook his whole body and for a long time prevented him from speaking.[38]

The minor-major pattern is enacted on a large scale in the overall design of the novel, which can be divided into two equal parts – before the betrothal, and after. Finally, it is enacted in the contrast between Levin as we first meet him, agitated and uncertain, and the spiritually redeemed or at least uplifted Levin (let us not enter into the probably meaningless question of whether he backslides 'afterwards', but content ourselves with the structural fact of the non-ironically affirmative full close) whom we leave at the end. None of this optimistic structuring is acknowledged in Lukács; nor does he have anything to say of the episode in which Kitty and Levin nurse the dying Nikolai Levin, though it is not only a climactic moment in the novel, but highly characteristic of the author in its preoccupation with the spiritual impact of dying upon both the sufferer himself and those who attend him. No critic is obliged to say everything about a work; but Lukács is affirming a theory of 'true artistic totality', not simply extracting illustrations of individual historical points, or offering to supplement existing readings; and this is clearly inconsistent with so decidedly partial an analysis. If the affirmative elements in *Anna Karenin* are meant to be acknowledged in Lukács' reference to 'Tolstoy's illusions ... without exception rooted in the specific position of the Russian peasantry' – and this generalisation would need to be considerably elaborated if Tolstoy's treatment of birth, femininity and death were to be convincingly tied down to a specialised socio-historical origin – then Lukács ought to concede that the 'completeness of the picture ... of the essential social factors' in *Anna Karenin* is far more radically modified by these 'illusory' elements than he indicates; is, in fact, outweighed by them.

My second example is also taken from *The Historical Novel*. Here Lukács discusses the conception of history which informs *War and Peace*.

It is part of Tolstoy's greatness that he has no confidence in the 'official leaders' of history, neither in the open reactionaries nor in the liberals. But it is a limitation – the limitation of the growing revolt of the peasant masses – that this historically justified mistrust stops short at a passive mistrust of all conscious historical action, that Tolstoy completely fails to understand the movement of revolutionary democracy already beginning in his time. This failure to understand the role of conscious action by the people leads Tolstoy into an extreme and abstract denial of the significance of conscious action by the exploiters, too. His abstract exaggeration thus does not lie in his criticism and repudiation of the social content of such action, but in the fact that it is denied any significance at all.[39]

Once again, Lukács' frame of reference cuts so narrowly across the substance of Tolstoy's work that even what he celebrates in it is, in fact, hardly there; and what he regrets as a limitation is, properly understood, one of the foundations of Tolstoy's imaginative world. It is certainly true that *War and Peace* depreciates the importance of the 'official leaders'. But to say that Tolstoy 'has no confidence' in them is to imply that the statesmen and commanders of the novel are judged and found wanting according to ordinary criteria of political virtue or effectiveness – an implication reinforced by the contentious gloss, 'neither ... the open reactionaries nor ... the liberals', with its implication that a judgement of a politically analytical kind has been made – and this is, at best, a half-truth. It would be truer to say that these criteria are represented as being themselves illusory, and that Tolstoy is much more enthusiastically concerned with a quite different plane of human experience. Lukács presents Tolstoy's low valuation of 'conscious historical action' in entirely negative terms, as a blind spot, or an excessively wholesale disillusionment; but this 'extreme and abstract denial' is the obverse of a positive, and centrally Tolstoyan vision. Here, for example, is the celebrated passage in which Prince Andrei, whose admiration for Napoleon has been made clear, and who has just been wounded in an act of heroic leadership, at last encounters his hero.

'That's a fine death!' said Napoleon, looking down at Bolkonsky. Prince Andrei grasped that this was said of him, and that it was Napoleon saying it. He heard the speaker addressed as *Sire*. But he heard the words as he might have heard the buzzing of a fly. Not only did they not interest him – they made no impression upon him, and were immediately forgotten. There was a burning pain in his head; he felt that his life-blood was ebbing away, and he saw far above him the remote, eternal heavens. He knew it was Napoleon – his hero – but at that moment Napoleon seemed to him such a small, insignificant creature compared with what was passing now between his own soul and that lofty, limitless firmament with the clouds flying over it. It meant nothing to him at that moment who might be standing over him, or what was said of him: he was only glad that people were standing near, and his only desire was that these people should help him and bring him back to life, which seemed to him so beautiful now that he had learned to see it differently...

'Well, and you, young man,' said he. 'How do you feel, *mon brave?*'

Although five minutes previously Prince Andrei had been able to say a few words to the soldiers who were carrying him, now with his eyes fixed steadily on Napoleon he was silent.... So trivial seemed to him at that moment all the interests that engrossed Napoleon, so petty did his hero with his paltry vanity and delight in victory appear, compared to that lofty, righteous and kindly sky which had seen and comprehended, that he could not answer him.

Everything did indeed seem so futile and insignificant in comparison with the stern and solemn train of thought induced in him by his lapsing consciousness, as his life-blood ebbed away, by his suffering and the nearness of death. Gazing into Napoleon's eyes, Prince Andrei mused on the unimportance of greatness, the unimportance of life which no-one could understand, and the still greater unimportance of death, the meaning of which no-one alive could understand or explain.[40]

There is visibly more in this than an absence of confidence in Napoleon – is he an 'open reactionary' or a 'liberal', by the way? – as an 'official leader' of human destiny. The episode is an example of a compositional device in which Tolstoy specialises: a sudden, dramatic and total shift in the object of desire, mediated through the perspective of a sympathetic character. What was intensely important to Prince Andrei has become trivial, and what was trivial intensely important. The transformation is effective for the reader because the appeal of Prince Andrei's obsession with martial glory has already been subtly subverted, both through its own disturbing hypertrophy ('Death, wounds, the loss of my family – nothing holds any terrors for me. And precious and dear as many people are to me – father, sister, wife – those I cherish most – yet dreadful and unnatural as it seems, I would exchange them all immediately for a moment of glory, or triumph over men');[41] and through the unflattering presentation of the Russian commanders and their councils. If this were an isolated moment, without thematic relevance to the rest of the novel, or to Tolstoy's work in general, it might be possible to dismiss it as a passing mystical excrescence on an essentially historical argument; but on the contrary, its Schopenhauerian indifference to temporal strivings, and celebration of joyful pure perception, represent a version of an ideal of spiritual liberation which Tolstoy repeatedly sought to realise. Throughout his work a tension and opposition is maintained between two types of aspiration, two ideals of happiness. One is the ideal of egotistical success and satisfaction, worldly and therefore contingent, artificial, complex and self-regarding – as with Karenin's pride in getting an unimportant reform approved by the Commission, or Vronsky's pleasure at the figure he cuts, as the romantic pursuer of a married woman, in the eyes of fashionable society. The second, and preferred, ideal is characterised by self-abandonment, spontaneity, simplicity and *caritas*. As the young, repudiated Lukács rightly says in *The Theory of the Novel*,

> Tolstoy's great and truly epic mentality ... aspires to a life based on a community of feeling among simple human beings closely bound to nature, a life which is intimately adapted to the great rhythm of nature, which moves according to nature's cycle of birth and death and excludes all structures which are not natural, which are petty and disruptive, causing disintegration and stagnation.[42]

This type of ideal is closely associated with the supposed religious and ethical serenity of the Russian peasant (a decisive element in Levin's final enlightenment), with the Schopenhauerian renunciation of will and of the *principium individuationis*, the differentiation between the self and others,[43] and with Christian compassionate forgiveness, as when Karenin forgives Anna and Vronsky when the former is gravely ill, and experiences a 'blissful spiritual condition that gave him all at once a new happiness he had never known',[44] or when Pierre is overcome with pity for Natasha after his initial revulsion at her elopement attempt – an episode immediately followed by his beneficent, soothing, exalting vision of the comet (Book 2, Part 5, 22). (These Christian and Schopenhauerian influences lie behind what is perhaps an anomaly in Tolstoy's opposition of values, his tendency, especially marked in later works such as *Resurrection* and *The Kreutzer Sonata*, to ascribe sexual feeling – of any intensity – to the first, artificial and egotistical, rather than the second, spontaneous and loving, category of preoccupations; so that in *Anna Karenin*, for example, sexual pleasure is the diversion of the *homme du monde*, Oblonsky, while Levin's simpler and more natural existence is associated with a stable family life in which the sexual element is relatively muted. In this way the great difficulty in identifying the natural with the good – that there are some things which are undoubtedly natural (or so one might think) but can hardly be called unproblematically good – is sidestepped.) The affirmative developments and climaxes in Tolstoy often take the form of a revelatory escape from the first kind of aspiration into the second: both Prince Andrei and Pierre experience delusory attractions towards satisfactions of the first kind, the former in his longing for martial glory, the latter in yielding to social pressures (and to sex) in making his first marriage, before each finds liberation – Prince Andrei in the will-renouncing serenity of his deathbed, Pierre in a marriage founded in compassion.

Over the course of Tolstoy's career, this opposition between the ideals of egotistical satisfaction and of compassion and self-abnegation comes to be increasingly starkly presented, and increasingly firmly aligned with that other opposition, whose roots are in Tolstoy's Apollonian-Dionysiac personality, between a longing for hedonistic, especially sexual gratification, and a longing for liberation from the self and its turbulent desires. In *War and Peace* aspirations of the ego are generally treated with sympathy and good humour. Pierre's and Prince Andrei's moments of epiphanic illumination may have an exceptional value, but there is no implication that the other characters, with their worldly concerns, their vanities and deceptive daydreams, are simply treading the primrose path to the everlasting bonfire. The enthusiasm of Petya and Natasha Rostov for the war may, by comparison with the disillusionment of Prince Andrei, be shallow and even tragically mistaken, but it is also charming:

Petya was in high spirits because he had left home a boy and returned (so everyone told him) a fine young man, because he was at home, because he had left Byelaya Tserkov, where there was no prospect of taking part in an early battle, and come to Moscow where any day there might be fighting, and above all because Natasha, whose lead he always followed, was in high spirits. Natasha was gay because for too long she had been sad and now nothing reminded her of the cause of her sadness, and she was feeling well again. She was happy too because she had someone to adore her – the adoration of others was a lubricant necessary if the wheels of her mechanism were to run quite smoothly – and Petya adored her. But above all they were gay because there was a war at the very gates of Moscow, because there would be fighting at the barriers, arms were being distributed, everybody was rushing here and there, and altogether something extraordinary was happening, and that is always exciting, especially for the young.[45]

How damning the references to Petya's pride in manhood and Natasha's egotistical need for adoration would be in the morally monolithic structure of *Resurrection*, and how touching they are permitted to be here! In *Anna Karenin*, too, the *homme moyen sensuel*, Oblonsky – that it comes naturally to characterise him in French phrases reminds us of the part which the opposed images of 'Europe' and 'Russia' play in realising contrasts of aspiration in Tolstoy's work – remains for all his failings an appealing and vital figure, while Kitty as well as Anna is allowed to take pleasure in her own physical attractiveness. In the later fiction, however, the negative presentation of the interests of the ego, their employment as objects of aversion, becomes the dominant, even overpowering quality. By the time of *Resurrection*, Tolstoy has not only withdrawn all sympathy from worldly characters and their foibles – could the earlier Tolstoy have referred, even in passing, to a minor character's 'nonentity of a wife',[46] or offered his hero's contemptuous dismissal of Petersburg society as a rare instance of spiritual enlightenment? – but lost the ability, or the willingness, to present self-transcendence positively, through visions of spiritual joy and liberation. The comprehensive negativity of *Resurrection*, the continual soliciting, through episode after episode depicting unrelieved suffering and unredeemed wickedness, of a revulsion on the reader's part which Tolstoy cannot leave to his responding sensibility but must go on to articulate for him in dogmatically-formulated abstract terms, deprives it of the emotional force of contrast: where all is dark, nothing is seen to be dark. The somewhat earlier *Death of Ivan Ilyich* makes, to be sure, very effective use of contrast, in an emotional progression reminiscent of the hell-fire sermon: an extended picture of suffering and terror, calculated to excite acute aversion in the spectator, concluded by a vision of escape through self-surrender and *caritas*.

The dying man was still shrieking desperately and waving his arms. His hand fell on the child's head. The boy seized it, pressed it to his lips and burst into tears.

It was at this very moment that Ivan Ilyich had fallen through the hole and caught sight of the light, and it was revealed to him that his life had not been what it ought to have been but that it was still possible to put it right. He asked himself: 'But what *is* the right thing?' and grew still, listening. Then he felt that someone was kissing his hand. He opened his eyes and looked at his son. He felt sorry for him. His wife came up to him. He looked at her. She was gazing at him with open mouth, the tears wet on her nose and cheeks, and an expression of despair on her face. He felt sorry for her.

'Yes, I am a misery to them,' he thought. 'They are sorry but it will be better for them when I die.' He wanted to say this but had no strength to speak. 'Besides, why speak, I must act,' he thought. With a look he indicated his son to his wife and said:

'Take him away ... sorry for him ... sorry for you to ...' He tried to add 'Forgive me' but said 'Forego' and, too weak to correct himself, waved his hand, knowing that whoever was concerned would understand.

And all at once it became clear to him that what had been oppressing him and would not go away was suddenly dropping away to one side, on two sides, on ten sides, on all sides. He felt full of pity for them, he must do something to make it less painful for them: release them and release himself from this suffering. 'How right and how simple,' he thought. 'And the pain?' he asked himself. 'What has become of it? Where are you, pain?'

He began to watch for it.

'Yes, here it is. Well, what of it? Let the pain be.'

'And death? Where is it?'

He searched for his former habitual fear of death and did not find it. 'Where is it? What death?' There was no fear because there was no death either.

In place of death there was light.

'So that's what it is!' he suddenly exclaimed aloud. 'What joy!'[47]

This climax is a triumph of imaginative intensity, and yet, precisely because of the ruthless simplicity of its rhetorical design, *The Death of Ivan Ilyich*, like *Resurrection*, lacks the affective richness and subtlety we associate with Tolstoy's greatest works, in which coherence is reconciled with abundance and variety. In *War and Peace* and *Anna Karenin*, the contrasted types of aspiration which I have schematically and simplistically analysed – the self-regarding and the self-transcending – are like magnetic poles, exercising a shaping or gathering influence over the material, and consequently over our responses to it, without absorbing every incident into a rigid structure. In the broad equatorial regions of these novels are countless details and episodes (the wolf-hunt in *War and Peace*, for example) to which we can respond freely (siding with the wolf or the hunters, or both) without feeling that the emotional coherence of the work is imperilled. Indeed a distinctive kind of 'realism' here generates a distinctive kind of response. The variability and surprisingness of the Tolstoyan world, to which an inhabitant of a variable and surprising primary world returns lively recognition, become themselves stimuli to desire: that Nikolai should survive and Petya be killed, that Koznyshev should not after all propose to Varenka, that Maria Bolkonsky should after all be happy, more or less, that Levin should hit one snipe and miss another, and his valet neglect to leave him a clean shirt for his wedding, induces a kind of aching gratitude which is the stirring of the appetite for life itself. In *The Death of Ivan Ilyich*, on the other hand, everything is assimilated to the poles; the internal opposition truly *is* schematic and simplistic. For once Tolstoy does provide a dogmatic and (in intention) didactic representation, of the sort that Lukács would have us 'learn from' once he has sorted out for us the truths it has to tell. Tolstoy still imitates the plausibility and consistency of reality, but what he no longer imitates is its contingency and unpredictability; for the reader a level of recognition, and hence a level of response, is lost. The palpable design of the story, its restriction to material with a strong and unequivocal emotional charge, works powerfully upon the mind and yet is liable to engender, in the reader fresh from the earlier novels, a qualifying dissatisfaction at the missing dimension. In approaching more closely to the puritanically-defined *desiderata* of Lukács, Tolstoy's fiction loses something of its distinctive mimetic richness, and in consequence something of its distinctive ability to enliven the sensibility, to revive our sense that life is for a thousand reasons worth living.

3

Objections from Moral Realism

I

In the last chapter I defended my central argument against objections arising from some types of historical realism. I turn now to the second group of objections posed at the end of Chapter 1, those which address themselves to the ethical implications of the argument, and to the question of the relationship between literary and moral evaluation in the process of criticism.

It is certainly possible to question the ethical status of literature conceived as a body of works which quicken and order desire. Neither the arousing of a desire in another person, nor the pursuit of such arousal oneself, is a self-evidently creditable act. Desire, as contrasted with judgement or knowledge, makes no necessary discrimination between the real and the illusory, the wise and the foolish; consequently the quickening of desire, as contrasted with the sharpening of judgement or the augmentation of knowledge, makes no evident contribution to a person's fitness in his dealings with the external world, only to his self-consciousness and his emotional energy. And the terms of my main thesis, it may be added, offer no assurance that even this contribution will be an ethically positive one; though the aesthetic structure is said to provide a 'paradigm of governance', it is not suggested that this represents a dampening down, or catharsis, of the aroused desire; on the contrary, it was insisted in the first chapter that the experience of a work leaves the reader with a residue of unrest, in the form of ungratified desire. 'The perceiver brings his own wishes and anxieties to the work (even if it is the work itself which draws them to the surface of his mind) and they are returned to him at the end whether he likes it or not, and whether the work in its own terms meets or denies them.'[1] It seems to follow from this that some literature must, by quickening selfish and anti-social desires, be definitely harmful in its tendency; and that literature as a whole cannot be the refining, educative, civilising influence it has sometimes been optimistically supposed to be, but must simply be a reflection, or an extension in the medium of language, of the confused plurality of wishes and preferences in human minds. And if we hold, with Plato, that the calming rather than the quickening of emotions is to be approved of, then imaginative literature must on balance be morally deleterious.

Inferences of this kind must dispose the most sympathetic reader to reject the view of literature I have put forward. But they are, I believe, erroneous inferences, in part: 'in part', because *any* claim of complete moral purity or innocuousness for literature is surely unsustainable. Certainly literature conceived as a stimulant acting upon the psyche cannot be exempt from the possibility of doing harm. But neither can literature conceived as polemic; nor even literature conceived as the transmission of knowledge. For who is to say that the possession of knowledge is always beneficial to the possessor, or to his fellow-men? It may fill him with anxiety, or even despair, and diminish his capacity for affection, or for work. Even if literature were conceived as the very opposite of psychically stimulating, as cathartic or anaesthetic, it would be open to the reproach that certain emotions (indignation against injustice, for example) ought *not* to be purged or deadened, ought rather to be encouraged to flow into action. All these reservations stem from the fact that literature is the property and tool of a morally fallible and inconsistent being, man, and partakes of his imperfections.

It remains true, however, that if literature quickens desire we cannot finally discount the possibility – though it is notoriously difficult to prove in any particular case – that a work may arouse a destructive wish that would otherwise have remained dormant, and that the reader may subsequently translate the wish into action. But several considerations militate against the appropriateness of holding the literary work fundamentally responsible if such a sequel does occur. Firstly, desire is no guarantee of action, even when we would like it to be – as, for instance, when we wish to complete a piece of work by a deadline. For desire to be translated into action, or an attempt at action, other mental faculties, powers of volition and decision, must be brought into play, and it is surely these faculties which are the proper object of moral judgement. The fact that I am prompted to desire strawberries (or rather, made more lucidly conscious of my existing though possibly dormant appetite for strawberries) does not mean that I will have the energy to go out and pick some, the extravagance to go out and buy some, or the unscrupulousness to go out and steal some. And if I do steal, the greater part of the responsibility lies with my unscrupulousness. It is true that I would not steal strawberries if I did not desire them; but virtue traditionally consists, after all, not in being free from temptations, still less in imagining that one is free from them, but in resisting them. If a literary work promotes my desires to commit a harmful act, and I actually commit it, it may be fair to direct some condemnation towards the work and (where he could reasonably be expected to have foreseen the consequences) its author; but before laying the weight of blame too heavily in that quarter, it should be admitted in the work's defence (a) that it could not (according to the hypothesis under discussion) promote a desire which was not already present in my psyche, and (b) that whatever influences may have been exerted it is in the last resort I myself – presumably a moral agent and not an automaton – who have actually willed and performed the act.[2] In any case, the passivity and repose usual in the act of reading are likely to work against the possibility of intemperate consequent action.

Secondly, one may become conscious of a desire and yet be perfectly aware of its badness and determined not to yield to it – as with the desire (quite common, I believe) to throw oneself off the roof of a tall building in order to find out what falling from a great height feels like. Here we have a possible course of action towards which both an attraction and an overriding repugnance are felt; and there are plenty of analogies in literature. An example with unimpeachable moral implications is the predicament endured by Godfrey Cass in *Silas Marner*: the sympathetic reader is both caught up in Godfrey's desperate hope that his secret marriage will not come to light and ruin his chances of a respectable union with Nancy Lammeter, and at the same time made to feel (partly by the juxtaposition of this theme with, on the one side, Marner's stolid endurance of cruel misfortune, and, on the other, Dunstan Cass's complete surrender to destructive selfishness) that such an evasion is intolerable as a foundation for subsequent happiness: a conflict of desires which generates a third desire – that the dilemma may be resolved in some humanly acceptable way – which is ultimately gratified within the novel. In this case, of course, a desire felt and repudiated is absorbed into a larger structure; the work itself supplies a counter-stimulus to the ethically suspect wish. It is a more difficult matter when the quickening effect of a work as a whole is under suspicion, for the same material may quicken a positive desire (of attraction) in one reader, and a negative desire (of revulsion) in another, or both, simultaneously or alternately, in the same reader – a point implicitly acknowledged by moralists who, while asserting that such-and-such a work is 'disgusting' or 'repulsive', nevertheless insist that it may entice readers into emulating its action. Probably many, or most, kinds of immoral act are, in fact, at once attractive and repugnant to most persons. From this variability or ambivalence of response springs the frequent difficulty in determining whether a work containing emotionally highly-charged material is salutary or corrupting in its effect, a difficulty exemplified in recent years in the discussion of a number of artistically ambitious films (*Straw Dogs, A Clockwork Orange, Apocalypse Now*) which include scenes of enthusiastic violence and destruction. Debates of this kind seem inherently irresolvable. The most morally-conceived material can be alchemised into corruption in the mind of the beholder: no doubt there are sadists who derive excitement from the blinding of Gloucester in *Lear*. Conversely, works written with the intention of arousing the least edifying of human instincts may actually, on occasion, repel, and indeed be defended with the spurious (but not all that easily refutable) argument that their purpose and effect is precisely to repel. The safest conclusion seems to be that literature does no harm without the co-operation of original sin; and that the arraignment of individual works is fraught with forensic difficulties.

Thirdly, the 'foregrounding' of desire, its propulsion into the limelight of self-consciousness, may, to put it modestly, do as much good as harm. *Know thyself* is a moral as well as an intellectual imperative, the more so since it has become generally accepted that wishes which remain unconscious can nevertheless exert an influence over our behaviour. Indeed literature may be very loosely and speculatively likened to psycho-analysis, which does not attempt to extirpate desires but to render them fully conscious and consequently less subversively harmful; to substitute, where necessary, a conscious condemning judgement on a futile or anti-social desire for an unconscious repression which may do little more than convert it into a different but equally disruptive symptom. That there is a psychologically therapeutic effect in the foregrounding of painful emotions through art seems to be borne out by the fact (I believe common experience will support this observation) that in depression or grief we tend to turn, not to art remote from our mood which might be supposed to counteract it, but to art close to it, which at once intensifies it (sometimes activating the relief-mechanism of tears) and confers upon it some temporary order and definition. In the same way, feelings of anger and resentment may well be less disruptive when they take the form of a fully conscious affect than when they lurk, inarticulate, below or partly below the level at which the will and intellect can supervise them.

Though these three points are intended to protect my hypothesis against the suspicion of immoralism, or covert disparagement of literature, or support for censorship,[3] they do not of course lead to the conclusion that all works of literature are morally neutral or of equal value, merely to a scepticism about confident assertions that specific works or types of work will tend to deprave and corrupt. Authorship remains a moral act like any other. Even if it could be proved that through some cathartic or compensatory effect the works of the Marquis de Sade were more beneficial in their influence than those of George Eliot, we should still wish to praise the latter for their appeal to altruism and honesty. And this brings me to a further possible objection against my hypothesis: that it fails to provide for any moral component in our evaluation of literature. For if the function of literature is to quicken desire, then a work which succeeds in quickening trifling, selfish or abominable desire has presumably fulfilled its function as well as any other.

It would be easy to dismiss this problem with the remark that a work which quickens lofty spiritual aspirations is, naturally, *ipso facto* superior to one which quickens base material appetites. But unless it can be shown that such superiority is manifested in a palpable difference of style, structure or some other specifically literary quality, this remains a purely moral judgement, analogous to the judgement that a surgeon's scalpel is a better thing than a soldier's bayonet, irrespective of craftsmanship. If we wish to express a relationship between moral and literary judgement, we have the options of saying, in the terms of this analogy, (i) that though a scalpel may be a better thing morally, a bayonet may sometimes be a finer work of craft, (ii) that, on the contrary, the only true or significant craft lies in the manufacture of implements of positive moral value, such as scalpels, or (iii) that the very process of making a scalpel always, or usually, or often, exacts a higher standard of craft than that of making a bayonet, so that moral and technical goodness can be allied. By the first version of the analogy, we maintain that literary and moral value are entirely distinct; by the second, that they are identical; and by the third, that there is a contingent association between them. My central argument, without further elaboration, would naturally be taken as implying the first; I turn, therefore, to the question of whether anything can be said for the second or third.

It is clear, I think, that there can be no *identity* between moral and literary evaluation, if only because the latter must attach some importance to efficacy of presentation. Even F. R. Leavis, who comes closer than almost any other critic to asserting the identity of the two values, concedes this much; writing (on the whole favourably) of L. H. Myers, he remarks, 'Myers hasn't the great novelist's technical interest in method and presentment; he slips very easily into using the novel as a *vehicle*. That is, we feel he is not primarily a novelist.'[4] This implies that the 'presentment' and the matter to be presented are distinguishable elements, and that the first as well as the second must be in good order if the novel is to be a successful work of art; so that a writer with whose attitude to life Leavis is in sympathy can still be found wanting by him as a novelist. (Leavis is less ready to admit that a writer with whose matter he has no particular sympathy can nevertheless excel in 'method and presentment', as his dismissal of *Tom Jones* – 'There can't be subtlety of organisation without richer matter to organise, and subtler interests, than Fielding has to offer'[5] – illustrates.) Common sense will support this degree of distinction. There is nothing on the face of it unreasonable or unhelpful in saying, for example, that *Rasselas* is a saner and wiser work than *Gulliver's Travels*, but that *Gulliver*, however cynical and obsessive, is funnier, livelier in narrative circumstantiality, and richer in speculative inventiveness and symbolism. This particular judgement may be disputed, but the type of judgement is surely legitimate. The question of which is ultimately 'better', like the question of whether a dull scalpel is better than a glittering bayonet, depends on the point of view from which they are considered; to adjudicate on it is less important than to enumerate and analyse the specific qualities which each possesses. If, on the other hand, we reject the separate evaluation of 'method and presentment', we are obliged to say that the best moralist is always the best writer; that, for example (assuming St Augustine to have had a moral insight at least equal to Dante's), if St Augustine had bothered to write a poem it would certainly have been as great as the *Divine Comedy*. This is a long way from common sense.

It seems impossible, then, to sustain a belief in the complete identity of literary and moral values. But if the two are not *identical*, may there not be a degree of *association* between them?

The most obvious, and on the surface attractive, answer to this question is that ethical goodness is simply one of the many qualities we value in literature. Just as we can praise a novel for being exciting or amusing, so (the argument would run) it comes equally naturally to praise it for its virtuous ethical tendency; we like to be amused, we like to be excited, and we also like to see good and evil justly represented, the former made desirable and the latter repugnant. As a general observation this is perhaps unobjectionable, but it is of little help in establishing a connection between literary and moral values which can be sustained in critical practice. For one thing, it leaves undetermined the relative importance of moral qualities in comparison with others. No-one, I suppose, will dispute the view that a morally perceptive and improving work is better, all other things being equal, than a morally imperceptive and corrupting one. But the problem of associating moral and literary evaluation in practice can hardly be said to have been solved unless we have provided a formula for assessing those hard cases in which, for example, a morally questionable tendency is arguably accompanied by high literary merits of a different kind.

A second difficulty arises from the variability of moral judgement. If moral values were a known and universally recognised commodity, it would be a simple enough matter to assess their presentation in a particular work, and to credit the work with whatever merit it could be held to derive therefrom; but in fact (needless to say) notions of virtue vary widely from reader to reader. (So, indeed, do notions of what is amusing or exciting, though on these lighter matters we are usually more ready to agree to differ.) For this reason, all attempts to validate an authoritative or systematic association between literary and moral goodness are likely to founder on the instability of both terms. The two kinds of value will not, as it were, stand still for long enough for us to align them; for if the literary value of an ethically contentious work is assumed for a moment to be agreed, then it will appear to one reader to be in direct proportion to its moral value, to another reader to be in inverse proportion, and to a third to bear no special relation to it at all; and a converse problem will arise if we take as our constant the *moral* value of a work whose *literary* merit is disputed. The only escape-route from this impasse (an escape-route which is almost invariably taken) is towards making one kind of value subordinate to the other, according to whether we are moralists or aesthetes; and to do this is to abdicate from the task of demonstrating an intrinsic association between them.

A still more serious objection to the simple inclusion of ethical goodness in a checklist of approvable literary qualities is that the analogy with other qualities (for example with humour and excitement) breaks down on a crucial point. To make a novel amusing or exciting requires certain compositional skills – verbal inventiveness and economy, convincing imitation of speech-mannerisms in dialogue, management of situation and suspense, and so forth – the functioning of which can to some extent be analysed critically, for the benefit, at any rate, of those readers who admit that the novel *is* amusing or exciting; here the relation between the affects and the techniques is clear, granted some initial consensus as to the existence of the former. It is much less clear that there is any analysable *technical* skill (as distinct from moral insight) required to give one's work a satisfactory moral burden. This seems to be a matter of choice rather than technique; one can *decide*, in a sense, to build in a moral implication, but one cannot (in the same sense) *decide* to be amusing. Amusement is an irrational, irreducible condition explicable only by the action of a complex stimulus, while moral approval is a rational state derived from pre-existent convictions and capable of being transferred from a concrete presentation to an abstract epitome. The moral attitudes embodied in *Pride and Prejudice* can be paraphrased in a few sentences – very imperfectly of course, but well enough to retain the assent of the approving reader; its humour, on the other hand, cannot in any sense be condensed from the full presentation of the novel without ceasing to be amusing. Two things, certainly, are missing from an abstracted moral 'argument': first, the authentication, the making self-consistent, of the invented world within which the moral values unfold; and second, the sequence of conceptions (of actions, characters, situations and objects) which engages the reader's sympathies for the moral *desideratum* (as distinct from the merely intellectual assent which can be secured by propositions and which hardly requires the conceptional complexities of fiction). Both these related processes are difficult and call for compositional skills; but neither has anything to do with the moral quality itself, since these technical difficulties would be exactly the same if it were proposed to invent a world for the purpose of immoral values, to engage sympathies in an immoral cause. Hence there can be no direct relation between the worth of a fiction and its exhibiting these skills.

It may be suggested, lastly, that the compositional skill peculiarly associated with moral worth is a mimetic skill, that of conforming one's picture to the moral complexity of reality. It is true that in a work which is otherwise closely mimetic of primary experience a jarring note may be struck, the reader's ease of recognition and response undermined, by an improbably simplified representation of a moral choice or dilemma – as is sometimes felt to happen in *Bleak House*, for example, where Jarndyce and his wealth perhaps play too often for conviction the part of a problem-shelving *deus ex machina*. But this, strictly speaking, is a failure not of ethical rightness but of plausibility in the presentation of psychology and situation, since the final moral value of a work clearly resides not in the *representation* of a morally problematical act or condition (which could be accomplished by an intellect highly perceptive but itself amoral) but in the implicit or explicit *judgement* upon it, or rather in the way in which the reader's sympathies are guided in relation to it; it would be quite possible to depict a moral crux with perfect mimetic conviction, and yet to promote the wrong response to it (as F. R. Leavis complains of James's *The Golden Bowl*).[6] Again, therefore, it is impossible to establish any logical relation between the quality of the literary skill and the quality of the moral import, unless we assert that the first is entirely dependent on the second, an option we have already rejected.

The ethical value of a work cannot, then, be shown to require any compositional skill strictly peculiar to itself; and therefore a direct association between the moral and the literary value of a work is out of the question. It might be tempting to rest my case at this point and to remark that, since the amorality of literary merit has been so clearly suggested the hypothesis that literature quickens desire can do little worse in driving out ethical considerations from the act of criticism. Nevertheless it goes against the grain to accept that the artistic superiority of (say) *Middlemarch* over

Fanny Hill must be argued exclusively according to the criteria of technical or compositional skill, range and resource, and that any mention of the former's moral superiority must as it were be tacked on afterwards, with apologies for including such an irrelevancy in a piece of literary criticism. It cannot, we are likely to feel, be utterly a coincidence, or a product of prejudice, that a high level of compositional skill should so often appear to coincide with a high level of moral sensitivity. And it is not in fact necessary to draw such a conclusion, and accept such a self-denying ordinance. There is, I suggest, a partial and indirect association between moral and compositional excellence; not an authoritative and systematic association, not an association so exact that in making a literary evaluation we can be assured that we are implicitly making as much moral judgement as needs to be made, but an association which justifies us in saying that the discrimination of the literary critic is in a general way a morally positive activity.

This association is grounded in the distinction between evoking (to put it crudely) simple and complex, long-term and short-term desires; desires which entail a shutting out of context and those which entail, and are defined by, an extended field of relations. (This schematic division is of course a mere expository convenience; it is really a matter of degree.) A distinction of this kind has already been hinted at above, in the reference to *Silas Marner*. The desire 'ultimately gratified within the novel' – that Godfrey Cass's predicament should be resolved without his being degraded by lifelong deception – is a product of two contradictory aversions: a shrinking from the exposure and ruination of a character presented as (in comparison with some others) generally sympathetic, and a rejection of that character's ignoble hope of escaping by dissimulation and good luck from a situation essentially of his own making. These aversions are called into being by the expository opening chapters and held in tension for a time in the reader's mind: compelled painfully to acknowledge each other's existence and to seek a compromise. In relation to them, the synthetic desire they generate is complex and they are simple: but they themselves might in turn be analysed as compounds of evoked preferences and sympathies; we would not, for instance, sympathise so readily with Godrey's marital ambitions (or at least not in quite the same way) if Nancy Lammeter were a less approvable object for them, or if Godfrey's domestic circumstances were less contrastedly wretched. The compositional dialectic which shapes the story – indeed the whole imagined world – to bring out these tensions and counter-tensions corresponds, not exactly to an extension of moral scope and subtlety (for we are encouraged to be concerned with the characters' happiness as well as the rightness of their conduct) but at all events to an extension in the field of desire, in time (from the short- to the long-term) and in complexity (from the isolated attraction towards or revulsion from a particular object or state, to the awareness of that attraction or revulsion as a force confirming or conflicting with other preferences in a complex conception of a desirable or repellent end). And this, considered generally, must tend to be a morally positive progression, since to be confined to instantaneous, self-sufficient attraction to or revulsion from a singly-considered entity is bound to be morally (and practically) disabling; however uncertain our subsequent ethical explorations may be, we cannot, indeed, be morally engaged at all until we transcend the infantile state of simply liking or disliking this or that now.

The point may be made more forcefully, perhaps, by looking at extreme cases. The sexual activity which pornography posits as the object of desire is characteristically confined to the transitory moment or occasion, freed as far as possible from subsequent, or extra-sexual implications. This is partly because the reader normally wishes to reach a peak of arousal fairly rapidly, without having to sit through a lot of tiresome scene-setting or character-development, and partly because the attendant minor (or major) desires which complicate and enrich the kind of erotic ambition dealt with by such as Tolstoy and Dickens – affection, attraction towards the strangeness of another personality and its appurtenances, appetite for shared non-sexual pleasures, ambition to raise a family, aspiration towards the marriage of true minds – inevitably introduce a sense of responsibility, and of an extended time-scale, which is inimical to the sensual abandonment on which the reader of pornography wishes to have his imagination concentrated. Consequently the kind of elaborately developed (and technically exacting) representation of sexual passion which we find in *Le Rouge et le Noir*, *Anna Karenin*, *A la recherche du temps perdu* or *Lolita*, and which brings out its interaction with other drives and preoccupations of the personality, is unnecessary and indeed counter-productive for the pornographer: complications and long perspectives are anaphrodisiac. Hence the tendency of pornographic books to fall into short anecdotal sections held together like beads by a vestigial thematic or narrative string;[7] to employ devices such as 'memoirs' (as in *Fanny Hill*) or 'confessions', which not only confer the immediacy of first-person narration but allow a more or less infinitely extensible series of episodes; and to be largely displaced (for who reads pornographic *books* nowadays?) by mass-circulation magazines whose verbal content comes in lengths which make no enormous demand on the reader's patience. This does not mean that it is easy to write pornography, but it does mean that there are compositional subtleties which it does not call into play and cannot, in fact, tolerate; and when we pronounce it an inferior *genre* we are, I suggest, noting both the absence of these subtleties, and a reason for their absence from which moral inferences can be drawn.

Conversely, the desires which are most expansive in time and complexity – to find a point of view from which life appears worthwhile, to live in harmony with a human community, to reconcile our passions with our affections and responsibilities, to re-discover the ground of a happiness we feel we have lost – cannot be evoked through literature without a certain controlled comprehensiveness of imagination, and a patient skill in the authentication of background and context. To feel the attraction of membership in a community, for instance, we must have a representation of a community set before us with sufficient plausibility, and sufficiently various appeal to the needs and incompletenesses which make us social animals, to compel recognition and response; and this imposes on the author a complex compositional task. Again, a great work may realise with exceptional imaginative lucidity the act or experience of a moment, precisely by preparing around it that context of causes, implications, ideas, memories and associations which defines its experiential quality: Proust, most obviously, specialises in rendering this play of ambient influences upon the experience of the present. Similarly, the essential difference – a difference which we recognise as both morally and artistically significant – between the acts of violence in Dostoevsky and the 'gratuitous' violence of, say, a Harold Robbins novel lies (as the well-worn adjective admirably suggests) in the latter's separation of the act from any context, save that of a plot whose sole function is to provide an occasion for the act. The murder in *The Brothers Karamazov*, by contrast, is not the climax to a loosely-connected series of 'sensational' incidents (another suggestive adjective), but the dramatic focal point of a nexus of aspirations, urges, fears and despondencies in which a variety of hypotheses as to what makes life worth living are imaginatively put to the test: a focal point which comes ultimately to seem almost unimportant, so thoroughly has the possibility of happiness or misery through events been displaced in our attention by the possibility of happiness or misery through ways of considering the world, the importance of the momentary act by the importance of the reflecting, connecting, interpreting spirit.

I conjecture, then, that there may often be a measure of correlation among the following: (i) the complexity or expansiveness of the desires engaged by a novel, (ii) the subtlety of its composition, and (iii) its moral value – (ii) and (iii) being both, and separately, consequent upon (i); so that in the case of some works we are justified in believing that our literary and our moral evaluation are more than accidentally allied. Naturally there are compositional skills quite unconnected with complexity of concern: no complication or expansion of sensibility, however amply embodied in the overall design, can save a work whose author writes incomprehensible prose, or cannot render clearly the individual details out of which the structure is built. Equally plainly, not all simple or short-term desires are morally questionable, nor all complex and long-term ones admirable. Yet it seems plausible, at any rate, that what we wish for here and now, with past and future and extended relations shut out from our awareness, may tend to be less admirable than what we wish for *sub specie mortis*, or with something of the variety and contingency of life before our minds. If this is false, as it may be – it is not really a question for literary critics – then we are driven back upon a complete separation of literary and moral judgement. And this is perhaps in any case the best policy for the practising critic, since if one thing does not *inevitably* follow from another (and here it is only a limited and contingent association that is suggested), it is more scrupulous, and more courteous to one's readers, to go to the trouble of establishing them separately.

II

To turn from critical theory to critical practice in this chapter is to confront formidable, or at least belligerent, antagonists, for the most influential tradition of moral realism in post-war English criticism is, of course, that sponsored by F. R. and Q. D. Leavis. In reading any criticism by the Leavises we must make a distinct effort to keep our nerve, and the essay I propose shortly to discuss in detail – Q. D. Leavis's on *Great Expectations* – is no exception to the rule. On the one hand, we must prepare ourselves for side-swipes at other critics (occasionally specified, but usually not), undergraduates of the present 'brutally callous generation', and misguided 'people' generally from which few readers can escape unintimidated; and for reductive passing dismissals of other writers ('Kafka, able only to describe and project in fiction his own neuroses'[8]), which are deplorable not so much because they insult the author – who after all is usually past caring – but because they insult the author's admirers, implying, without bothering to substantiate the point, that they are barking up a tree which is not only wrong but rotten. On the other hand, we are offered – though the essay in question is by no means the worst offender on this point in the Leavis canon[9] – adjectival assertions of merit which brook no qualification and yet seem often to lack clearly-focused meaning: 'infinitely suggestive and complex work of art', 'Shakespearean genius as a creator', 'wonderful plot', 'remarkable', 'accomplished'. The danger is that these incidentals will be so mesmerising to those who take them seriously, and so irritating to those who do not, that insufficient presence of mind will be retained to appraise fairly and watchfully the essential content of the criticism.

To some extent this intemperateness in both praise and condemnation is a besetting vice of literary criticism in general, avoidable only by exceptional self-restraint. Partly because of its chronic methodological uncertainties, its shortage of hard data of agreed interpretative and evaluative relevance, there is a vacuum at the heart of literary criticism into which animosities and ill-formulated enthusiasms which would be better reserved for private conversation are always liable to rush; they cannot be easily refuted, since in this discipline even more than in others the acceptable level of logical or empirical argument (even, indeed, the necessity of such argument) is imperfectly established, and if they answer to the impressions or prejudices of a sufficient number of readers they will get a hearing. There is plainly, however, a further and ideologically specialised motive at work in the case of the Leavises. One senses behind their polemical savagery the force of their conviction that the pursuit of literary discrimination is identical with the pursuit of moral wisdom, and that failure in the first pursuit is to be the more mercilessly condemned because it is failure in the second as well. Denying that George Eliot is exceptional among great novelists in being 'addicted to moral preoccupations', F. R. Leavis writes:

> Is there any great novelist whose preoccupation with 'form' is not a matter of his responsibility towards a rich human interest, or complexity of interests, profoundly realised? – a responsibility involving, of its very nature, imaginative sympathy, moral discrimination, and judgement of relative human value?[10]

And of Conrad he declares:

> He is a greater novelist than Flaubert because of the greater intensity of his moral preoccupation.... To appreciate Conrad's 'form' is to take stock of a process of relative valuation conducted by him in the face of life: what do men live by? what *can* men live by? – these are the questions that animate his theme.... The dramatic imagination at work is an intensely moral imagination, the vividness of which is inalienably a judging and a valuing.[11]

The prerequisites of the great novelist, in other words, are perception and rendition of (Leavis's 'interest in' presumably includes both these concepts) the true complexity of human life ('what do men live by?'), and a discriminating moral valuation of the possibilities within that complexity ('what *can* men live by?' – meaning, no doubt, live by above a merely selfish or animal level, just as the 'complexity of interests' in the preceding extract does not, we sense, including smoking, gambling and running after women). Hence the critics who misrepresent the value or purport of a work are not simply aestheticians in error, but the knowing or unknowing apologists for some false and deplorable set of values, some human untruth. Writing in her *Great Expectations* essay of American critics' objections to Pip's refusal of Magwitch's patronage, Mrs Leavis is capable of saying, 'Perhaps a Victorian gentleman's view of having such a patron attached to him as father and house-mate cannot really be understood nowadays, particularly in a country that has accepted violence as a way of life.'[12] This is only an especially startling expression of the Leavises' consistent implication that the works of the great novelists are a lifeline of moral health, in a culture thoroughly hostile to 'life', for which there is almost nothing to be said.

'How we must read *Great Expectations*'[13] is a complex appraisal, not to be easily summarised, which undoubtedly brings out much of the work's psychological subtlety. Yet from the title onwards Mrs Leavis's moral polemicism, her refusal to acknowledge directions in the movement of the novel which do not lead to 'a judging and a valuing' (in her husband's words), betrays her into obscurities and forced readings. In the essay itself she unquestionably sets out to describe the novel as it truly is, and would certainly not accept that a different account could be equally truthful to the text. The title, however, is *prescriptive*, implying that other readings are, as a matter of fact, possible, but that this one has a virtue such that we ought to accept the injunction to follow it alone. Thus the question of whether the literary-ethical rightness so uncompromisingly insisted upon lies entirely in the novel itself (to be extracted therefrom by anyone with a clear and thorough knowledge of the work), or to some extent in the prior qualifications (of knowledge, conviction, and judgement) which the reader ought to bring to the work, is blurred from the beginning. (This will be recognised as a version of a problem already discussed with reference to historical realism,[14] the fallacy of treating literary works as *sources* of enlightenment while reserving the right to apply to them prior convictions about what is and is not enlightening.) The obscurity is deepened by passages such as the following:

> Dickens sees people as at once the products and symptoms of their society and the producers of it. Similarly he shows his interest in ethical matters by exploring the behaviour of characters, chosen for the purpose, in such a way as to undercut the theory and extend our views by presenting situations in a new light, disturbing our preconceptions and prejudices. Where judgement on behaviour is in question Dickens puts before the reader facts that must be taken into consideration before forming such judgement, facts that would otherwise have lain outside our perceptions even.[15]

There is a three-way confusion here between what the novelist thinks, what he renders in his work, and what truly exists in the primary world. The first verb, 'sees', is a good example of Mrs Leavis's imprecision, hinting as it does at three meanings simultaneously: 'sees' in the strict sense of having a perception of some phenomenon, real or deceiving (as in 'I see that the weather is taking a turn for the better'); 'sees' in the sense of 'conceives, interprets' (as in 'I see inflation as essentially a political rather than an economic problem'); and 'sees' as a conventional synonym in reported discourse for 'describes, represents' (as in 'Gibbon sees barbarism and religion as principal causes of the decline of Rome'). The ambiguity serves to insinuate into the reader's mind the suggestion that what Dickens *represents* in his novel is in no way different from what he strictly *sees*, the actual human and social phenomena that strike upon his intellectual retina. (Indeed, the abuse of this one verb, so commonly used by teachers and students of literature, could stand as an epitome of the realist fallacy.) A still stranger choice of words comes in the next sentence. Clearly, characters in a novel are not (except in the most naive imaginable *roman à clef*) 'chosen', but invented. They may be invented in accordance with what the author believes to be reality, but that is a different matter. And an author might, I suppose, be thought to conceive of a number of characters and then 'choose' which should go into his final text, but there are no grounds for suspecting this here. This suggestion that characters are somehow pre-existent to the literary invention (a suggestion reinforced by 'exploring' in the same sentence) further blurs the distinction between fiction and reality, and is evidently designed to anaesthetise the reader against the absurdity of 'facts' in the final sentence: for while facts may with some propriety be *chosen* to demonstrate a point, even the most ardent Leavisite might be expected to cavil at the notion of a judgement supported by 'invented' facts. The passage might more neutrally and less ambiguously be rewritten thus:

> Dickens represents people as being at once the products and symptoms of their society and the producers of it. Similarly he shows his interest in ethical matters by inventing characters who behave in a way which undercuts theory, and situations which we cannot evaluate in the ways we are accustomed to. Where judgement on behaviour is in question Dickens tells us stories which must affect the way we make such judgements, stories which we would not otherwise have thought of even.

This revised formulation discloses the logical crack which the imprecisions of the original conceal. If a novel presents 'facts' about behaviour which 'must be taken into consideration before forming ... judgement', we are indeed receiving from it a kind of moral education which may be counted as a part, perhaps the essential part, of its literary value. But if it merely tells stories which may or may not correspond to any facts, then we are by no means obliged to accept any moral valuations contained in or implied by the work; far from receiving an education, we need to possess one already in order to know whether the characters and situations presented conform to any human reality. Plainly, stories can only affect our judgements (our rational judgements at any rate) in so far as we believe them to correspond to real states or events; and if we are in a position to know whether or not they do so correspond, we are capable of drawing conclusions from the real states and events – which seems to render the stories, for this purpose, superfluous. We assess the moral realism of a novel, in other words, by applying to it criteria externally derived; it cannot itself directly enhance our moral insight. In practice this is the principle on which the Leavises often appear to work; when Dr Leavis dismisses Sterne's work as 'irresponsible (and nasty) trifling',[16] there is no evidence that he is doing anything other than applying externally-derived moral criteria to the texts. The prescriptive title of Mrs Leavis's essay suggests too, as I have hinted, an awareness of the inevitability of imported criteria. But when , as in this essay, an admired work is undergoing exposition, a quite different principle comes into play, whereby the work is conceived as a self-sufficient, educative source of moral valuations which are inseparable from its innermost nature ('The dramatic imagination at work is an intensely moral imagination, the vividness of which is inalienably a judging and a valuing'); which validate, and are in turn validated by – are indeed the essence of – its literary merit. This means that there can be no significant error in interpreting the work which is not at the same time a turning away from the light of moral sensitivity, human value, life and growth; and conversely that there can be no extra-moral, no ethically uninstructive readings of an approved work (or the approved parts of a partially approved work) which are not perversions of its true meaning. To suggest that *Great Expectations* (for example) has significant qualities quite apart from the realisation of moral insights – to suggest that moral *desiderata*, in this as in most novels, are accompanied by, and do not wholly subsume, other *desiderata* to do with pleasure, success or happiness – is to suggest that it defects from the profound seriousness of art, and this (granted the novel's greatness) must be a misrepresentation. This attitude to Dickens's novel leads Mrs Leavis, as I shall now try to demonstrate, into a good deal of forced interpretation.

Essentially, as we would expect, Mrs Leavis takes the novel as a kind of *Bildungsroman*; she dissents perceptively and convincingly from the view which sees Pip's progress as a simple loop, into snobbery and out of it, and stresses the complication of moral guilt and social shame in Pip's feelings, his persistent misgivings and self-reproaches, and the ways in which his natural open-heartedness tempers his social defensiveness – as in his growing sympathy for the returned Magwitch, or in his feeling little objection to Joe's meeting Herbert or Matthew Pocket but 'the sharpest sensitiveness' to his being seen by the contemptuous and contemptible Drummle. No-one, to be sure, will deny that in *Great Expectations* Dickens is preoccupied with the 'growth of moral sensibility' in his principal character, and that this is perhaps the novel's central theme. But to satisfy herself of the consistent seriousness of Dickens's purpose, Mrs Leavis finds it necessary to maintain that the condition which Pip attains at the end of the novel, that of a morally chastened, sensitive and cultivated gentleman, is not only a good, but a normative and indeed, so far as the society depicted is concerned, exclusive good, in comparison to which other conditions are 'placed' as in some degree inferior and inadequate. And this entails showing not only that Pip is acting quite honourably when he finally chooses to separate himself from the world of forge and village, nor simply that he is compelled to do so because he has become remote from it in habits, tastes and education, but that he would be acting wrongly, in an absolute sense, if he were to return to that world, since it is inferior, in an absolute sense, to the one he now inhabits.

Dickens has made his point repeatedly, that he believes that education and the society of educated people with high standards of integrity like Matthew and Herbert Pocket, represent, other things being equal, a more desirable social habitat than a village–market-town society of Gargerys, Wopsles, Trabbs, Pumblechooks, Hubbles and Orlicks. Dickens has intimated that there are real distinctions to be made, based not

on money or birth but on cultivation and intelligence and talent.
Joe is described by Pip as 'this gentle Christian man', which is
neither a gentleman nor even a wholly satisfactory practical
character; it seems to represent an uneasy gesture of the
novelist's towards making a special status for Joe, to get over the
difficulty Joe now presents in having outgrown the original role
of a 'good-natured foolish man'.[17]

Mrs Leavis loads the dice here by picking out, as if typical of their
'social habitat', the two most ethically admirable members of the
educated metropolitan society Pip is raised to, and setting against
them a list in which Joe and Biddy (the most ethically admirable
members of their society) are almost lost amid their grotesque
neighbours. The 'high standards of integrity' of the Compeysons,
Drummles, Jaggerses, Sarah Pockets and Havisham relations do
not spring quite so readily to mind as proofs of the superior virtues
of education and gentility; yet these, as much as the Pockets father
and son, comprise the 'social habitat' to which the village–market-
town society of Pip's infancy can properly be contrasted. It is true,
as Mrs Leavis suggests, that Joe Gargery lacks qualities which are
possessed by, say, Herbert Pocket; but they are qualities of
subtlety and practicality the absence of which is felt only outside
his accustomed field of action; the question of whether that field is
inferior to Herbert's remains undecided. Herbert, conversely,
lacks not only Joe's talent for hammering iron but his imperturb-
able saintliness – we feel that he could perform a misguided,
though not a mean, action occasionally, whereas Joe, as Pip says, 'is
always right'.[18] Mrs Leavis points out that after pronouncing the
dictum 'lies is lies', Joe does in fact lie to Mrs Joe, conveying
flattering compliments from Miss Havisham which were never
spoken; and she goes on:

> Dickens really needs to make no comment on the inadequacy of
> simple-minded people thereafter. He has deliberately made his
> point thus, and it is unmistakable; yet it seems not to have been
> taken by readers, another instance of the unintelligent reading
> he habitually receives.[19]

But Joe's harmless, almost playful deception does not really
undermine either the justice or the sincerity of his general advice
to Pip. Pip's lies about the wonders of Satis House are told

through a mixture of childish confusion and egotism; Joe's are told to make up the deficiencies of Miss Havisham's courtesy, and to soothe Mrs Joe's irritability and social inferiority feelings – one can imagine Herbert Pocket behaving with similar good breeding. (Indeed Joe's lapse from truthfulness is by most standards less grave than the equivocations and illegalities practised by Pip, Herbert, Wemmick and Jaggers for the protection of Magwitch: in both cases the altruistic purpose redeems the act, and we do not feel that the character's honesty is fundamentally vitiated.) Joe's goodness consists in any case not in adhering precisely to the letter of the moral law, but in his essential incorruptibility (evidenced, for example, in his refusal of compensation for Pip's departure from the forge), and in his unremembered acts of kindness and of love (as when he forgives the convict – 'poor miserable fellow creature'[20] – for stealing his file and victuals). If readers 'habitually' acquire the impression that Joe has as good a claim as any character to stand for an ethical ideal, it is perhaps not because they are unintelligent but because they read the novel without a predetermining wish to find support for the belief (possibly correct, but that is not the point) that lack of education must tend to imply deficiency in a person. Mrs Leavis herself does not seem quite sure whether Dickens, or the novel, is on her side. Does the 'uneasy gesture' towards the elevation of Joe count as part of the novel, or not? Is the 'difficulty' presented by Joe's allegedly 'having outgrown [his] original role' a difficulty for the cohesion or comprehensibility of the work, or a difficulty for Mrs Leavis's diminishing view of the character? (Joe is introduced as 'a mild, good-natured, sweet-tempered, easy-going, foolish, dear fellow – a sort of Hercules in strength, and also in weakness';[21] and it does not seem implausible to represent such a person as behaving, subsequently, with exemplary decency in moral crises, particularly if we reflect that the word 'foolish' can conventionally suggest 'innocent, free from corruptive sophistication' as well as merely 'stupid'). Similar uncertainties are raised by another passage in Mrs Leavis's essay, in which she argues the radical unsuitability of Biddy as a wife for Pip.

As soon as Pip began to educate himself by systematic study she lost contact with him, and once he returns from London makes this clear by calling him 'Mr.'; her letter, sent to inform Pip of

Joe's impending visit, nicely defines the degree of her literacy and her difficulty of communicating with Pip on all grounds. George Eliot, whose authority cannot be questioned here, shows a village schoolmaster of great natural intelligence and superior abilities, Bartle Massey, who is yet highly respectful to the excellent Rector and never expects to be treated as an equal socially. Bartle, like Dinah the Methodist preacher in the same novel, speaks in the dialect, and so would Biddy have been tied to the Gargery kind of idiom if Dickens had not falsified her in this respect, thus obscuring another difference from Pip – the outward sign of a real cultural difference and a limitation of interests, experience and knowledge. Dickens cheats over her ability in these circumstances to deflate Pip by having Joe explain that she is exceptionally quick, but she is still not plausible in her role. A coarser style of repartee would have carried more conviction in her case (as it does in Susan Nipper's), but then Pip's idea of going back to marry her would have been more obviously impracticable. Dickens avoids idealizing Biddy and so should the modern critic.[22]

But Dickens, according to Mrs Leavis's own argument, *does* idealise Biddy in some ways, falsifying her (where 'her' presumably refers to one of those pre-existent real personalities that novelists are required, according to the realist fallacy, to inform us about) by cheating over her cultivation and articulateness; so perhaps the modern critic should follow Dickens on this point, or at least refrain from citing what may be accurate historical information as if it were material to the meaning of a work which does not acknowledge it. The passage is further confused in that it fails to distinguish clearly between a class impossibility of marriage with Biddy (which is what the analogy with Bartle Massey – 'great natural intelligence ... superior abilities ... never expects to be treated as an equal socially' suggests); an impossibility owing to disparity of intellectual level – notice, here, how Mrs Leavis's shift from 'dialect' to (Gargery) 'idiom' covertly disengages from the Bartle Massey analogy which would now be inconvenient; and a moral impossibility owing to Biddy's belonging to a social habitat less desirable than Pip's – which is what Mrs Leavis must establish if she is to show that remaining in the world of gentlemen is not merely a choice or a practical necessity for Pip but a moral

imperative derived from the 'inadequacy of simple-minded people'. Energetically arguing for the first two, Mrs Leavis says
nothing to convince us of the third. We are well aware that Joe and
Biddy are socially 'lower' than Pip now is, and much less educated,
so that he would probably be unhappy living in their world; the
whole point of the issue, however, is whether or not these limiting
characteristics are represented as precluding a life which can be as
highly valued as any other. And surely the final effect of the novel
is as much one of Pip's being disqualified from the peculiar virtues
and rewards of Joe's and Biddy's existence as of their being
disqualified from the virtues and rewards of his; Pip significantly
remarks that 'it would be natural' for their child to grow up a much
better man than he himself did[23] – a valuation which tends, if
anything, to reverse Mrs Leavis's. Pip cannot marry Biddy, not
because she represents something inferior to the condition he has
attained – on the contrary, the slightly artificial prepared speech of
repentance he never manages to deliver ('I would show her how
humbled and repentant I came back . . . I would remind her of our
old confidence in my first unhappy time . . .')[24] puts him again
briefly in the embarrassingly self-dramatising and presumptuous
role which demonstrates her relative maturity and tact – but
because, with a sense of congruity more sober than his, she has
already opted for a more suitable partner.

Another obligation imposed upon Mrs Leavis by her fastidiously
ethical conception of artistic seriousness is to show that Dickens
makes no concessions to extra-moral concerns, to sentiment or the
desire for a happy ending – allows no wish-fulfilments which are
not rigorously justifiable in terms of the total moral import. This
second necessity meets an obvious obstacle in the revised and now
generally accepted ending to the novel, in which Pip chances to
meet Estella (hitherto uniformly cold and unyielding) amid the
ruin of Satis House, and they go off together hand in hand. This is
so plainly the 'if only' of heart's desire rather than the stern 'this is
so' of moral realism (it is carefully made clear that neither Estella
nor Pip has been there during the latter's eleven years of working
in Cairo, so that the accident of their meeting takes on the quality
almost of a miraculous grace) that one might expect Mrs Leavis to
choose the option of upholding the original version, in which Pip is
finally able (in her phrase) 'to relegate the Estella who showed such
odious characteristics'[25] to the past. Instead, she attempts a
resourceful defence of the revision.

Dickens's second thoughts produced the right, because the logical, solution to the problem of how to end without a sentimental 'happy ending' but with a satisfactory winding-up of the themes .... What is essential is that Estella should be stripped of the attributes which made her both desired by Pip and out of his reach ....

We are not surprised to find Estella [at Satis House] too; it seems inevitable, as she belongs to the place in his memory. That Pip should marry Estella without the jewels that had enhanced her beauty for him (that is stripped of her pride, social superiority, aristocratic grace, youth and fortune, and also of the illusions Pip had had, lost when he heard of her parentage) shows him to have recovered from the spell Satis House had cast over him. Estella is now saddened, a poor widow, has passed through Drummle's distasteful hands, and has nothing left but the site of Satis House. The old Pip would have shuddered away from her, and he says she is almost unrecognisable. But for the first time she is not walking away from him – he notes 'She let me come up with her'. She has gone through a process comparable with Pip's self-knowledge and humiliation so that they can truly come together at last. Her appeal for Pip now is that they have this experience in common, as they have had a common past history, both having been made use of and having much to regret.[26]

This amounts to saying that Pip is united with Estella because she has ceased to be what he originally desired. It is true and obvious that Estella could not accept him without being driven to abandon her aloof attitude, which has played some part in exacerbating his passion. But Mrs Leavis implies, further, that there is virtually no continuity between the present Pip's desire for the present Estella, and the past Pip's desire for the past Estella – indeed that the former depends upon the expiration of the latter. 'The old Pip would have shuddered away from her,' we are told, 'and he says she is almost unrecognisable.' But there is no textual evidence for the first part of the sentence – a puzzling hyperbole at best, serving to gloss over the simple continuity of sexual attraction; and as for the second, it is Estella who claims to be unrecognisable and Pip who on the whole mentally dissents. They do not recognise each other at once, but this is explained by the twilight and the mist, and is clearly in part contrived for the sake of a moment of poignant suspense.

> A cold silvery mist had veiled the afternoon, and the moon was not yet up to scatter it. But, the stars were shining beyond the mist, and the moon was coming, and the evening was not dark. I could trace out where every part of the house had been, and where the gates, and where the casks. I had done so, and was looking along the desolate garden-walk, when I beheld a solitary figure in it.
>
> The figure showed itself aware of me, as I advanced. It had been moving towards me, but it stood still. As I drew nearer, I saw it had the figure of a woman. As I drew nearer yet, it was about to turn away, when it stopped, and let me come up with it. Then, it faltered as if much surprised, and uttered my name, and I cried out:
>
> 'Estella!'
>
> 'I am greatly changed. I wonder you know me.'
>
> The freshness of her beauty was indeed gone, but its indescribable majesty and its indescribable charm remained. Those attractions in it, I had seen before; what I had never seen before, was the saddened softened light in the once proud eyes; what I had never seen before, was the friendly touch of the once insensible hand.[27]

The emphasis, here and throughout the rest of the chapter, is rather on what has been added to Estella than on what had been subtracted. She is now sadder and wiser enough to express in open affection what she could previously only express in the 'sudden checks' of tone[28] which betrayed a suppressed pity for him. Far from separating this meeting with Estella from the longings of his past, Pip goes out of his way to associate the two:

> 'You have always held your place in my heart .... To me, the remembrance of our last parting has ever been mournful and painful.'[29]

Besides, unless we assume some novelistic sleight-of-hand whereby a discontinuity in Pip's feelings nevertheless permits a continuity in the reader's, Mrs Leavis's view, I venture to suggest, contradicts the reader's experience. What reader who responds at all to the union in the last chapter does not find it to be the resolution of a tension which has been developed throughout the novel? It is the climax to a long history of frustration, contradicting the painful quality of all that has gone before and paradoxically deriving its force of completeness precisely from this contradiction, which brings the frustration to an end. We are glad that Pip gets Estella because we have been sympathetically engaged throughout by his aspirations towards her – not, surely, because we have felt those aspirations to be entirely regrettable and misguided, and are now relieved that a reformed Pip will marry a reformed Estella on the strength of common experiences and compatibility of temperament.

Mrs Leavis cites Pip's repeated defeats by Estella at 'Beggar my neighbour' as symbolic of the inevitable fruitlessness of his attachment to her (though it is only fruitless in an ultimate sense, of course, if we suppose that it is not this attachment that the ending gratifies).

> The situation between them could not have been exemplified more concisely and yet naturally. The relation is re-enacted to enforce the conclusion, which we have no excuse therefore for not arriving at, that there can be no profit for Pip in his adoration for Estella and that we are not to expect a love-interest in this novel (a remarkable sacrifice for a novelist and a risk for one writing for a Victorian public). It is a guarantee that Dickens has a serious object more consistently in view than anywhere else but in *Hard Times*.[30]

The *non sequitur* here is glaring. An adoration in which there can be no profit does not preclude a love-interest. On the contrary, the tendency of an infatuation to be intensified by the inaccessibility of the object, and to manifest itself in a self-fulfilling conviction of weakness and unworthiness, is common, almost usual, particularly among children and adolescents;[31] and respectable Victorian readers, accustomed to pre-marital chastity, and fresh from *Jane Eyre* and *Villette*, might be thought especially likely to recognise it. Mrs Leavis suggests that 'Satis House and its inmates' provided Pip with imaginative stimulus, an alternative to the dull life of the forge and the village, and that Estella's attraction lies in her symbolising this imaginative enrichment.

He doesn't love *her*, she is unlovable and unloving, he only loves what she represents for him.[32]

But – passing over the point that Pip shows great imaginative vitality long before visiting Satis House (see the first page)– it is, again, commonplace in early sexual experience for the beloved to become associated with a sense of heightened communion with the ambient world.[33] That Pip's feelings are sexual is borne out by the repeated references to Estella's beauty: he does not fall in love with Miss Havisham, or any other inmate of Satis House. Mrs Leavis's irrefutable-sounding formula plays with the imprecisions of the word 'love': to say that one cannot 'love' an 'unlovable' person is verbally symmetrical but in its readily-understood meaning absurd.

Perhaps the most extraordinary passage of all in Mrs Leavis's essay is her treatment of Pip's outburst at the news of Estella's betrothal to Drummle.

> The rhetorical outpouring is generally held against Dickens as though he endorsed it, whereas in fact it is in keeping with his keen exposure of Pip's case: Estella embodies Pip's aspirations ('You are part of my existence, part of myself', etc.) and it is made clear that he is not so much wretched at losing her (he never expected to win her) as humiliated that she should degrade his dream by marrying a stupid brute like Drummle. [The speech seems to me to be reminiscent of Catherine's similar rhetorical speech about her feelings for Heathcliff in *Wuthering Heights* ('I am Heathcliff. If all else perished and he remained', etc.) and if so shows Dickens's intelligent use of a passage that had lodged in his memory once]. Pip in fact makes the suitable comment on his speech himself: 'The rhapsody welled up within me like blood from an inward wound, and gushed out', he says. The idealization has been exposed as an illusion even to Pip's reluctant mind.[34]

Here is the speech, and the following paragraph.

> 'You are part of my existence, part of myself. You have been in every line I have ever read, since I first came here, the rough common boy whose poor heart you wounded even then. You have been in every prospect I have ever seen since – on the river, on the sails of the ships, on the marshes, in the clouds, in

the light, in the darkness, in the wind, in the wood, in the sea, in the streets. You have been the embodiment of every graceful fancy that my mind has ever become acquainted with. The stones of which the strongest London buildings are made, are not more real, or more impossible to be displaced by your hands, than your presence and influence have been to me, there and everywhere, and will be. Estella, to the last hour of my life, you cannot choose but to remain part of my character, part of the little good in me, part of the evil. But, in this separation I associate you only with the good, and I will faithfully hold you to that always, for you must have done me far more good than harm, let me feel now what sharp distress I may. O God bless you, God forgive you!'

In what ecstasy of unhappiness I got these broken words out of myself, I don't know. The rhapsody welled up within me, like blood from an inward wound, and gushed out. I held her hand to my lips some lingering moments, and so I left her. But ever afterwards, I remembered – and soon afterwards with stronger reason – that while Estella looked at me merely with incredulous wonder, the spectral figure of Miss Havisham, her hand still covering her heart, seemed all resolved into a ghastly stare of pity and remorse.[35]

Note that Miss Havisham is impressed by the 'rhetorical outpouring' even if Mrs Leavis is not. Note, too, that there is no reference to Drummle in this speech. It is true that a page earlier Pip expresses great distress at the betrothal, which is hardly surprising since he has just been told of it; and it is both natural and conventional in these circumstances that the last appeal should be directed towards the question of the beloved's future happiness rather than one's own. 'Put me aside for ever – you have done so, I well know – but bestow yourself on some worthier person than Drummle .... There may be one who loves you even as dearly, though he has not loved you as long, as I. Take him, and I can bear it better, for your sake!'[36] Nothing in this calls into question the intensity of his wretchedness at losing her. The sequence of Pip's wishes is quite straightforward: having, since his last meeting with Estella, been robbed by Magwitch's revelations of any serious hope of winning her, he stakes everything instead on the attempt to divert her from Drummle (marriage with whom must entail more material evils than the degradation of Pip's dream). Mrs

Leavis obscures this sequence by saying in plain contradiction of
the plot and the very text of two pages earlier ('My long mistake
... induced me to hope that Miss Havisham meant us for one
another'[37]) that Pip has never expected to win her.

As for Pip's 'suitable comment' on the speech, it does not seem
to me to prove, or even suggest, what Mrs Leavis infers from it. A
haemmorrhage is not, after all, considered and meretricious, like
rhetoric, but spontaneous and distressing, like sincerity; and the
tendency of this image to validate, rather than undermine, the
sentiments of the speech is reinforced by the preceding sentence
(where 'ecstasy', of course, suggests not pleasure but, derivational-
ly, loss of self-control) and by the echoing of the 'wound' image
from the speech ('poor heart you wounded ... blood from an
inward wound'). The analogy with *Wuthering Heights* proves
nothing, unless we first accept that Catherine's speech is itself
rhetorical, unendorsed by the author in the sense of being 'placed'
as the expression of an illusory idealisation – a point which would
require to be argued at some length; and then only if we are
convinced that Dickens understood and emulated this irony. As a
matter of fact, Pip's speech *is* rhetorical, or over-composed – the
kind of thing that might be *written* in a moment of passionate
inspiration, but hardly *spoken* on the spot – but in this it resembles
many speeches in Dickens which are undoubtedly meant to be
taken seriously.[38] Pip's ransacking of his experiences ('the
marshes ... the streets ... the strongest London buildings') for
expression of his fixation, and the self-perception in 'part of the
little good in me, part of the evil', suggests an attempt to portray
genuine feelings – these are not *merely* stock phrases, but have
some grounding in the story; but we may feel in reality the list
could hardly be so exhaustive, or the reasoning so balanced, or the
cadences so stately: the inversion and blank-verse rhythm near the
end ('let me feel now what sharp distress I may') are particularly
unconvincing. The falsity of the speech lies in its being, from every
point of view except that of plausibility on its immediate occasion,
too poetically effective; the falsity is not that of blurred reasoning
or inapposite images which arises when (knowingly or self-
deceivingly) we try to express one kind of feeling while actually
experiencing another. The lapse is a technical one on the part of
Dickens, a failure of mimesis, which might almost be passed over
by a reader sufficiently engaged, imaginatively and emotionally,
by this crisis in the 'love-interest', the existence of which Mrs

Leavis denies. In defending Dickens against the charge of maintaining a slightly sentimental love theme alongside his keen interest in the representation of a developing moral sensibility – a charge so little damaging to the enjoyment and admiration of most readers, and so fatal to the astringent pedagogic Dickens required by the exclusivity of her moral realism – Mrs Leavis strains the meaning of the text, and narrows the amplitude and variety of the tale as cruelly as any unsophisticated reader seeking only entertainment.

4

Objections Concerning Language

The third principal group of objections to the main thesis are concerned with the proposition, or indisputable fact, that 'novels are primarily *verbal* creations' – to quote the blurb of a book by Roger Fowler to which I shall shortly devote some attention.[1] The idea I have been proposing – that the essential characteristics of the experience of reading fiction are the quickening of desire and the establishment, by virtue of the structuring to which the material of the work has been subjected, of a sense of psychological mastery over it – is evidently at least plausible, and I have tried to show that it is defensible, if we confine our attention to 'gross and overall effects' such as plot and character. We do indeed find ourselves taking an interest in the events and personalities of a novel which it is natural to describe in terms of wishes – of 'kinetic' emotions as Stephen Dedalus might call them. We respond with attraction and aspiration to the career of David Copperfield, with aversion and anxiety to that of Uriah Heep. When we turn, however, to the level of what is sometimes called 'style', the argument becomes more problematical. In Chapter 1 it was suggested that the smallest units of language, whether by engendering conceptions of objects, actions, states or qualities (as do nouns and verbs), or by creating expectations of such conceptions (as do articles, conjunctions, and certain other lexical items) initiate the 'kinetic' process, the quickening of desire being founded upon the insufficiency of the conception by comparison with the thing conceived – that is, upon the very nature of language itself.[2] The difference between the small-scale and large-scale levels of conception is, on this view, simply one of amplitude and complexity. But, as we shall see, there are contrary views, which would by no means accept this way of regarding the language of fiction. One view, drawing on some techniques of contemporary linguistics, and at the same time reviving a traditional critical distinction, allocates to 'style' a role different in kind, not merely in degree, from that of plot, character, and other 'overall effects'. Another view, while repudiating the traditional notion of 'style', insists on the priority of language as the origin and medium of literature, and draws certain methodological conclusions from that priority. These arguments will be discussed separately in due course, but for the moment they may be consolidated into a single methodological objection to any critical theory which gives prominence to the consideration of affect, as mine may be supposed to do. This is that critical activity should attend first to causes rather than to effects: to the visible material of language – initially at the most detailed level – rather than to the imaginative content it creates, let alone to the affects which the content may be supposed to create.

One way of attempting to answer this objection would be to argue that style, or more broadly the detailed deployment of language in a work, is essentially a means to an end – namely the imaginative substance or content, which is commonly described in such terms as 'plot', 'character', and 'theme'. In support of this view it might be pointed out that very few – if any – stylistic features can be acquitted of making some contribution to imaginative content. The rarity of complete synonyms, for example – or at least the difficulty of establishing beyond dispute that two words are completely synonymous – is notorious. If an author opts for the word 'peril' rather than 'danger', we can only designate this as a purely stylistic choice, and our response to it as a response exclusively to style, if we can be sure that there is not a subtlety of meaning or suggestion involved ('peril', perhaps, implying a slightly greater urgency than 'danger', or helping to sustain an archaic/Gothic/romantic setting and atmosphere). Moreover, since reading a novel is an experience in time, never reducible, even when we know a work intimately, to a single simultaneous apprehension, every decision about the *order* in which the components of a sentence, a paragraph, a chapter, a novel shall appear must be considered as affecting, however minimally, the total apprehended imaginative conception. When everything which engenders or contributes to an imaginative conception is subtracted from a unit of language, nothing in practice is left but its sounds and its visual appearance as an arrangement of symbols on the page – if even these can indisputably be declared imaginatively inert; and these sensory qualities are not what one normally understands by an author's 'style' or his 'use of language'.

If, then, stylistic choices can normally be accounted for as being instrumental to imaginative content, and if the pleasure or interest we derive from an author's use of language resolves itself into pleasure or interest in the conceptions engendered thereby, it could reasonably be argued that critical analysis should begin with the 'ends' (the engendered conceptions, or content), since only when these have been stated can a function be assigned to the 'means' (the deployment of language). But in the course of the argument this distinction between 'ends' and 'means' has lost all practical value. For if, as I have argued, the smallest linguistic unit contributes to content, then the 'ends' begin at the lowest level of detail anyway – these lower-level 'ends' becoming the 'means' towards higher-level 'ends'. And if we consequently insist upon attending in the first instance to the highest-level 'ends', then the distinction again appears suspect, and our procedure begins to offend common sense. If the highest-level 'end' of Homer's *Odyssey* is 'the story about Odysseus's eventful return journey to Ithaca', it scarcely justifies critical scrutiny, since it is also the 'end' of a hundred children's books adapted from Homer; one might even suggest that this broad conception is in Homer rather a 'means' towards the 'end' of poetic treatment, a string for the beads of eloquence and invention. Yet if, on the other hand, we wish to say that the highest-level 'end' of the *Odyssey* is not the story but a profound imaginative vision of life, we are compelled to return to the lower levels of conception in order to build up a description of what that imaginative vision is.

The conclusion to which we are being impelled is that in reading a work of fiction we encounter many interacting levels of conception, all of which, immediately or ultimately, arise from the action of language upon our minds. One conception, for example, might be designated 'the personality of Leopold Bloom'; another, 'Leopold Bloom's discovery that he has locked himself out of 7 Eccles St'. The latter can be traced to a single sentence, the former to perhaps half the entire text of *Ulysses*. Conceptions at all levels modify and enrich one another, generating super-conceptions such as the one which might be designated 'the unsurprisingness, in view of his already apprehended personality, of a certain error on the part of Leopold Bloom and his subsequent non-violent and comparatively short-lived vexation'. Since conceptions are interdependent, and potentially interact in all directions – it is far from being the case simply that the lesser generate the greater, or the earlier the later – no level or type of conception is in principle prior to, or more deserving of critical attention than, any other. (Not that I am offering this talk of 'levels of conception' and 'super-conceptions' as a model for critical analysis – it is simply an attempt to articulate in a philosophically acceptable way the constructive complexity of the reading experience, which is misrepresented by simple models opposing 'means' to 'ends', style to content, language to plot.) If this picture of the functioning of a work of fiction is correct, then my main thesis faces no particular difficulty, since conceptions at all levels, the smallest-scale as well as the largest-scale, can be conceived as quickening desire in conformity with the argument advanced in Chapter 1. There is no obligation to attend first to the small-scale conceptions, since these are not logically prior to the large-scale ones; and if it is true that they arise out of 'language', that is also true of the large-scale conceptions.

I now propose to test and certify the argument of the present chapter by confronting it with two arguments which both, though on rather different grounds, maintain the central importance of the analysis of language in the criticism of fiction. One is taken from Roger Fowler's *Linguistics and the Novel*, already mentioned; the other from David Lodge's *Language of Fiction*.[3]

II

Linguistics and the Novel uses the postulate of transformational grammar – roughly, that the 'surface' structure of a sentence represents a special formulation, or 'transformation', of an underlying 'deep' structure of meaning which might have been formulated in different ways – to support a revalidation of the concept of 'style'.

In terms of the linguistic theory employed here, features of tone and style are controlled by the relationship between the surface structure and the deep structure of sentences. I think it will be realised that the distinction between these two levels of structure is a version of the established belief that in linguistic communication there are available 'different ways' (surface structures) 'of saying the same thing' (deep structure). This thesis is basic to traditional stylistics as well as to contemporary linguistics.[4]

To illustrate the difference between deep structure and surface structure, Fowler offers the following example:

John broke the window.
The window was broken by John.

These two sentences have the same deep structure (action, agent, object) corresponding to the cognitive content they share; but their surface structures, which have nothing to do with cognitive content, differ. Fowler goes on as follows:

> To say that surface structure features have no semantic function by no means entails that they have no communicative function whatsoever; on the contrary they are of great significance in stylistic and rhetorical analysis, as we shall see. It is precisely a writer's choice of surface structures from among possible alternatives for expressing his intended deep structures which governs the 'connotations' or 'reverberations' which the experienced reader discerns in a literary text.[5]

In other words, a clear distinction can be drawn between *meaning*, in the sense of cognitive content, and *style*, which imparts attitudes or perspective towards the cognitive context. Fowler later elaborates this point, with a further example.

> Language is a powerfully committing medium to work in. It does not allow us to 'say something' without conveying an attitude to that something. . . .
> First, as a result of the perspective effect of transformations mentioned above, language inevitably slants the presentation of 'content'. Our sentences chop up the events and processes and people we refer to, analyse them according to certain models of how the world works which our culture, and our biologically given mental structure, make available to us. If I say 'William got himself mugged', I signal an entirely different view of human responsibility from the view that is coded in 'William was mugged': in the former, I regard William as responsible for his own misfortune. The choice between these two close

alternatives may be made below the level of consciousness; my sentence-structure betrays a value-judgement of which I may be unaware, but which is available to anyone else who reads or hears the sentence: available either by analysis or subliminally, as an effect of 'tone'.[6]

Now I would not dream of disputing (and I am not competent to dispute) the value of transformational grammar in illuminating the nature of languages and the relationship between language and thought. But I submit that the inferences concerning literary experience that Fowler draws from it are unfounded.

The argument we must conduct here is a rather complex one. Let us look first at the two 'John' sentences. It is easy to say that they 'mean the same', and express this meaning 'in different ways'. But what do we understand, or what *could* we understand, by 'meaning'? Three considerations, I suggest, could be drawn upon:

(1) the fact to which both sentences refer;
(2) the constituents of deep structure: action (breaking), agent (John), object (window);
(3) the mental representation produced by the sentence.

It will perhaps be contended that (1) has nothing to do with meaning. But before accepting this contention we should ask ourselves very carefully whether our conviction that the two sentences *must* 'mean the same' is not derived from the reflection that they designate the same – and, therefore, a single – fact. Each sentence is then conceived as a kind of flag stuck in the same little morsel of fact: one flag may be red and the other blue (and this represents style, or surface structure), but both are unquestionably stuck in the same spot (and this represents content). Here we do indeed have a clear distinction between a thing and the way it is presented – a distinction which could assume considerable interest in the case of two sentences describing, say, a composition by Stockhausen or the death of a hunger striker. But this distinction is meaningless in the case of fiction, since sentences in fiction do not designate facts, and therefore two sentences cannot be different ways of designating the same facts. All that corresponds to a sentence in fiction is the conceptions to which it gives rise. Thus, if the 'John' sentences occurred in a work of fiction, it would be false to say that they 'meant the same' unless the conceptions, or mental representations (3), they produced were identical. Those mental representations might, it is true, in each case overlap or interlock with the representations produced by other sentences in the fiction, such as 'John gazed at the hot cross buns in the baker's window'; but this shared contextual appropriateness does not prove that the 'John' sentences mean the same, since the representations produced by quite alien sentences, such as 'John sloped off feeling wretched', would as well interlock with those produced by the 'hot cross buns' sentence.

It may be argued, then, that the mental representations produced by the two sentences are indeed the same, and that the difference between the sentences is merely a formal or stylistic one. But a little introspection will show, I submit, that they produce slightly different representations. That produced by the first can be indicated as follows:

| (moving picture) | John striking, or casting a heavy object into, a window which shatters with a great star-shaped splash | + TIME-PERSPECTIVE 'PAST' |

The representation produced by the second sentence would look like this:

| (still picture) | a window with a great star-shaped hole in it; John at hand, his posture making it evident that he has done the deed | + TIME-PERSPECTIVE 'PAST' |

More simply, the first gives a picture mainly of John, the second a picture mainly of the window. This is a difference in representational focus which is acknowledged by the metaphorical distinction between 'active' and 'passive' voices in traditional grammar. Now if the sentences occurred in a non-fictional context (say in court testimony) the differences in representation would be of absolutely no importance, and would certainly be overlooked. But in fiction, where no correspondent facts exist, there can be no motive for overlooking the difference, or justification for characterising the sentences as 'different ways of saying the same (factually identical) thing'. They are, quite simply, slightly different sentences generating slightly different conceptions – though the difference in this example is, of course, utterly trivial.

It will be protested, next, that though the 'John' sentences in a fictional context do not have a correspondent fact (1) in common, they do have a deep structure of cognitive content (2) in common, and are still, therefore, 'different ways of saying the same thing': they share a semantic value (content), to which they give subtly different expression (style). But the semantic value of the proposition in deep structure is composed of two elements: a logical structure (action, agent, object); and an identification of certain things (the act of breaking, John, a window). Clearly, if the two sentences 'say the same thing', this cannot be because of the logical structure that underlies them, since the same logical structure underlies innumerable other sentences which certainly do not say the same thing, such as 'Pandora opened the box'. They can only 'say the same thing' if the things they identify are the same in each case, that is, the things identified by the proposition in deep structure. But the things they identify can only, in the fictional context, be the representations to which they give rise: since on the one hand, there are no external (factual) things for them to identify; and on the other hand, to disregard the *details* of the representations and claim that the sentences only identify 'the same three things' as the deep-structure proposition is to perpetrate an obvious circular argument, imposing the logical structure (action, agent, object) upon the content of the sentences in order to prove that that is all the content they have. We have seen that the representations produced by the two sentences are slightly different. Therefore they do not, in fiction, 'say the same thing' – unless by virtue of that convention whereby, for simplicity's sake, we pretend that a plurality of sentences in a fiction all relate to a thing exterior to themselves: 'Will Ladislaw', say. (That this *is* a conventional pretence is demonstrated by the fact that when we doubt the consistency of a character – doubt, in other words, that the various conceptions engendered by a number of sentences (or paragraphs, or chapters) are consonant with one another – we do not for a moment consider the defence that the fictional statements have at least this sort of coherence, that they are 'about the same person'). Consequently, Fowler's use of transformational grammar as an instrument for separating style from content, on the grounds that surface structure provides the stylistic slanting of a content

which remains unchanged, is essentially inappropriate in the case
of fiction. One suspects that it has been unconsciously influenced
by a notion, illegitimately transferred from such fields as political
rhetoric, of facts being 'coloured' by devices of rhetorical presentation. Even when he deals with non-fictional discourse, Fowler's
preoccupation with this theme leads him to rather odd conclusions. An example is his treatment (quoted above) of the two
'William' sentences, 'William got himself mugged', and 'William
was mugged'. These are supposed to illustrate the point that 'as a
result of the perspective effect of transformation . . . language
inevitably slants the presentation of "content"'. Yet a moment's
reflection will reveal that these sentences differ in their cognitive
content – they are saying different things *about what happened*. (Or if
they are *not* saying different things about what happened – 'got
himself' being on this reading cognitively interchangeable with
'was' – then they do not, as Fowler alleges, 'signal' different views
'of human responsibility').[7] Fowler apparently assumes that the
sentences have the same content because they describe the same
event. But their dissimilarity from this point of view has nothing to
do with transformations – it is simply a question of accurate or
inaccurate reporting. The same confusion is evident in his remark
that 'language . . . does not allow us to "say something" without
conveying an attitude to that something'. Here the first 'something' plainly refers to the deep-structure proposition, and the
second 'something' to the object or event which the proposition
denotes. This confusion allows Fowler to offer as self-evident an
assertion which is by no means evident to common-sense, namely
that a linguistic formulation of an idea effects no alteration in the
content of the idea, yet does, and inevitably, contribute an attitude
towards the thing which is the subject of the idea. If this assertion
is questionable in non-fictional contexts, it is doubly so where
fiction is concerned. In the case of, say, political utterance, it may
be helpful to say that the linguistic formulation cannot add
'content', if by 'content' we understand – and this is a useful
definition in the context – fact, such as information or substantive
policy; in this situation a clear distinction between 'content' and
'presentation' can therefore in principle be drawn. But in the case
of fiction a limiting definition of 'content' in terms of fact is
meaningless, and all conceptions engendered in the reader's mind
by whatever means – even by a choice of word-order – are equally
'content' in the only useful sense, and so equally legitimate. Thus,

in the case of fiction, though not of politics, the truism that Fowler seeks to overturn – that style and content are essentially inseparable – is usefully true.

All this is not to say that a critic who wishes to do a thorough job can dispense with the analysis of 'small-scale' conceptions and the means by which they are brought into being. It is merely to say that attempts to conduct this analysis in terms of a special agency called 'style', the workings of which can supposedly be demonstrated with quasi-scientific reliability through the application of linguistic techniques, are likely to prove misleading. Here, to illustrate this point, is a passage from *The Mill on the Floss* which Fowler chooses to discuss in some detail.

It was a heavy disappointment to Maggie that she was not allowed to go with her father in the gig when he went to fetch Tom home from the academy; but the morning was too wet, Mrs. Tulliver said, for a little girl to go out in her best bonnet. Maggie took the opposite view very strongly, and it was a direct consequence of this difference of opinion that when her mother was in the act of brushing out the reluctant black crop, Maggie suddenly rushed from under her hands and dipped her head in a basin of water standing near – in the vindictive determination that there should be no more chance of curls that day.[8]

Fowler's commentary runs as follows:

Consider ... the way in which the arrangement of clauses in the surface order of this very ordinary paragraph from George Eliot's *The Mill on the Floss* (1860) splits up the information given into its more and less prominent parts, focusing the reader's attention on the feelings and actions of Maggie Tulliver and subordinating what are from the point of view of this particular narration inessential and contingent details .... The syntax manages to 'foreground' both the severity of Maggie's feelings and the violence of her actions, and to 'background' their causes and their consequences. Two crucial clauses are transformed into ponderously striking noun phrases which can be placed in the attention-catching 'left-hand' syntactic positions – 'heavy disappointment' at the beginning of the first sentence and 'vindictive determination' after the dash; contrast the less emphatic

untransformed versions 'Maggie was disappointed/vindictive/
determined'. In addition to this positional prominence, the
sonorous polysyllables of the words concerned also highlight the
importance of the meanings conveyed by them. (Polysyllabicity
is of course very concrete, a pure feature of surface structure.) In
the first sentence, expression of the cause of Maggie's disappointment dwindles out to the right in subordinate clauses.
For the remainder, Maggie has a monopoly of active, finite verbs
in prominent positions. 'Mrs. Tulliver said' is parenthesized,
placing the action of saying below, in importance, even the
feeble substance of what she says. Contrast the active directness
of the first clause of the next sentence: 'Maggie took the opposite
view.' Actually, 'taking the opposite view' isn't an action, but
the archetypal subject-verb-object sequence manages to suggest
that it is, a surface-structure implication vindicated by the
subsequent active finite verbs: 'Maggie suddenly rushed ... and
dipped her head in a basin of water ...' The syntactic
mechanisms of the centre of this sentence forewarn the reader
that these major semantic nuclei are to come: 'it was a direct
consequence ... *that*' announces a main clause to come, and
'*when* her mother was ...' indicates clearly a suspension of
major meaning for one more subordinate clause. By such devices
the syntactic structure leads the reader through the semantic
centres of the prose, emphasizing and playing down as
appropriate.[9]

There is a good deal of truth in Fowler's remarks, but there are also
some unproved assumptions, at least one apparent contradiction,
and (perhaps most important) a tendency, consequent upon his
stylistic theory, to overlook comparatively major considerations of
content (in my non-factual sense) in favour of minor questions of
grammatical form and syntactical arrangement. He is surely right,
for example, about the emphatic quality of 'took the opposite
view'. Another critic, though, would perhaps see the effect as
being derived as much from the way the adult idiom of the phrase
(as employed by philosopher or barrister) suggests Maggie playing
the grown-up in her own eyes, as from syntactical parallelism. He
might note, further, that this momentary promotion of our
conception of Maggie's consciousness to the adult plane suggests
(as when a child is referred to as 'her ladyship') an ironic
perspective on someone's part – whether the parents' or merely

the narrator's is uncertain – towards her self-important sense of outrage. These are, of course, linguistic points – or points which one approaches through a close scrutiny of language; but they concern matters of content (the precise nature of Maggie's demeanour or self-image, and perhaps the impression she makes in adult eyes), and they require neither a specialised linguistic vocabulary to articulate them nor specialised linguistic tests to verify them.

Other aspects of Fowler's account are distinctly puzzling. His assumption that left-hand syntactic positions are prominent and confer importance sounds plausible but soon becomes problematical in practice. In the case of

To be or not to be, that is the question

one is readily convinced. But the longer the sentence one considers, the more one is inclined to say that, as in the case of this sentence, or the opening one of *Pride and Prejudice*, syntactical techniques for arousing expectation can direct emphasis towards the right-hand position. Indeed, near the end of his commentary Fowler suggests that the second (and last) sentence of the Eliot passage throws considerable emphasis to the right by means of syntactical devices which 'forewarn the reader that ... major semantic nuclei are to come: "it was a direct consequence ... *that*" announces a main clause to come....' If this is true, however, it is not clear why the opening phrase of the first sentence – 'It was a heavy disappointment to Maggie *that*...' – does not throw emphasis on to what follows, instead of (as Fowler actually suggests) 'foregrounding' Maggie's disappointment by virtue of its left-hand placing and leaving the rest of the sentence to dwindle out in subordinate clauses – which, incidentally, are by any standard major semantic nuclei and of which the first ('she was not allowed ...') is actually a main clause. One begins to suspect that Fowler's left-hand/right-hand topography gives a crude and inconsistent picture of the play of emphasis within a sentence: play which can nevertheless be picked up largely instinctively by a reasonably attentive reader or listener. As for Fowler's observation that the 'sonorous polysyllables' *disappointment* and *determination* 'highlight the importance of the meanings conveyed by them', one can only ask what grounds there are for the general principle which this implies. Some would say that polysyllabicity, however 'concrete' (is monosyllabicity less concrete, less a feature of surface struc-

ture?) can just as often serve to deflect the reader's attention from
the meaning being covered. The obvious reason for the conversion
of 'Maggie was (or 'Maggie felt') disappointed' into 'It was a ...
disappointment to Maggie', is to permit the insertion of 'heavy' –
'Maggie was heavily disappointed' being ugly and unidiomatic; it
is, above all, the image in 'heavy', with its direct evocation of a
quasi-physical pain and sense of burden, which generates our
conception of how Maggie felt. More trivially, 'vindictively
determined' becomes 'in the vindictive determination' for reasons
of euphony and in order to avoid false parallelism with other
verbs: the two past tense verbs ending in -*ed* and the dangerously
close present participle which refers to the basin of water.
Finally, Fowler's comment on the treatment of Mrs Tulliver's
pronouncement illustrates his tendency to obscure one point in
the act of making another. The parenthesising of 'Mrs. Tulliver
said' may indeed downgrade the importance of 'the action of
saying' (though this again implies a dubious and unsupported
general principle – cannot parenthesis sometimes direct attention
to what is parenthesised?). But what it also does is to present us
with the statement 'the morning was too wet' fractionally before,
or in a syntactically prior position to, the phrase which informs us
that this statement was merely Mrs Tulliver's judgement; and this
priority subtly but perceptibly conveys the force, definitive rather
than simply opinionative, enjoyed within the household by the
mother's judgement on such matters. Fowler's reference to 'the
feeble substance of what she says' is thus somewhat misleading.

Now it may well be that on all disputed points concerning the
Eliot passage Fowler is right and I am wrong. What should be
clear, however, is that the justice of the analysis in either case
depends upon the sensitivity of the analyst's interpreting (and
necessarily subjective) imagination – to be attested by the
assenting response of other readers – rather than upon the
application of objective linguistic techniques which are well suited
to the codification of possible grammatical structures within a
given language but less well suited to the task of accounting for
the effect of particular statements, within the discourse-
conventions of fiction, upon minds experienced in literature.[10]
I believe it is clear, too, that Fowler's analysis is more hindered
than helped by his determination to uncover features of pure style
(identified with 'surface structure') which are independent of
semantic 'content'; in this attempt the sense of the intimate

interdependence of the small-scale and the large-scale in a literary work is blurred, and compositional resource at the level of the phrase or sentence comes close to being presented as a kind of box of tricks designed to beguile our perception of meanings (imagined objects or events) which pre-exist 'style'. In the next section I shall consider a book which, developing the tradition of the New Criticism, insists that style and content are indeed inseparable.

III

In the first section of this chapter I argued that the language of a work of fiction is instrumental to its content; but that 'content' must here be understood to include the smallest-scale conceptions, generated by the most localised details of diction and phrasing: that all conceptions, from the smallest- to the largest-scale, are equally the product of language. The second section was devoted to repudiating the notion that literary works possess features of style which are independent of the conceptions.

The methodological conclusion I wish to draw from these arguments is that it is natural and proper to begin critical analysis with the conceptions, and as permissible (since all levels of conception interact with one another) to begin with the large-scale (plot, character and the like) as to begin with the small-scale. But there is a contrary view to be disposed of first. This view contends that to begin analysis with the conceptions is methodologically unsound; it maintains that language in a work of fiction is not merely a disposable ticket to something more important, a set of conceptions, but is in David Lodge's phrase the 'all-inclusive medium'[11] of the fiction; that conceptions have no imaginative reality, and therefore no affective value, unless it is conferred upon them by their precise realisation through particular words on the page; that a favourable judgement on a plot, a piece of characterisation, a moral perception, is at root a favourable judgement on the language in which it is set forth; and that therefore a critic's analytical attention should first be directed towards those 'verbal configurations' which create the work's 'solidity, concreteness, interest, power to move'[12] – again I quote from Lodge.

These two views – that critical analysis may begin with conceptions (at any level), and that it should properly begin with language itself – are not, perhaps, in practice so easily distinguishable as I have striven for dialectical purposes to make them appear.

If we consider in detail the passage in *Language of Fiction* from which I have already rather unfairly lifted a couple of phrases, the tendency of each to merge into the other in spite of itself becomes still more evident.

> Reading a novel critically is a very delicate and complicated activity. One begins it with an open mind, but one hopes to finish it with a mind which is at least provisionally closed – closed, that is, upon an articulate sense of its meaning and value. While reading one is both involved and detached: involved in the stream of 'life' presented by the novelist, yet able simultaneously to stand back from it and perceive how it acquires its solidity, concreteness, interest, power to move, from certain verbal configurations, from the way it is communicated. One seeks all the time to define what kind of novel it is, and how successful it is, and often one does so against the background of critical opinion already gathered around the text, or of one's own previous readings. Constantly one makes notes (which may be mental or written) about local detail: *this* is significant or irrelevant – *this* works or doesn't work – *this* connects with or contradicts *that*. Such notes are necessarily provisional, particularly in the early stages, for further acquaintance with the text may lead us to revise our criteria of significance and relevance. The novel unfolds in our memories like a piece of cloth woven upon a loom, and the more complicated the pattern the more difficult and protracted will be the process of perceiving it. But that is what we seek, the pattern: some significantly recurring thread which, however deeply hidden in the dense texture and brilliance of local colouring, accounts for our impression of a unique identity in the whole.
>
> It is my own experience that the moment of perceiving the pattern is sudden and unexpected. All the time one has been making the tiny provisional notes, measuring each against one's developing awareness of the whole, storing them up in the blind hope that they will prove useful, and then suddenly one such small local observation sends a shock like an electric charge through all the discrete observations heaped up on all sides, so that with an exciting clatter and rattle they fly about and arrange themselves in a certain meaningful order. If this account seems too metaphorical, let me borrow the plainer words of Rene Wellek:

> In reading with a sense for continuity, for contextual coher-
> ence, for wholeness, there comes a moment when we feel that
> we have 'understood', that we have seized on the right
> interpretation, the real meaning. It is a process that ...
> proceeds from attention to a detail to an anticipation of the
> whole and back again to an interpretation of the detail.[13]

The general emphasis here is certainly upon the observation of the
verbal detail, conceived as the *primum mobile* of meaning and value
in fiction; we are to register suggestive local details until they are
seen to form a 'significantly recurring thread' – a thread the
thickness, we presume, of a phrase, an image. When, in the
following section which closes the theoretical half of *Language of
Fiction*, Lodge identifies 'the perception of repetition' as 'the first
step towards offering an account of the way language works in
extended literary texts',[14] and instances Charlotte Brontë's use of
fire imagery in *Jane Eyre*, and Conrad's use of *cynicism* as a focal
word and concept in *Under Western Eyes*, this emphasis seems to be
confirmed. But Lodge seems also at two points to acknowledge the
force of an objection to this procedure. The points I have in mind
are in the sixth sentence quoted:

> Such notes are necessarily provisional ... for further acquaint-
> ance with the text may lead us to revise our criteria of
> significance and relevance ...

and at the end of the Wellek extract:

> It is a process that ... proceeds from attention to a detail to an
> anticipation of the whole and back again to an interpretation of
> the detail.

The objection may be stated as follows. The 'verbal configurations'
of a literary work and its 'solidity, concreteness' and so forth do in
an obvious enough sense stand in a relation of cause and effect.
Without the former the latter would not exist. But from (say) the
second sentence of a novel onwards, this relation of cause to effect
ceases to be a simple one, for such solidity and concreteness as the
first sentence has created in the reader's mind begins to exert an
influence over what the verbal configurations of the second
sentence can reasonably be taken to mean, or are felt to imply. That

this is literally so, a couple of examples – the first from Nabokov's *Invitation to a Beheading*,[15] the second from Beckett's *Murphy*,[16] will demonstrate.

In accordance with the law the death sentence was announced to Cincinnatus C. in a whisper. All rose, exchanging smiles.

The sun shone, having no alternative, on the nothing new. Murphy sat out of it, as though he were free, in a mew in West Brompton.

The first example scarcely requires comment: the spirit in which we respond to its second sentence – perhaps, even, the physical and psychological character of the 'smiles' we are likely to conceive (smug bureaucratic smiles, not jolly Pickwickian ones) – must be largely determined by our awareness of the situation the first sentence has suggested. In the second example, the cosmic fatalism and *ennui* implicit in the first sentence confer special resonances of existential anxiety upon the parenthetical clause in the second. (That these resonances are to some extent mocked and modified by what follows only demonstrates that the influence may be exerted backwards as well as forwards; even the verbal configurations of a first sentence are not immune from having their intellectual and emotional burden modified by conceptions which subsequently form in the reader's mind.) Here, then, what was an effect – a conception produced by language, or more strictly by our understanding of the signification and implication of a piece of language within the conventions of fiction – has become in turn a cause, a determining influence upon the understood signification and implication of subsequent pieces of language. And, in a multitude of ways, our understanding of, and response to, a word or phrase may justifiably be conditioned by our understanding of, and response to, 'gross and overall' products of the language of fiction such as those we describe as 'character', 'setting', 'theme', 'ideology', or 'narrative tone'. Consistent narrative irony, for example, alters our perception of certain effects of diction and phrasing. 'He lay, sprawled, too wicked to move, spewed up like a broken spider-crab on the tarry shingle of the morning': not a Mervyn Peake grotesque, but Jim Dixon waking with a hangover in Kingsley Amis's *Lucky Jim*:[17] our familiarity with the narrative posture of the novel (which is closely related to Dixon's own self-querying consciousness) helps us to distinguish the parodic unseriousness, mingled with a certain relish, in the heroic diction. Character can modify even the understood signification of a single word. In normal usage a 'table' is (primarily) an item of domestic furniture; in the light of our apprehension of a fictional character's mental process, it may be the tee in a game of golf:

> Through the fence, between the curling flower spaces, I could see them hitting. They were coming towards where the flag was and I went along the fence. Luster was hunting in the grass by the flower tree. They took the flag out, and they were hitting. Then they put the flag back and they went to the table, and he hit and the other hit. Then they went on, and I went along the fence.[18]

If, to conclude with an example Lodge himself uses, the word 'darkness' in Conrad's *Heart of Darkness* comes to unite certain threads of thought, feeling, incident and detail in the story, it is because these threads have been sewn into it by the contexts in which it is used, not because of any intrinsic structuring power in the signification of the word itself. It is (in Lodge's revealingly vague information) 'further acquaintance with the text' which determines the significance and relevance of the key-word.

It is not enough to reply to this that since the words on the page, in their initial unmodified significations, remain the *primum mobile* in which the reciprocal process of cause and effect has its origin, this reciprocal process is a secondary affair, so that the Lodgean emphasis on the primacy of 'verbal configurations' retains its validity. It is true that if the possession of a conception which we can label 'the mind of Benjy Compson' enables us to translate 'table' as 'golf tee', that possession is nevertheless ultimately the product of the 'language' of the novel. If there were no 'language', there would be no conceptions, indeed no novel. But the word 'language' in these correct statements has a sense quite different from that generally implied in Lodge's notion of the 'language of fiction'. Our conception 'the mind of Benjy Compson' is, certainly, derived *ultimately* from this word and that word and the other semi-colon: from what is unquestionably 'on the page'. This is the sense in which it is finally and definitively attributable to 'language'. But it is derived *immediately* from smaller-scale conceptions (the product of words singly and in complex combination) which stand in a reciprocal relation of influence and modification to yet other conceptions and may indeed themselves be reciprocally modified by the 'Benjy Compson' conception. In practice it is this interaction among conceptions, greater and lesser, and not the initial cause-effect relation between words and the as yet unmodified conceptions which they immediately generate, which Lodge identifies as giving meaning and value to a work. Now for some analytical purposes it may be convenient to refer to the smaller-scale, more localised, levels of conception in a novel as 'language', while the larger-scale are categorised as 'plot', 'character' and so on. By this means attention can be concentrated on the part which slender structures describable as, say, 'imagery', or 'rhetorical devices', play in building up the totality and unity of a work, and this Lodge does very fruitfully in the second half of *Language and Fiction*, without, on the whole, overlooking in practice the contribution which the larger structures make to the quality and significance of the smaller. But in view of the reciprocal interaction between the smaller-scale and larger-scale levels, there can be no justification for crediting 'language' in *this* sense with the status of *primum mobile* or 'all-inclusive medium'. On the contrary, its utility as a critical term, in this sense, depends precisely on its *not* being all-inclusive, on its isolating one aspect of a work – to the extent that this is possible and expedient – from the rest. It is only 'language' in the first, banal sense of 'the words on the page, in their initial unmodified significations', which is always a cause and never an effect – only 'language' in this sense which is all-inclusive, being the sufficient (and obvious) origin or all that the work is, including that which in the second sense may be isolated as 'language'. The central flaw in Lodge's theory lies in his claiming for the second kind of 'language' – a heuristic critical concept – the causative priority of the first.

By using the term 'language' in these two senses, one somewhat specialised and one all-inclusive, Lodge enjoys the luxury of combining a characteristic and perfectly valid critical strategy – roughly, an analysis of the part which verbal devices (recurrent images, normative terms, departures from, or conformity to, the patterns of colloquial speech, and so on) play in bringing the imaginative and moral complexity of a novel to life – with the freedom to support his arguments by referring to elements in a work which have to do with 'language' only in the sense that it is in language, not music or binary notation, that they are written about. In his chapter, 'The Rhetoric of "Hard Times"', for example, Lodge argues that

> when all the contradictions, limitations, and flaws in Dickens's argument [have been] extrapolated, *Hard Times* remains a novel of considerable polemical effectiveness. The measure of this effectiveness, it seems to me, can only be accounted for in terms of Dickens's rhetoric .... I shall try to show that *Hard Times* succeeds where its rhetoric succeeds and fails where its rhetoric fails ....
>
> If *Hard Times* is a polemical novel that is only partially persuasive, it is because Dickens's rhetoric is only partially adequate to the tasks he set himself.[19]

To a large extent Lodge makes out his case for the special prominence of those small-scale conceptions he designates as 'rhetoric'. Dickens is, certainly, a writer who specialises in the use of repeated images, symbols and locutions to remind us of moral polarities and central points of characterisation; and the analysis of such devices as the association of Bounderby with images of metallic and above all 'brazen' surfaces, or the application of organic metaphors to machinery and mechanical metaphors to humanity, does indeed yield access to the novel's most crucial concerns. Yet the dangers of omission and overstatement in a doctrinaire assertion of the priority of 'rhetoric', and the tendency of false emphases obstinately to right themselves in practical analysis, are also evident in Lodge's chapter. To begin with an omission, it seems to me that the polemical effectiveness of the novel is partly undermined, not by misfiring 'rhetoric', but by certain glaring improbabilities at the level of plot about which Lodge says very little. An outstanding example is Stephen Blackpool's stolid and needless acceptance of ruin in consequence of his promise to Rachael that he will not join the Trade Union. (His refusal leads, it will be remembered, to his ostracism by his colleagues and eventually to his dismissal by Bounderby.)

> Rachael burst into tears. 'I didn't seek it of him, poor lad. I prayed him to avoid trouble for his own good, little thinking he'd come to it through me. But I know he'd die a hundred deaths, ere ever he'd break his word. I know that of him well.'
> Stephen had remained quietly attentive, in his usual thought-

ful attitude, with his hand on his chin. He spoke in a voice rather less steady than usual.

'No one, excepting myseln, can ever know what honour, an what love, an respect, I bear to Rachael, or wi' what cause. When I passed that promess, I towd her true, she were th' Angel o' my life. 'Twere a solemn promess. 'Tis gone fro me, for ever.'[20]

Dickens shows no convincing reason why Stephen should not have consulted with Rachael when it became clear, as it must have begun to do a little before the episode in which Slackbridge singles him out as a solitary recreant, that not joining the Union would get him into trouble; or why at the point just quoted she could not release him from his promise (or would not have done so already, as soon as she learned that he was suffering by it) in order to permit him to make peace with his fellow-workers and his employer. (Four days lapse between the ostracism and the interview with Bounderby which ends in Stephen's sacking and precedes the episode quoted above. Dickens tries to cover the interval by making Stephen avoid Rachael, for fear of bringing her into disgrace with her fellow-workers who, he observes, are 'changed to him' (*Hard Times*, II, 4; p. 176). But if this is so, then the news that he has been sent to Coventry must be current among the female employees; why, then, does Rachael not seek him out? Her home is 'but a minute' (I, 13; p. 125) from his.) Perhaps recantation, at this stage, would not have saved Stephen; but to evade this possibility altogether, and to imply, as Dickens does, that the unsought promise remains eternally binding in the minds of both parties despite Rachael's evident and natural distress at its consequences, is psychologically absurd unless both characters are destitute of common-sense, which is not how Dickens generally depicts them. The implausibility weakens the polemical force of the novel, since if we take the story seriously at this point we are compelled to consider Stephen not so much downtrodden by an inhuman industrial Utilitarianism as undone by his own and Rachael's muddle-headedness. This is plainly first and foremost a lapse in plot-construction, which no verbal realisation would be likely to redeem for an attentive reader. (In an earlier chapter of *Language of Fiction*, Lodge points out that if the brilliantly-contrived plot of *Tom Jones* had been handed to another writer to execute as a novel, the result 'would not have been ... necessarily, a good novel'.[21] He might have added that if a terribly ill-contrived plot had been handed to Henry Fielding to execute, the result would have been, necessarily, not a good novel – or at least a gravely deficient one.)

Much of what Lodge does say about *Hard Times* is entirely convincing; yet his analysis can often be taken as readily to contradict as to support his proposition that the novel's successes and failures are successes and failure of rhetoric.

> A . . . significant failure of Dickens's rhetoric is to be observed in the treatment of Tom Gradgrind. In this connection, I must register my disagreement with John Holloway's opinion that 'the gradual degeneration of Tom . . . is barely (as in fact it is treated) related to Dickens's major problems in the book, though it is one of his best things'. It is gradual (though not very extensively treated) up to the beginning of Book II, by which point we have gathered that Tom, so far from drawing strength of character from his repressive and rationalist upbringing, is turning into a selfish young man prepared to exploit others for his own advantage. He is still a long way, however, from the depravity that allows him to connive at the seduction of his own sister and to implicate an innocent man (Stephen Blackpool) in his own crime. This moral gap is rather clumsily bridged by Dickens in the second chapter of Book II, where he suddenly introduces a key-word for Tom: 'whelp' . . . .
>
> 'Whelp' is a cliché, and it will be noticed that the word is first used by Harthouse, and then adopted by the novelist in his authorial capacity. When a novelist does this, it is usually with ironical intent, suggesting some inadequacy in the speaker's habits of thought. Dickens plays on Gradgrind's 'facts' to this effect. But in the case of Harthouse's 'whelp' he has taken a moral cliché from a character who is morally unreliable, and invested it with his own authority as a narrator. This gives away the fact that Tom is being forced into a new role halfway through the book. For Tom's degeneration *should* be related to the major problems with which Dickens is concerned in *Hard Times*. According to the overall pattern of the novel, Tom and Louisa are to act as indices of the failure of Mr. Gradgrind's philosophy of education . . . .
>
> Perhaps Dickens was misled by feeling the need to inject a strong crime-interest into this story, of which Tom was a handy vehicle; or perhaps he lost his head over the preservation of

Louisa's purity .... Whatever the explanation, 'the whelp',
unlike those key-words which organize and concentrate the
represented character of individuals and places, acts merely as a
slogan designed to generate in the reader such a contempt for
Tom that he will not enquire too closely into the pattern of his
moral development – a pattern that will not, in fact, bear very
close scrutiny ....

Dickens falters in his handling of the character of Tom
Gradgrind because he uses a device for fixing character (*whelp*) to
express a process of change.[22]

There is little at the level of detail to quarrel with here (though one
might argue in defence of the borrowing of *whelp* from Harthouse
that its use helps to underline the villain's psychological ascend-
ancy over Tom; to my mind it is not its origin but the sheer
number of repetitions which renders the phrase exasperating and
drives us to reflect on the inadequacy of the character-exposition
behind it). But the passage does not really support Lodge's general
point, that the success or failure of the argument depends upon
that of the rhetoric. Dickens, certainly, uses an inert cliché here:
whelp has little exploitable suggestiveness as an image beyond a
generally derogatory implication. But is it exactly true to say that it
is used 'to express a process of change'? Surely, as Lodge in effect
admits, there *is* no process of change to express; there is a 'moral
gap' (that is, a gap in Tom's moral development) where it ought to
be. The error lies not, then, in the *choice of expression* (for we may
doubt whether any expression would be able to tie together
threads which are not there anyway); it lies, ultimately, in
Dickens's assumption that the initial signification of a well-chosen
word will serve a purpose which in fact only the realisation of a
developed character-conception, interacting appropriately with
the other conceptions generated by the novel, can fulfil. It lies,
that is to say, in Dickens's trusting all too readily to the potency of
'language' in the specialised Lodgean sense of small-scale conceptions engendered by small-scale verbal configurations, such as
single words. If the failure had been a failure of rhetoric, it could
have been made good by rhetorical means; actually, as Lodge
clearly recognises ('not very extensively treated ... a pattern that
will not... bear very close scrutiny'), it could only be made good
by painstaking thoroughness and consistency in realising the
contribution of Tom's development to 'the overall pattern of the

novel'. Tom would either have to remain within his minor original role as victim of his father's desiccated version of education (which is what Lodge probably implies by his suggestion that Dickens may have been 'misled by feeling the need to inject a strong crime interest into the story') or have to be given a plausible sequence of motives to account for his transformation into a moral monster far removed from the sister who has shared his upbringing (which is what Lodge regrets the lack of in his 'moral gap'). And both these alternatives concern the achievement of large-scale conceptions ('role', 'sequence of motives') quite distinct from – though of course reciprocally related to – Lodge's specialised domain of 'language'. As practising critics we may applaud Lodge's observation of these 'gross and overall' deficiencies; but as theorists we are bound to note that it is only by authorising himself, through his alternative, all-inclusive concept of language, to cite any evidence whatever from the novel without consciously infringing his own methodology, that he is entitled to observe them in the context of his theoretical argument for the primacy of the 'language of fiction'.

(A brief comment on Lodge's later chapter on *Hard Times* ('How successful is *Hard Times?*', *Working with Structuralism*, Routledge & Kegan Paul, 1981, pp. 37–43) may be offered in passing. The chapter largely concerns itself with narrative structure, and with the affinity of much of the action and characterisation to theatrical forms such as melodrama and pantomime. Its main point of interest for our purposes is an implied, almost casual, reformulation of the role of 'language'. Lodge speaks of the novel's 'characteristic style or rhetoric' as its 'surface structure', and declares his intention of 'examining the novel's structure at a deeper level, that of narrative technique' (p. 38). This seeming misapplication of terms from transformational grammar (for narrative technique as Lodge treats it – the use of suspense, ironic reversals and so on – is surely *broader* rather than *deeper* than 'style', and has at all events nothing to do with Chomskian 'deep structure') reveals a new perspective on the role of 'style'. From being seen as the *origin* of all that the novel is ('it acquires its solidity, concreteness ... from certain verbal configurations') it has become the *final*, or *surface, expression* of 'deeper' qualities. The two perspectives are not, however, at all incompatible; Lodge is simply shifting his attention from the reader's experience, which begins with the text, to the compositional process, which ends with it. And the points I have made about the former apply equally to the latter. Each is a mirror-image of the other; just as the reading of a novel consists in the apprehension of interacting conceptions, large and small-scale, each of which modifies or rather helps to constitute others, so in the act of composition (it is reasonable to assume) the final text is arrived at by collaboration and compromise between local and more general intentions.)

IV

In the first three sections of this chapter I have attempted to refute, first in general terms and then in reply to the arguments of Fowler and Lodge, the view that 'style', or 'language' in the sense of the functioning of small-scale verbal configurations, is the best or necessary starting point for critical analysis. In this last section I shall try to show that the contribution made to the effect of a work by 'language' in this specialised sense can be accounted for in terms of the general thesis I have put forward. It is perhaps time to recapitulate that thesis, and to note one or two elaborations of it which have arisen by the way and may prove relevant to the following discussion.

It was argued in Chapter 1 that a work of imaginative literature draws desires to consciousness, or to a greater degree of definition; that these desires, temporarily averted from the exterior world, become implicated in the unfolding fabric and pattern of the work; and that when the reading is over, or the reader is obliged to withdraw his attention from the work, these become again, for the (usually brief) period in which they linger in consciousness, desires seeking gratification in reality. From this reversion arises the psychic unrest we experience in relinquishing a work which has engaged our interest, however satisfactory, aesthetically or in terms of the resolution of the tensions in its content, its final effect has been. (Indeed it would follow logically from this description that the more effectively a work combines quickening desires with implicating them in a satisfying aesthetic order, the greater the unrest produced by the mental reversion to the *status quo ante* must be, and I am inclined to venture the generalisation that this is in fact so.) Despite the attendant unrest (the argument continues), we value the experience of literature for two reasons: firstly because a lucid and acute awareness of desire contrasts favourably, through the sense of spiritual vitality it confers, with the comparatively low-level, or at least fitful, charge of our hour-by-hour consciousness; and secondly because by drawing desires into an apprehensible pattern (through the correlative fabric of the invention) the work offers us a model, a paradigm, of possible psychological sovereignty over them. The painfulness of quickened desire is compensated for by a sense of having briefly escaped that uncertainty of emotional direction and control, that vulnerability to somewhat arbitrary and incoherent fluctuations of feeling, which accounts for a good deal of the anxiety and dissatisfaction of daily experience.

This description suggests, then, that there are two aspects to the impact of a literary work upon its reader: first, the arousal of desires (or aversions, which are simply desires with a negative added) through the *nature* of its material, the conceptions, or conceptional complexes, it engenders; and second, the establishment of an effect – or illusion, if you prefer – of psychological sovereignty over the quickened desire through the *ordering* of its material. Two remarks need to be added. The first is that, since in a structure of the slightest complexity its nature and its ordering cannot sensibly be separated – the truth of this is particularly obvious in the case of a story, but one might say even of a one-word composition that it had an ordering, namely the ordering which results from the decision to isolate one from all other words – these two functions must be seen as simultaneous rather than consecutive; to render any material intelligible (and therefore capable of quickening desire) requires at least some elementary order in its presentation. Lucidity is both an intensifier of affect and a quality of structure; in a successful work it is the lucidity of the total conception (the conceptional whole) which engenders our impression of complete psychological control, just as we infer a person's authoritative knowledge of an arcane subject (and in literature the work is in the position of sole presenter of a body of 'information' peculiar to itself) from the clarity with which he expounds it. The second additional observation is a restatement of a point made in Chapter 2. Much of the content of a work of fiction serves the purpose (among, as a rule, other purposes) of acting as 'facilitating material' – material whose presence in the work is justified not so much by the immediate stimulus it offers to the reader's sympathy or sensibility (though like other verbal material it must have some tendency to provoke response, and may in fact be strongly flavoured emotionally in its own right) as by the economy and effectiveness with which it facilitates the apprehension of material which is psychologically more highly charged. Scene-setting, cultural or historical signposting, the introduction of secondary characters, the elucidation of complicated but essential plot-devices such as lawsuits, wills, unusual family relationships, coincidental encounters, political or military manoeuvres and the like, are areas in which relatively inert exposition is liable, though by no means certain, to occur. This is simply another way of saying that in any extended literary work there are zones of high and low intensity; and the point should not in any case be overstated – for since all the conceptions of a work reflect upon, confirm or modify one another, the difference between material which itself stimulates response and material which rather clarifies and expedites the stimulus given by other material is a difference of degree or emphasis, not of kind.

In the present chapter I have argued that the smaller-scale and larger-scale conceptions generated by a literary work – those we loosely assign on the one hand to 'style' or 'language', and on the other hand to 'plot', 'theme', 'character' and so forth – interact, and are mutually dependent for their intelligibility and effectiveness; that they constitute a complex unity. If this is so, any rationale offered for the larger qualities should also be seen to hold for the smaller. I wish now to review briefly the qualities we respond to and value at the level of verbal detail, and to attempt to show that their functions and affects can be as plausibly discussed within the terms adumbrated above as can the more obviously affect-producing larger-scale qualities.

We are moving into an exceptionally complex field of analysis, in which a considerable amount of schematisation will be necessary. This is inevitable for two reasons. Firstly, as I have already remarked, the two suggested aspects of a work's impact upon its reader are so closely related that to discuss a phrase or a sentence in terms of only aspect has a suspicious appearance of omission about it, like describing the painfulness of going to the dentist without mentioning its medico-cosmetic benefit, or *vice versa*. Secondly, the various qualities of verbal detail that I propose to refer to – qualities of expository clarity, of imagery and metaphor, of tone and diction, of senuous beauty or the opposite – can seldom if ever be located in isolation, and often several may be predicated of the same word or phrase; for example, a metaphor (say the 'spring of a beast' that is the irruption of Quint's ghost into the domestic idyll in *The Turn of the Screw*) may serve at once to evoke more exactly or pungently a particular quality of an imagined experience, to present an image with an emotional charge consistent with and appropriate to that experience (and connected, perhaps, with other such images elsewhere in the work), and to contribute to a strongly characterised narrative voice. To single out one of these functions is to fall short of doing justice to the polyphonic subtlety and complexity of what the reader actually experiences. Accordingly, some allowance should be made, in considering what follows, for a certain instability in, and overlapping between, the analytical subdivisions proposed.

Here, as a source-passage for illustrations, is the episode in *The Turn of the Screw* just alluded to.

It was plump, one afternoon, in the middle of my very hour: the children were tucked away and I had come out for my stroll. One of the thoughts that, as I don't in the least shrink now from noting, used to be with me in these wanderings was that it would be as charming as a charming story suddenly to meet someone. Someone would appear there at the turn of a path and would stand before me and smile and approve. I didn't ask more than that – I only asked that he should *know*; and the only way to be sure he knew would be to see it, and the kind light of it, in his handsome face. That was exactly present to me – by which I mean the fact was – when, on the first of these occasions, at the end of a long June day, I stopped short on emerging from one of the plantations and coming into view of the house. What arrested me on the spot – and with a shock much greater than any vision had allowed for – was the sense that my imagination had, in a flash, turned real. He did stand there! – but high up, beyond the lawn and at the very top of the tower to which, on that first morning, little Flora had conducted me. This tower was one of a pair – square, incongruous, crenelated structures – that were distinguished, for some reason, though I could see little difference, as the new and the old. They flanked opposite ends of the house and were probably architectural absurdities, redeemed in a measure indeed by not being wholly disengaged nor of a height too pretentious, dating, in their gingerbread antiquity, from a romantic revival that was already a respectable past. I admired them, had fancies about them, for we could all

profit in a degree, especially when they loomed through the
dusk, by the grandeur of their actual battlements; yet it was not
at such an elevation that the figure I had so often evoked seemed
most in place.

It produced in me, this figure, in the clear twilight, I
remember, two distinct gasps of emotion, which were, sharply,
the shock of my first and that of my second surprise. My second
was a violent perception of the mistake of the first: the man who
met my eyes was not the person I had precipitately supposed.
There came to me thus a bewilderment of vision of which, after
these years, there is no living view that I can hope to give. An
unknown man in a lonely place is a permitted object of fear to a
young woman privately bred; and the figure that faced me was –
a few more seconds assured me – as little anyone else I knew as
it was the image that had been in my mind. I had not seen it in
Harley Street – I had not seen it anywhere. The place, moreover,
in the strangest way in the world, had, on the instant, and by the
very fact of its appearance, become a solitude. To me at least,
making my statement here with a deliberation with which I have
never made it, the whole feeling of the moment returns. It was
as if, while I took in – what I did take in – all the scene had been
stricken with death. I can hear again, as I write, the intense hush
in which the sounds of evening dropped. The rooks stopped
cawing in the golden sky and the friendly hour lost, for the
minute, all its voice. But there was no other change in nature,
unless indeed it were a change that I saw with a stranger
sharpness. The gold was still in the sky, and the clearness in the
air, and the man who looked at me over the battlements was as
definite as a picture in a frame. That's how I thought, with
extraordinary quickness, of each person that he might have been
and that he was not. We were confronted across our distance
quite long enough for me to ask myself with intensity who then
he was and to feel, as an effect of my inability to say, a wonder
that in a few instants more became intense.

The great question, or one of these, is, afterwards, I know,
with regard to certain matters, the question of how long they have
lasted. Well, this matter of mine, think what you will of it, lasted
while I caught at a dozen possibilities, none of which made a
difference for the better, that I could see, in there having been in
the house – and for how long, above all? – a person of whom I
was in ignorance. It lasted while I just bridled a little with the

sense that my office demanded that there should be no such ignorance and no such person. It lasted while this visitant, at all events – and there was a touch of the strange freedom, as I remember, in the sign of familiarity of his wearing no hat – seemed to fix me, from his position, with just the question, just the scrutiny through the fading light, that his own presence provoked. We were too far apart to call to each other, but there was a moment at which, at shorter range, some challenge between us, breaking the hush, would have been the right result of our straight mutual stare. He was in one of the angles, the one away from the house, very erect, as it struck me, and with both hands on the ledge. So I saw him as I see the letters I form on this page; then, exactly, after a minute, as if to add to the spectacle, he slowly changed his place – passed, looking at me hard all the while, to the opposite corner of the platform. Yes, I had the sharpest sense that during this transit he never took his eyes from me, and I can see at this moment the way his hand, as he went, passed from one of the crenelations to the next. He stopped at the other corner, but less long, and even as he turned away still markedly fixed me. He turned away; that was all I knew.[23]

I will take it as agreed that this is an impressive and highly-charged passage, productive of excitement and admiration, and will attempt to relate the qualities that make it so to my argument.

1 *Qualities of successful exposition* – precision of vocabulary, concise and pungent phrasing, lucidity of phrase-, sentence-, or para-graph-structure – are in a sense coterminous with the adequacy of a work's total conception, since if any single conception (an object or an event, say) is not made clear, it cannot be said, from the reader's point of view (whatever the author may have conceived), to be part of the work's content at all. A work may, of course, for special reasons positively eschew precision, conciseness and intelligibility. The Eumaeus episode in *Ulysses* is not marked by exact and telling vocabulary, the speeches of Miss Bates in *Emma* are not concise, *Finnegans Wake* is not in any ordinary sense intelligible. But all such apparent exceptions may be drawn back under our general principle if we observe that the total conception of a work includes not only conceptions such as objects or events

but also, in many cases, governing or filtering conceptions through which these conceptions are perceived. Examples of such governing conceptions would be the consciousness of a character, or a parodic or dream convention. The imprecisions, redundancies and eccentricities in the works cited serve (when successful) to render precisely and economically both the governing conceptions and the more specific conceptions they govern. (When they fail in this task they are open to essentially the same criticisms as passages of straightforward exposition. A speech by a confused or loquacious character, for example, ceases to be effective when its length or disorder exceeds what is necessary to render a character-conception which interacts satisfactorily with the work's other conceptions. Thus one can imagine a 'Miss Bates' whose speech-mannerisms would depart so widely from the norm among other characters as to infringe the convention of (somewhat stylised) social realism maintained in the rest of the novel.) The expository virtues, then, are, strictly, all-embracing, and incorporate as specialisations all other virtues which have to do with the content of a work. (The possibility of 'stylistic' virtues unconnected with content has already been dismissed, with minor exceptions which will be considered at the end of the discussion.) Consequently I shall confine myself in this sub-section to general observations and to noting qualities which do not seem specifically to demand attention in the sub-sections which follow.

Expository clarity serves, I suggest, two functions which correspond to the two complementary aspects of the reading experience as I have described it. Firstly, it expedites the reader's access to the conceptions (of actions, objects, sensations, characters, and so on) and thereby facilitates immediacy and liveliness of response. A wasted word, a purposelessly convoluted sentence, or a formulation whose meaning in context has to be guessed at or inferred from other evidence, delays the movement of attention from conception to succeeding – and perhaps closely interacting – conception; it requires a profitless expenditure of mental energy on the reader's part, thus reducing fractionally his reserves of energy for the apprehension of necessary material and for emotional response. Or to put the positive version of the case: the subtler and more extensive an author's command of nuances of expression, the greater the range and delicacy of the conceptions, and consequent responses, he can secure; the more economical his use of language, the more – and more complex – response will be obtainable for any specified expenditure of energy by the reader, within any specified span of time or attention. In other words, the author aspires (if one may so express it) to minimise the tax on our vitality levied by the act of apprehension, in order to maximise the vitality available for responding to the conceptions which are apprehended; or, again, by compressing into a given quantity of language as much detail and substance of conception as is digestible, to make a relatively small effort of apprehension provide relatively high reward in psychic stimulation. (The implied distinction here between what at the level of verbal detail makes conceptions clear and what provides emotional stimulation corresponds, *in parvo*, to the larger-scale distinction, noted above, between 'facilitating material' and material 'psychologically more highly charged'; like that distinction it is one of degree, and always provisional.) An example may make the situation clearer. Suppose that in the bipenultimate sentence of the specimen passage James had originally written 'sideways movement' before substituting 'transit', with its precise denotation of lateral movement against a background, and its hints of incorporeality (cf. 'transitory', 'transient') and of literal (astronomical) unearthliness (cf. 'transit of Mercury'). One might express part of the artistic gain represented by this supposed revision by observing that through it James performs for us, releases us from, the intellectual exertion of combining two separately verbalised conceptions (movement and lateral direction) into one conceived action, and thereby leaves us more energy for responding to the psychic stimulus the conception presents; while at the same time, through the associative connections 'transit' makes with other, broader conceptions in the story (Quint's being a ghost, and the general atmosphere of uncertainty about the relationship between the apparent and the real), James reinforces these conceptions at no additional cost to us – or at any rate (since some energy is perhaps expended in extracting from 'transit' the conceptions compounded into it) at less cost than would be exacted if a separate form of words were set aside for the purpose. Ultimately these are varying applications of the same principle, namely that the differential between the energy devoted to apprehension and the energy devoted to response should be as favourable to the latter as possible; in this way the desires which constitute response are quickened, that is, freed as far as possible from the drain on their intensity which the conflicting claims of intellectual exertion impose. Conversely, where a form of words can be shown to be less concise than it might be, when all the delicacies and refinements of conception it accomplishes (including conceptions relating to the narrative *persona*) have been taken into account, then the comparatively unfavourable differential in energy between apprehension and response may be cited as the affective correlative of a compositional lapse.

The second function of expository clarity at the level of verbal detail is its contribution to the effect of psychological governance over the quickened desire. Lucid verbal formulations are localised equivalents – and indeed components – of a work's overall cohesion, and engender a similar impression of control. Why clarity or coherence in a literary work should engender in the reader's mind a sense of psychological strength and security with regard to a body of affect is not immediately clear, though that it has at least some tendency to do so will probably not be disputed. To some extent the process may be explained, in a manner already hinted at, as a kind of conscious or subconscious psychological inference; from the fact that a complex of conceptions has been made clear, we infer *intellectual* control in him who has proved capable of making it clear, and perhaps also *emotional* control, bearing in mind that the opposite quality, incoherence, is commonly a symptom of imperfectly mastered feeling. But this consideration seems insufficient to account for the infection of the reader's own consciousness by an illusion of sovereignty. If an inference about authorial control were the only factor, we would surely be able to admire James's, exhibited in, say, the firmly focused consistency with which, in the first sentence, the governess's complacency is rendered by a series of related indications – the homely 'plump', the quietly gleeful 'my very hour', the reassuring 'tucked away', the self-indulgent 'stroll' – and yet to feel, ourselves, entirely apart from these Jamesian qualities of control, to experience nothing ourselves but a series of emotional fits and starts, as the various conceptions draw out their responses. The reason this does not happen is that, as remarked above, the nature and the ordering of material cannot be experienced separately, and a reader cannot, therefore, receive and respond to conceptions independently of their precise sequence and arrangement; this sequence and arrangement impose their pattern upon the reading experience, and the intellectual and emotional control manifested through them becomes internalised by the reader, becomes for the time being a quality of his consciousness – with the crucial difference that a patterning which may have cost the writer immense intellectual and emotional effort becomes the reader's property at a much lower price, that of apprehending something which has already been made as apprehensible as possible. Hence, in comparison with the expenditure of psychic energy undertaken by the author, and the expenditure he himself would have had to undertake had he tried by introspection to draw out any body of his own desires into a coherent totality, the reader of a successfully functioning work of fiction, with whose content he is capable of some engagement, finds his desires pouring forth, interacting with one another, and assuming an apprehensible total pattern, with felicitous ease. Again, therefore, it is the exceptionally favourable *differential* between energy devoted to response and energy devoted to apprehension – the fact that a high level, or a formidable complexity, of desire appears to be compatible with a quite low outlay of intellectual exertion – which induces in the reader the impression that he has far greater psychic resources for understanding and marshalling his desires than normally appears to be the case.

2 *Qualities of imagery* – the denotation in simile and metaphor of imagined things, generally for the purpose of enriching more abstract or more complex conceptions (actions, attitudes, feelings) – constitute a large specific area of what we value and respond to at the small-scale verbal level, and are assimilated into my account in the following way.

Their contribution to the quickening aspect of our experience of literature can be divided into three elements. Firstly, they help to clarify the literal meaning, to particularise a conception, and consequently our response to it; from this point of view they are simply auxiliaries to direct statement, called upon because they can convey an idea more memorably and economically than literal exposition. Indeed the dividing line between direct and metaphorical statement is extremely difficult to draw – a fact well illustrated by our specimen passage, since James (here as elsewhere) tends to favour not so much the boldly evocative Shakespearean metaphor ('against a sea of troubles') or the Proustian analytical simile (There is a species of hymenoptera ...) as the word or phrase which though partially tamed to a literal meaning still retains some metaphorical colour; 'shrink', 'invoked', 'bridled', 'challenge', 'flanked'. 'Definite as a picture in a frame' is a relatively unusual case of advertised simile. Secondly, metaphorical qualities help to direct the reader's mind to the appropriate zone of feeling; to activate, and then to sustain in activation, a particular area of sensibility and prevent us from losing the fixity of our emotion: the prevalence of blood imagery in *Macbeth* is an obvious example. The boldest attempt in the James passage to call out through imagery a visceral emotional response in support of that evoked by the conceived action and situation is, of course, 'stricken with death'; but this is only the summit of several levels of subtle evocation: the repeated reminders of fading light and the 'hush'; the supernatural suggestion in 'visitant' and perhaps in 'transit'; and the nervous anxiety and agitation conveyed through the governess's frequent recourse, in recalling her sensations, to the 'strange', the 'sharp' and the instantaneous ('arrested me on the spot', 'in a flash', 'on the instant'). And, of course, what the author excludes – the comic or light- hearted or reassuring imagery he does not intrude into the treatment of Quint's apparition – equally conditions the overall emotional effect.

Through these two functions imagery works to confirm and refine the total affective quality of a work, or an episode in a work. Occasionally, however, one finds a metaphorical inventiveness which exceeds any integrative function of this kind. Some passages in Nabokov, for example, have the air of being miniature detachable prose poems (or indeed verse poems, as in parts of *The Gift* and *Pale Fire*): this should not disturb us once we acknowledge that the unity of a novel need not lie in all-subordinating plot or thematic centres, but can inhere at least partly in a diversity of interests radiating from a generous sensibility. The supreme specialist in such diversity is probably Proust, whose extended metaphors and similes, especially when considered *en masse*, betray a relish, and arouse a delight, which seems partially independent of the immediate contribution they make to the clarification of the thought or feeling which has ostensibly prompted them.

And just as the Japanese amuse themselves by filling a porcelain bowl with water and steeping in it little crumbs of paper which until then are without character or form, but, the moment they become wet, stretch themselves and bend, take on colour and distinctive shape, become flowers or houses or people, permanent and recognisable, so in that moment all the flowers in our garden and in M. Swann's park, and the water-lilies on the Vivonne and the good folk of the village and their little dwellings and the parish church and the whole of Combray and of its surroundings, taking their proper shapes and growing solid, sprang into being, town and gardens alike, from my cup of tea.[24]

The simile serves beautifully its purpose of elucidating (perhaps with a certain cosmetic stylisation) a mental event, but it also has an intrinsic appeal which is more than functional. We are grateful to Proust not only for making the experience clear, but for using this mediating conception to do so; and there are countless images of a similar kind throughout the novel. These images collectively embody, and implicate us in, a general appetency of the imagination. They draw out desires which are directed not centripetally towards the specific zones of experience which are the major preoccupations of the novel, but centrifugally towards the universe of knowledge; very often, indeed, the more extraordinary and specialised Proust's image, the more enchanted one is by it. Yet in the final analysis the very diversity of these centrifugal materials constitutes their unity, since this encyclopaedic pursuit of expressive images is itself an aspect of the total conception, a quality of the mind which we see objectifying itself in the novel. An isolated image of this kind would, I think, be experienced as a blemish, or at least an odd imaginative *cul-de-sac* – or possibly not be experienced at all in quite this way, since it is, perhaps, only because of their frequency that we attune our sensibility to respond to the encyclopaedic, the outward-facing, as well as the thematic, the inward-facing, tendency in Proust's extended images.

Finally, to describe the contribution of imagery to the second proposed aspect of the reading experience, the effect of psychological governance, it will suffice to repeat with slightly different emphasis points which have been made already, since the essential controlling qualities of clear and coherent presentation are as appropriately invoked in the case of imagery as in that of literal statement (in so far as the two are distinguishable). Effective images, considered singly, evince an imaginative resource and an intellectual acuteness which the reader internalises in the manner suggested in sub-section 1 above; while the repetition of images, and the development of image-complexes such as those of

sharpness and immediacy in the James passage, contribute to the
impression of intellectual and emotional control communicated by
patterning and likewise internalised. This does not, of course,
mean that it is necessary for the reader *consciously to register* the
repetition or interrelation of images; to do so is as superfluous to
the experience of aesthetic order in literature as a mental notation
of key-relationships to the experience of a musical work in sonata
form.

3 *Qualities of tone*, or 'voice', I take to include all qualities of
diction, syntax and rhythm, and all special effects of dialect and
idiolect, in so far as they contribute to a conception of the speaker
or narrator's personality or consciousness, rather than of the
subject-matter of his speech or narrative. The distinction is an
insecure one, since the consciousness of a fictional character or
narrative voice *is*, to a large extent, the things it is conscious of;
and the things it is conscious of are often – that is, when another
speaker or narrator does not refer to them – only accessible to the
reader through the fictional consciousness. Moreover, the speaker
or narrator may be his (or her) own subject-matter. Thus, when
the governess declares, 'I didn't ask more than that – I only asked
that he should *know*', she at once *describes* her state of mind, and
reveals it (in so far as her 'present' narrative can be taken to
correspond to her 'then' state of mind) through certain self-
depreciating turns of language – the priority given to the negative
clause, the 'only' – coupled with the pleading stress on 'know'.
We respond both to the description and to the revelation, or rather
to the conception of the governess's feelings co-operatively
engendered by both. Another insecure distinction might be drawn
between authorial (or, to avoid the intentional fallacy, let us say
'authoritative') voice and characterising voice. This distinction is
insecure because even narrative voices which enjoy the authority
of omniscience are to a greater or lesser extent unnamed *personae*
with characteristic attitudes and mannerisms towards which one
may feel degrees of sympathy or aversion. (This sympathy or
aversion is not to be confused (at least not logically – psychologically the confusion is easy) with approval or disapproval for the
fiction as a work of art. That the narrative *persona* of, say, *Howards
End* is more sympathetic than that of say, *Buddenbrooks* is a
legitimate critical observation about part of the overall effect of
each novel, but it does not entail the conclusion that *Howards End*

is the more admirable work.) The basic difference between the two types is that authoritative voice provides a norm, and is for better or worse inextricably associated with the novel's conceptional totality, whereas the conceptions immediately generated by characterising voice can be tested against, and modified by, others generated elsewhere, an obvious case being that in which a character's self-presentation is subverted by other characters' observations or by the main narrative voice or by assumed social norms in the world of the novel – or by all three, as befalls Mr Collins in *Pride and Prejudice* or Mrs Elton in *Emma*. Characterising voice will, in fact, normally be the voice of a character, though one can think of cases in which a non-personalised voice is 'placed' in this way – passages of parody, for example. Our extract from James combines the authoritative and the characterising (as first-person narratives almost inevitably do). To question the governess's narrative as an authoritative exposition of her subjective experiences (what she believes to have happened to her) would simply render the fiction null and void – as would questioning the ultimate authority of a third-person narrative (however sceptical it might authoritatively be);[25] but we are free to draw inferences about – derive conceptions of – her personality from her narrative and to feed these inferences into our overall conception of the content of the tale.

Qualities of tone, like qualities of imagery, serve to clarify and organise the content of a work and are, like them, specialisations of the qualities discussed in sub-section 1. But a couple of specific points may be made about them. Firstly, as already suggested, 'voice' arouses affect in the same way as any other conception; the naive precision, in our extract, of 'as charming as a charming story' and the coy imprecision of 'Someone' in the following sentence induce sympathy or anxious reservation or a mixture of both; while the composure displayed elsewhere (notably in the Jane Austen-like formula, 'An unknown man in a lonely place is a permitted object of fear to a young woman privately bred') impresses us with the governess's counterbalancing (and again, affectively somewhat ambivalent) prim strength of intellect and character. Secondly, tone well defined and constantly maintained plays a particularly obvious part in unifying narrative and thereby contributing to the effect of aesthetic order and psychological control: a more obvious part than imagery, since the impression of voice is more or less continuous, while the most an image or

image-type can do is significantly recur. Effective authoritative
voice is almost by definition homogeneous; characterising voice
may be homogeneous, as in *The Turn of the Screw*, setting aside its
introductory section; or may undergo fluctuation or metamorph-
osis in harmony with other conceptions, as in Beckett's *Malone
Dies* (most markedly at the very end); or may take the form of a
group of individually consistent and significantly interrelated
voices, as in *The Sound and the Fury* or *The Woman in White*.

4 *Qualities of aural, visual and formal beauty.* All the qualities so far
discussed have been seen as small-scale contributors to the content
of the work, the conceptions; and since, according to my account,
the conceptions are the stimuli to our desire, and their presentation
and arrangement the objective correlative to our sense of psychological governance, it is not surprising that it should have been
possible to elaborate on the relationship between these matters of
verbal detail and the proposed two-part description of our
experience of fiction. But despite my attempted refutation, above,
of the notion of stylistic qualities distinct from content, it may be
protested that there are at any rate a few linguistic qualities, of
varying importance, which are not related to content and consequently cannot be assimilated to my argument in this comparatively tidy fashion: beauty of sound, beauty of visual appearance (in
individual words or in layout), and small-scale formal beauty
(conceived as an aesthetic quality – inherent, say, in the internal
symmetry of a sentence or paragraph – independent of the
function of making conceptions clear).

The answer, I think, is essentially the same in all these cases. It is
impossible to deny that, all things being equal from the point of
view of the clarity, pungency and coherence of the conceptions, a
word, a phrase or sentence which is ornamental in one or more of
these respects might be chosen in preference to another. This
ornamental quality might be valued by the reader, quite justifiably,
for the simple reason that it is pleasant; and thus lie outside the
terms of my theory about the functioning of literature in relation to
the reader's experience. But there are reasons for supposing that
this dissociation of ornamental beauty from the functions I have
proposed is extremely rare. Beauty of sound, for example, would
surely dissatisfy us (unless used ironically or for the deliberately
disturbing effect of implicating the reader's sympathy in something abhorrent) in a description of a murder or a concentration

camp. Or to put it another and better way (since this last formulation holds good only if we assume a narrowly sensuous or epicurean notion of verbal music, and it may be objected that beauty can inhere in the harshest or dryest sonorities), the beauty must have a character such that it supports, or at least does not subvert, the affective quality of the content – in which case it may be assimilated into my account. Qualities of sound contribute to the evocation of physical phenomena (through onomatopoeia) and of states of mind (through association – a steady, easily-breathed rhythm suggesting physical, and by inference psychological, composure, and so on); and fluency and ease of delivery are manifestations of control which the reader is likely to internalise. When these functions related to the conceptions and their organisation have been discounted, it is difficult to believe that much of importance remains. The visual beauty of individual words, that slightest and most elusive of the aesthetic qualities of language, is subject to exactly analogous considerations, if indeed it does not resolve itself on examination into other qualities: is there, one wonders, a word in the language which is not beautiful to hear and does not denote a beautiful object and yet is beautiful to look at? Similarly, semantic patterning which helps to enforce the clarity and coherence of conceptions, as in a sentence already quoted

An unknown man	item
in a lonely place	+ condition
is	=
a permitted object of fear	item
to a young woman privately bred	+ condition

can be accounted for in terms of my argument, while a pattern with no such rationale (a sentence or paragraph, say, with an internal repetition of structure which did not correspond to a repetition in the relationships among conceptions being pre-sented) would be likely to present the same disagreeable and gratuitous appearance as an obviously contrived rhyme in poetry, if it did not in any case irritate us by impairing clarity of exposition. The same consideration applies to experiments with the layout of the words on the page, as in concrete poetry; if the visual pattern lacks conceptual point it strikes us as an affectation, unless we allow ourselves to apprehend it simply as a perceptual object, whose lines and loops and spaces happen incidentally to be those of linguistic symbols. But this effectively takes us out of the bounds of literature altogether, into the question of the aesthetic order attained by abstract art.

5

Objections Concerning Affect

I

In this final chapter of theory I propose to defend the main thesis against the objections commonly aimed at critical procedures which refer to affects. These objections are of two related kinds, one concerned immediately with critical practice, the other with methodological propriety. The first problem arises from the obvious fact that responses to literary works vary from reader to reader; not only may one person find repugnant what another welcomes (for example, Odysseus's acts of vengeance after his return to Ithaca), but even when two people happen to describe their responses in the same terms their experiences may, for all we know, be subtly different. How then (unless the discussion of literature is to be confined to the unadjudicated pooling of impressions amid 'the easy equality of friends'[1] – a civilised activity but hardly a collective discipline of study) can criticism be sensibly conducted with reference to the reader's responses – an index which can apparently point to any number of different conclusions simultaneously? Other approaches to literature, it may be said, have at least the merit of being grounded upon comparatively objective materials – historical evidence, letters and diaries, preliminary drafts, demonstrable literary conventions and linguistic usages, and literary texts themselves – whose content and validity can be agreed, or fruitfully argued, by critics in general, however much their respective values for literary-critical activity may be disputed.

The second objection puts essentially the same point in a different way. The purpose of literary criticism, it insists, is to discuss, analyse and assess literature. By directing attention to responses we are making a contribution to the study of psychology, but hardly to that of literature; we are falling into what Wimsatt and Beardsley call 'the Affective Fallacy', a 'confusion between the

poem and its *results* (what it *is* and what it *does*)'.[2] Admittedly, 'the
poem' itself is an elusive subject for analysis, since in the case of a
literary work the usual epistemological problem about knowing
any object (as distinct from one's own perceptions or impressions)
is compounded by the complex material-cultural-mental status of
this kind of object. Moreover, what a thing *is* can sometimes best,
or only, be inferred from what it *does* (as the size and structure of a
star can be inferred from the radiation it emits). If, then, responses
were a reliable indication of the nature of a literary work, such that
by noting the responses we might reasonably arrive at an account
of what was going on in the work, an affective methodology might
turn out to be the most efficient approach to the literary object. But,
as we have observed, no such trustworthy correspondence
between object and response can exist, because of the personal
factors which help to condition the response. If we treated
responses as radio signals we would be inclined to infer the
existence of many different *Odysseys*, many different *Hamlets* and
Golden Bowls and *Lolitas*.

These objections are, I believe, largely correct, and deliver the
death-blow to any thorough-going affective methodology which
would purport to reach an understanding of literary works by
scrutinising readers' responses. This conclusion does not, it should
be noted, do anything to invalidate the general theory advanced in
this book. What has been proposed so far – setting aside the
comments on other critical theories, which are just or unjust
whether or not the theory they are intended to clear the way for is
valid – is that the countless particular affects produceable by
imaginative literature have a specific common mode or characteristic: namely desire, rather than (for example) satisfaction or
emotional neutralisation. It would be no contradiction of this
general point to say that, because of certain practical difficulties in
treating highly personalised emotional responses as evidence, an
awareness of it is of no help in discussing particular works. (In a
similar way, one might truly assert as a general principle that the
physical characteristics of a human being are determined genetical-
ly at conception, without being able, by virtue of that principle, to
predict with any useful degree of confidence the characteristics
which a specific child of specific parents will have.) If we drew this
conclusion, we would be obliged merely to state our general point
and then dismiss it from mind in order to approach the literary
work from other, non-affective directions. For reasons which I will

come to shortly, I do not regard this renunciation as necessary, but hold that it is possible and fruitful to refer to feelings and responses when practising literary criticism. Nevertheless, it is quite vain, I suggest, to treat literary criticism as a species of psychological investigation, to attempt a kind of diagnostics or radio-astronomy of aesthetic response; if the central proposition of this book is to be of more than theoretical value, the recognition that literature quickens desire must be brought to bear, in a methodologically satisfactory way, upon the analysis of works themselves. 'Brought to bear', it is perhaps necessary to insist, not 'imposed as an all-sufficient explanation'. A general theory about a category of things, if true, refutes some other general theories; but it does not provide exhaustive descriptions of individual things – though it does exclude, or modify, descriptions founded upon the refuted general theories. For an exhaustive description of a literary work many techniques are needed, including plenty of entirely familiar ones; my proposal is to build in to critical activity a clear awareness of the affective function of literature – not to reduce critical activity to the study of affects.

Perhaps the best way of beginning to distinguish the present argument from the kind of affective theory it rejects is to indicate agreement with the terms in which Wimsatt and Beardsley, in the essay already mentioned, criticise the affectivist tradition which they associate particularly with I. A. Richards and C. L. Stevenson. Briefly, this tradition holds that literature employs a special, emotive function of language which is quite distinct from the cognitive or referential function. The distinction might be exemplified by the uses of the word 'fascism', which to a political scientist has a number of referential meanings concerned with the theory and practice of state organisation, but in general use possesses also a strong emotive import, of a negative kind, which is far from being a mere corollary of it referential meanings and can be used to induce an emotional attitude in contexts in which its agreed referential meanings do not arise, as when an English politician calls the IRA 'fascists' and is applauded. On this view of literature it is seriously misleading to discuss a literary work in terms of its 'meanings', if by 'meanings' we understand the referential values of words which we can check by consulting common usage or a dictionary; we must rather explore its *emotive* meanings or values. And since these are not publicly demonstrable and approximately fixed, as referential meanings are – there is no dictionary of emotive values in language, though there may be certain areas of consensus concerning them – we have some justificating for directing our attention in the first instance towards the emotional responses in which their effects are made manifest.

Against this view Wimsatt and Beardsley argue persuasively that the emotive import of a statement is essentially dependent upon what it referentially means, or at least suggests. Thus, the emotive force of 'fascism' as an insult is derived, if not necessarily from the full descriptive meanings a political scientist would acknowledge, at any rate from certain descriptive suggestions (cruelty, violence, hatred of contrary opinions, martial ostentation) which have legitimately become attached to the word. Accordingly, the publicly demonstrable meanings and suggestions of the literary text provide a perfectly workable basis for any analysis of its emotive force, and there is no need to resort to the tabulation of responses.

> The more specific the account of the emotion induced by a poem, the more nearly it will be an account of the reasons for emotion, the poem itself, and the more reliable it will be as an account of what the poem is likely to induce in other – sufficiently informed – readers. It will in fact supply the kind of information which will enable readers to respond to the poem. It will talk not of tears, prickles, or other physiological symptoms, of feeling angry, joyful, hot, cold or intense, or of vaguer states of emotional disturbance, but of shades of distinction and relation between objects of emotion.... The critic is not a contributor to statistically countable reports about the poem, but a teacher or explicator of meanings.[3]

At least in the case of Richards, however, the strictures of Wimsatt and Beardsley, though just, are insufficient to dispose of his argument completely. To some extent, indeed, he anticipates their point about the dependence of the emotive value of language upon its referential value.

> A statement may be used for the sake of the *reference*, true or false, which it causes. This is the *scientific* use of language. But it may also be used for the sake of the effects in emotion and attitude produced by the reference it contains. This is the *emotive* use of language. The distinction once clearly grasped is simple.

We may either use words for the sake of the references they promote, or we may use them for the sake of the attitudes and emotions which ensue. Many arrangements of words evoke attitudes without any reference being required *en route*. They operate like musical phrases. But usually references are involved as *conditions for*, or *stages in*, the ensuing development of attitudes, yet it is still the attitudes not the references which are important. It matters not at all in such cases whether the references are true or false. Their sole function is to bring about and support the attitudes which are the further response.[4]

Referential meaning, then, usually does make a contribution, sometimes an indispensable contribution, to emotive effect. This is a concession, rather than a complete answer, to the objection later articulated by Wimsatt and Beardsley, since despite apparently unambiguous statements earlier in the passage Richards suddenly reverts to positing (unfortunately without examples) 'arrangements of words' which 'evoke attitudes without any reference being required *en route*'. But there is a deeper, though less obvious, confusion in Richards's argument. In order to grasp it we must take careful note of his use of the term 'reference'. In Richards's writing, a 'reference' is not precisely *what a word refers to*, its descriptive meanings, nor the *act of referring* (on the part of the word, or its user), but rather the *movement of thought* which is stimulated by the word or statement, and may or may not arrive at the terminus of an actually existing object or event. A statement is said to 'cause' a reference. Now Richards's picture of the two uses of language could be expressed diagrammatically as follows:

Scientific Use
statement → reference

Emotive Use
statement → reference → emotion

But these two causal sequences are not quite comparable: the first is surely incomplete. The 'emotive use' terminates in the emotion; but the 'scientific use' does not in the same sense terminate in the 'reference' (as we are to understand the term). Scientific statements (even in Richards's broad sense) are not made 'for the sake of' the reference, in a sense comparable to that in which emotive statements are made 'for the sake of' the emotional effects; they are made for the sake of communicating a truth-claim. In writing a history of the English Civil War we do not say 'Charles I was beheaded in 1649' for the sake of the movement of thought which these words stimulate, but for the sake of getting across the assertion that the terminus of that movement of thought is something which actually happened. The reference, whether in 'scientific' or 'emotive' discourse, is a staging-post to some further phenomenon in consciousness. A more plausible diagram, therefore, might be the following:

Scientific Use

statement→ reference→ conviction
(or doubt)

Emotive Use

statement→ reference→ emotion

In each case the third item in the sequence depends upon a contribution made by the reader's mind: his faculty of evaluating truth-claims in the first case, his emotional predispositions in the second. This improved scheme, however, remains doubly unsatisfactory: it fails to explain how we recognise which use is in question; and it fails to acknowledge the obvious point that a believed truth-claim can itself be productive of emotion. Both of these issues can be resolved if we consider a case in which a reader or auditor is unsure of which use of language he is dealing with – that of a listener, for instance, who switches the radio on at random and hears a voice declaring that a hurricane is about to strike the region in which he lives. In this situation it is likely that the listener will experience both emotions and (tentatively at least) the thoughts which result from receiving an assertion that something is truly the case. The statement itself, therefore, is in itself not definitely either 'scientific' or 'emotive'; it contains the potential for both functions. It is only when the listener learns the *convention* – truth-telling or imaginative – within which the statement has been made that one of these responses can be decisively suppressed or subordinated: if the programme turns out to be a play, he can conclude that he has not received an assertion, and need neither check its veracity nor take consequent action; if it turns out to be the weather forecast, he may reasonably be expected to ensure that his emotion does not interfere with the speedy taking of consequent action. (Naturally the subordination of emotion in this circumstance may be difficult; the point is that it loses its conventional priority. And indeed some 'truth-telling' discourse may aim, for polemical purposes, to arouse emotion. But the emotion remains 'subordinate' in that it is instrumental (however illogically) to the end of conviction. The polemicist may structure his utterance to maximise its emotional impact, but his aim is assent to propositions about the primary world.)

With these considerations in mind we may venture an expanded diagram, as follows.

Truth-telling convention

statement → reference → conviction/doubt
(emotion conventionally
subordinated)

Imaginative convention

statement → reference → emotion
(conviction/doubt
conventionally suppressed)

Yet another way of expressing this distinction would be to say that while in the case of 'scientific' discourse we are induced to have beliefs (that a statement is true or false, that a question has or has not been settled), in reading imaginative literature we put conceptions to ourselves (or allow the work to put them to us) without believing them or indeed thinking that the question of belief arises, in order, as it were, to see what they feel like – much as we might entertain a daydream for the sake of its emotional stimulus without for a moment believing it. Now one consequence of this view of the experience of reading literature is that literature cannot in any straightforward sense be conceived as giving *satisfaction*: for if we have no belief in the conceptions presented to the imagination, if we know them to be, as it were, fantasies with which we are voluntarily associating ourselves, then any emotion we feel about them must be an incomplete and aspiring emotion, the kind appropriate to thinking 'suppose' (or 'if only') 'I inherited a million pounds', rather than to believing that I actually have

inherited a million pounds. The literary experience must, therefore, be essentially one of unproductive, and finally perhaps
somewhat frustrating, aspiration – unless we can show, as I
attempted to do in my first chapter, that it contains compensations
which justify our valuing it highly in spite of its dimension of
unsatisfactoriness. Richards comes tantalisingly close to performing this task himself in *Principles of Literary Criticism*, when he
ascribes to art a capacity for conferring upon 'impulses' (appetencies and aversions – my 'desire', in fact) an 'equilibrium' which
frees us 'from the bewilderment which our own maladjustment
brings with it' and permits a rewarding discrimination between
the more and the less important impulses.[5] But Richards's
evangelical view of art as a supremely effective form of psychological and even social therapy leads him to credit it, contrary to my
theory, with a capacity to satisfy, or at least appease, impulses as
well as to energise and interrelate them; and this in turn obliges
him, at the cost of Humpty-Dumpty-like eccentricities of terminology, to maintain the view that reading literature entails not merely
suppositions or fantasies, but beliefs.

> Very often the whole state of mind in which we are left by a
> poem, or by music, or, more rarely perhaps, by other forms of
> art, is of a kind which it is natural to describe as a belief ....
> When, through reading *Adonais*, for example, we are left in a
> strong emotional attitude which feels like belief, it is only too
> easy to think that we are believing in immortality or survival, or
> in something else capable of statement, and fatally easy also to
> attribute the value of the poem to the alleged effect, or
> conversely to regret that it should depend upon such a
> scientifically doubtful conclusion. Scientific beliefs, as opposed
> to these emotive beliefs, are beliefs '*that* so and so'. They can be
> stated with greater or lesser precision, as the case may be, but
> always in some form. It is for some people difficult to admit
> beliefs which are objectless, which are not about anything or in
> anything; beliefs which cannot be stated. Yet most of the beliefs
> of children and primitive peoples, and of the unscientific
> generally seem to be of this kind. Their parasitic nature helps to
> confuse the issue. What we have to distinguish are beliefs which
> are grounded in fact, i.e. are due to reference, and beliefs which
> are due to other causes, and merely attach themselves to such
> references as will support them.

That an objectless belief is a ridiculous or an incomplete thing is a prejudice deriving only from confusion. Such beliefs have, of course, no place in science, but in themselves they are often of utmost value. Provided always that they do not furnish themselves with illicit objects. It is the objectless belief which is masquerading as a belief in this or that, which is ridiculous.... These objectless beliefs, which though merely attitudes seem to be knowledge, are not difficult to explain. Some system of impulses not ordinarily in adjustment within itself or adjusted to the world finds something which orders it or gives it fit exercise. Then follows the peculiar sense of ease, of restfulness, of free, unimpeded activity, and the feeling of acceptance, of something more positive than acquiescence. This feeling is the reason why such states may be called beliefs. They share this feeling with, for example, the state which follows the conclusive answering of a question.[6]

The general point here – that one can be profoundly affected by a work of art without believing that what it represents is truly the case – is well taken, but Richards's equation of this affect with a kind of 'belief' is as untenable as it is eccentric. Three comments should be sufficient.

Firstly, one wonders how Richards can know anything about the beliefs of children, primitive peoples and the unscientific if they are beliefs which 'cannot be stated'. I should have thought that the characteristic beliefs of persons in all these categories were readily statable beliefs about, or in, things: Father Christmas, tree-spirits, walking under ladders. Secondly, Richards's distinction between 'beliefs which are grounded in fact, i.e. are due to reference, and beliefs which are due to other causes, and merely attach themselves to such references as will support them', is surely the distinction between justified beliefs, and prejudice or wishful thinking with its fig-leaf of factitious plausibility; and this has nothing to do with any distinction between a belief *that* so and so, and a supposed alternative type of belief. Richards seems to be confusing the notion of a belief which is 'objectless' in the sense that it has no object, that is, is not about anything, with a notion of a belief which is 'objectless' in the sense that its object does not in fact exist. (This confusion, between an object's presence or absence in thought, and its presence or absence in reality, runs parallel to another confusion which allows Richards in the just-quoted passage to co-ordinate 'reference' with 'fact', but in a passage quoted earlier to speak of a 'reference, true or false'.[7]) And thirdly there is something distinctly strange about a terminology which would require me to say that when reading about Uriah Heep or looking at the Tiepolo Venus in the National Gallery I am experiencing an 'objectless (emotive) belief': it would surely ring truer to say that I am experiencing an objectful aversion or desire. The object may be an image or group of images or other conception in whose correspondence to reality I have no belief (which is why I can only respond to it through the mode of desire, not through that of primary experience which, because it involves the possibility of action upon our persons and circumstances, can extend to 'finished' emotions of pleasure and pain), but it is an object nevertheless. Of course it is true that I do not have to have what Richards calls a 'scientific' belief in immortality in order to be moved by *Adonais*, and I would be a fool to be induced to have one by the invention of a poet; but it is not necessary to introduce a new, non-scientific kind of belief in order to account for my emotion, which can be adequately explained by saying that an invented world in which immortality is conceived to be the case (the world of the poem) has struck me as desirable, devoutly to be wished, when presented to my imagination. Richards, however, cannot rest content with a description of this kind since it leaves the emotion incomplete and unsatisfying; his untenable 'objectless belief' is added to the picture in order to validate his higher claim for the aesthetic affect – that it is (or can be) satisfying.

Richards's inconsistencies and eccentricities stem, therefore, in my view, from a quixotic attempt to demonstrate in the case of the arts a process of emotional satisfaction parallel to the process of intellectual satisfaction (sign→ statement→ reference → assertion→ belief) effected by science; an attempt to establish for the various stages between the linguistic sign and the reader's eventual response a distinction which is also an equivalence – a parity of value – between scientific and emotive uses of language. This tempts him (Wimsatt's point) to speak sometimes as if, or almost as if, referential meaning and emotional stimulus were functions arbitrarily united in a word or phrase or statement. It also prompts him (my point) defensively to ascribe to the experience of art a psychological conclusiveness, likened to 'the state which follows the conclusive answering of a question' and validated by a gravely problematical concept of 'objectless (emotive) belief', which in my view it does not possess and need not possess in order to have value.[8] These difficulties vanish if, as I have suggested, we hold that the distinction between 'science' and 'poetry' (to borrow Richards's terms for a moment) lies not in any difference in what may be said or in the meaning we initially attach to what is said – though certainly some statements may be more *likely* to occur in 'scientific' than in 'poetic' contexts, or *vice versa* – but in a conventional distinction between discourse which makes a claim to primary truth, and discourse which makes no such claim and is therefore to be construed quasi-hypothetically, like a fantasy, even though it is not hypothetical in form. According to this view, a statement in, say, a history, and the same statement in a novel, are in substance the same thing (subject to contextual modification), carrying the same potential cognitive and emotive force. The situations differ simply in that in each case we are conventionally called upon to suppress, or subordinate to an incidental role, an aspect of our possible response, as in the final version of my diagram (p. 139 above): in the case of a novel, our faculty of evaluating truth-claims; in the case of the history, our desires and aversions, to the extent that they might impede the evaluation of truth-claims. (We are not, for example, to allow our aversion to a conceived event to prejudice our judgement of a historian's claim that such an event happened; though if we accept the claim we are, naturally, at liberty to have emotions about it, as about anything else which we believe to be the case. With the fictional convention, on the other hand, it is the aversion (or desire) which matters; the acceptance or rejection of truth-claims is not in question.) The author, correspondingly, tends or tries to discharge such obligations as his chosen convention imposes, and exploit such opportunities as it permits. Tolstoy is not expected to, and does not, offer statistical justification for the statement about happy and unhappy families which opens *Anna Karenin*: he does, however, attend to continuities and contrasts in the story (in the triplicate presentation of the marriage relationship, for instance) which engage, and interrelate, certain emotional dispositions in the reader, and yet if offered within a truth-telling convention would have the appearance of gratuitous and implausible patterning. At the level of verbal detail the different priorities upheld by the two conventions are reflected in differences in characteristic diction and sentence-structure, and in the importance attached to such emotionally supportive elements and devices as rhythm, imagery and onomatopoeia. All this is thoroughly obvious and explains why in practice it is seldom necessary for a convention to be defined externally to the text; normally one can tell a novel from a history by a cursory glance at a random page. The warning label 'fiction' is only needed in these exceptional cases which effectively simulate the public media, as well as the private apprehension, of real experience: such as my hypothetical *The Diaries of Ronald Reagan*,[9] or (at the time of its publication) Poe's *The Facts in the Case of M. Valdemar*.

This distinction of convention seems to be sufficient to account for the characteristic differences in our response to literary and to non-literary discourse, and to preclude the need, in describing the former, for special categories of 'emotive' language, meaning or belief. To some extent, this is simply a terminological point, for it would be possible to redefine Richards's emotive categories as the products of convention acting upon language, by an argument analogous to that which points out that the cognitive 'meaning' of a word is conditioned, and rendered exact, by the context in which the word is used. But terminological suggestion can be very influential: such terms as 'meaning' and 'belief', translated provocatively from the cognitive to the emotive realm, tend confusingly to retain elements of their previously-acquired value, while the analytical bisection of the communicative functions of language into 'scientific' and 'emotive' hemispheres tends to imply a total, *ab ovo* separation between literary and scientific discourse, a specialised and arcane aetiology of aesthetic response. In critical practice this leads at worst to the discussion of responses in isolation from textual meanings of which Wimsatt and Beardsley complain (Housman's bristling beard, or the emotional attitudinising of the sentimental reviewer, or the laboratory investigation of somatic reactions to art), and, at best, as in much of Richards's own criticism, to a preoccupation with what is elusively, delicately and ambiguously stimulative in the action of the work upon the reader, at the expense of due attention to the work's amplitude, its internal perspectives, its overt and essential qualities. An emphasis on the sovereignty of convention serves to remind us of what is common to our experience of literary and non-literary discourse: the act of apprehending the cognitive, publicly demonstrable meanings and suggestions of the text, which are what they are whether we further interpret them as assertions or as imaginative suppositions.

II

I have argued so far that a criticism which asserts the existence, and importance, of a characteristic literary affect should nevertheless be grounded upon the publicly demonstrable meanings and suggestions of the text (construed within the conventions of literary discourse), and should not attempt to substitute for this the analysis of responses. But this leaves us with a serious problem of methodological theory. How are we to engage in public discourse (criticism) about public objects (literary works) while incorporating reference to private events (affects) which are far from consistent or universal in their relation to the objects? If we refuse to do this, our general thesis about the nature of the literary affect, even if correct, remains in practice useless. If we attempt to do it, on the other hand, we perpetually risk the charge of subjectivism, of laughably confusing personal sensations with the demonstrable properties of public objects. (Compare the late Hans Keller's remark about 'Mr. Joseph Kerman's recent autobiography on the Beethoven quartets'.)

The first point to be made about this problem is that it arises out of the very nature of literature and the arts in general. Human states of mind are, if not the alpha and omega of art, at least necessary attendants at its ritual. Nobody is going to sit through *King Lear* or *War and Peace* who does not in some sense 'care' about what happens to the characters; nor is anyone likely to read, or at any rae enjoy, even an imagist poem without some engagement of feeling. The most delicate shivering of sensibility is still an affect, and the dryness, reticence, chastity or whatever we choose to call it of a poem by T. E. Hulme, or a work of Stravinsky's neo-classical period, or a painting by Mondrian, corresponds to a psychic state just as the most rapturous passage of Wagner or Shelley does, though a psychic state as far removed from our normal condition in the direction of serenity and contemplativeness as *Tristan* or the *Ode to the West Wind* in the direction of fervour and passion. But emotional responsiveness – more specifically, the disposition to feel certain things, conditions and events as desirable or distressing – varies not only between one person and another but between one moment and another in the same person's life. Marvellian gardens (and the attitudes to them of Marvellian *personae*) may come to seem as appealing as Wordsworthian mountains; Leopold Bloom as sympathetic as Stephen Dedalus (or more so); the sufferings of Leontes and Hermione as poignant as those of Romeo and Juliet (and – which is to say the same thing – the correlative disturbances in oneself as necessary, or healthy, to seek governance over). It is therefore no more to be wondered at that responses to a literary work should vary than that two men in the same circle, or one man at different times, should fall in love with different women – which is not to say that the lovers' feelings, or rather their perception of certain qualities as causes of their feelings, are irrelevant or unhelpful in understanding the women. (And the weakness of the analogy is a significant one. Women do not exist for the benefit of their admirers; works of art do exist for the benefit of *their* admirers – whose feelings may therefore be of more than incidental relevance to the question of why the works are as they are.)

To maintain a viable affect-related criticism while acknowledging these conditions poses certain difficulties, but to give up the attempt entirely is impossible in practice and unnecessary in theory. It is impossible in practice because even non-affective modes of criticism implicitly refer to affects in their very vocabulary. We cannot proceed very far with the analysis of *King Lear* without observing that it is a 'tragedy', which in turn means assuming that its outcome is in some important sense productive of negative emotions, loosely describable as pity, terror, gloom, pathos or whatever. (One might perhaps argue that the term 'tragedy' simply indicates the presence of certain characteristic plot-components, and makes no assumptions about affects. But this would leave us wondering why, if not because of their corporate affective tendency, these components should belong to 'tragedy' and not to 'comedy'. Their grouping can hardly be accidental, and to say that it has developed historically is only to push back slightly the question of its fundamental cause.) We cannot get much further with *King Lear* without referring to relationships among its parts in a way which assumes certain affective values. To remark, uncontroversially, that 'the breakdown of the social order leads to an escalation of violence and cruelty, culminating in the blinding of Gloucester', is to note the exploitation, for thematic and structural purposes, of a more or less universal affective tendency, a quite exceptional fear and sensitivity about the notion of injury to the eyes. The episode could not be the *culmination* of a dramatic progression, could not perform the service of finally and irrefutably destroying the possibility of partial sympathy for the villains, and thus preparing the way for the moral clarity and certitude of the conclusion, if it did not strike us, in this and in other respects (such as the age and dignity of the victim) as belonging to a peculiarly horrifying category of acts. Similarly, when Edgar calls Edmund 'a most toad-spotted traitor'[10] we recognise the epithet as abusive, and appropriate to its context, because we share in a consensus about the resemblance between two affect-situations: toads are disgusting (except to toad-fanciers), and so, in the remotely similar sense which is all that is necessary, has Edmund's behaviour been. 'Leopard-spotted' would not do half so well.

To abstain in criticism from referring to such personal and disputable things as affects is needless theoretically because there are plenty of precedents for fruitful discussion arising from – though not confined to – personal and disputable feelings and experiences. If I agree with three friends that our common acquaintance X has a rather frosty personality, only to hear a fourth assert that he has always struck her as a very warm person, this does not mean that the conversation is bound to be fruitless: on the contrary, the dissenting opinion may prompt us all to a careful review of our recollections. It is true that if certain ground rules are neglected the conversation will not progress beyond blank mutual contradiction. One such rule might be that each participant should do his best to cite relevant facts about X's behaviour, since the differences in response may result not from irremediable differences in attitude or temperament but from entirely remediable lapses of memory or failures of knowledge. (In a similar way an obtuse person who declared Shakespeare incapable of arousing pity or terror might be wooed back to the consensus view by a reminder of the blinding in *Lear*: one function of critical discussion is to carry us beyond opinions based on what we happen to feel or remember at a random moment into a capacity for judgement which more nearly commands the full range of what we have felt and what we have the power to feel.) Another necessary rule would be the acceptance of a notional equality among responses, a prohibition on statements saying (explicitly or in effect), 'I'm more sensitive than you are to what people are really like, so I'm right' or, 'Your impression doesn't count', or 'You are insincere'. Such statements would certainly render the discussion fruitless and rebarbative. Better, perhaps, let a disagreement stand and acknowledge the possibility of an ambiguity

or complexity in the object or person under discussion which the
present participants have been unable to articulate definitively.

In some cases an expressed difference of response to all or part of
a literary work can largely disappear with a more exact apprehension, by one or both parties, of the work's content. In other cases
the difference genuinely arises from conflicting judgement or
temperament and cannot be resolved. This kind of conflict often
entails a disparity in evaluation as well, since, as we have noted,
the structure of a work, to say nothing of its details, is likely to
deploy certain affective values, and to appear seriously distorted or
gratuitous to a reader or spectator who cannot endorse the
affective structure. It is difficult to think very highly of a thriller if
you find the heroes as loathsome as the villains and consequently
could not care less who gets the better of whom; in this situation
the suspense which is the essence of the work's dynamic structure
loses all but an intellectual interest. Disparaging evaluation tends
to follow at the heels of affective disengagement. Logically it
should be possible to admire the craftsmanship which controls the
exploitation of emotional preferences in an assumed audience,
while dissenting from and perhaps even condemning some or all
of those preferences; but in practice we are generally content to
denounce a work whose structuring attitudes we find repugnant,
and either take its compositional inferiority for granted, or dismiss
the possible effectiveness of its appeal to the sympathetic as a
matter too trivial or distasteful to think about. It is usually only
when a work enjoys a secure prestige that we are prepared to enter
speculatively into the attitudes to which its structure and details
seem to refer and correspond, and to separate our admiration of
compositional skill, of imaginative resource and coherence, from
our rejection of what is disagreeable or worse in attitudes. An
example already alluded to is Odysseus's revenge upon the
disloyal members of his household in Book XXII of the *Odyssey*,
particularly the hanging of the maidservants and the torture and
mutilation of Melanthius. (It is true that it is actually Telemachus
who decides to hang the women instead of merely killing them
with his sword; but if we are to rejoice that Odysseus is again
master in his own house, we must surely hold him morally
responsible for what is done under his sovereignty.) A fair
proportion of modern (that is, Christian and post-Christian)
readers are likely to find their sympathies swinging away from
Odysseus here to an extent which vitiates the sense of triumphantly

restored fitness and harmony which the original auditors may be presumed to have felt, and which is so unmistakably foreshadowed and prepared by the symmetrically corresponding Books I–IV, also centred on Ithaca. Few, however, would, I fancy, translate this alienation of sympathy into a criticism of Homer as an artist.

At this point the ardent non-affectivist might step in to assert that my Homeric example proves his own case against the legitimacy of discussing responses. Post-Christian sensibilities are all very well in themselves (he might argue) but they have nothing to do with the study of Homer. There is one and only one correct response to – or rather reading of – this aspect of Book XXII, and that is a reading founded upon a knowledge of the ethical and other assumptions of Homer and his original auditors. It is to be arrived at by a study of the poem and of relevant historical evidence, not by introspection on the part of the critic. If (to put it another way) Homer expects us to rejoice at Odysseus's revenge, and has structured his poem with that expectation (derived from contemporaneous moral and aesthetic norms) in mind, then we are fully entitled to dissent, but not to offer our dissent as literary criticism. And the same applies to works less remote from ourselves. If our sensibilities differ from those implied in a work, what service is it *to the study of the work* to obtrude them? And if they agree, what interest does that have for anyone but ourselves? On the other hand, contextual information, biographical, historical, cultural, linguistic, can, when prudently deployed, purify and enhance our understanding of a work.

To assert the absolute priority in the critical act of objective information over subjective response, indeed the superfluity and illegitimacy of the latter, looks sensible, self-denying, and scholarly; but it is, I believe, open to four serious objections. The first is that it leaves us virtually speechless when information about the author is lacking or information about the ambient society thin. To restrict a discussion of *Beowulf*, for example, to the clarification of its cultural setting or its religious attitudes would be to overlook constituents of its meaning and appeal (present and past) which need no special gloss because they are related to unchanging, or only slowly and subtly changing, human wishes and anxieties: the night-walking monster, the comfort of the lighted hall, the dark pool, the dragon, the pyre. With Homer the position is still worse, since most of our knowledge about the feelings, tastes and beliefs of the poet and his auditors is itself inferred from his works. As

well as noting the circularity which this tends to impose upon the
'objective', cultural-historical approach, we may reflect that these
inferences about Homeric sensibility could often not be drawn if
we did not first apply our own sensibility. If, as E. V. Rieu
suggests,[11] Polyphemus is the object of a pity on Homer's part
which temporarily diverts sympathy from Odysseus, this can only
be inferred from the affects induced in us by the events and
speeches of the episode (the blinded Cyclop's petting of his
favourite ram, for example), since there do not appear to be any
explicit expressions of pity for the monster in the poem: rather the
reverse. In this kind of situation it might actually be more scholarly
and scrupulous simply to indicate frankly that we are registering a
subjective response (though in any case, if it were proved
tomorrow by irrefutable historical evidence that neither Homer nor
any of his contemporaries felt the slightest pity for Polyphemus,
would anyone really care that his own sympathetic reading was
anachronistic, or feel obliged to forgo it?) In practice, even our best
efforts at historical authenticity in interpretation are bound to
betray the influence of latter-day sensibility, and we should beware
of claiming too much for them.

Secondly, an exclusively 'objective' approach is, necessarily,
partial and often superficial, since while knowledge about authorial intention, social and cultural background, audience expectation or linguistic usage may help to illuminate themes and
ideologies, and explain a variety of circumstantial details (why
Molly Bloom menstruates, where the wilderness of Wirral might
be), there are levels in every work which only introspection, the
observation of what the work is doing to our minds, can uncover.
Objective modes of criticism can inform us about Jacobean theories
of kingship, but cannot explain why

> Tomorrow, and tomorrow, and tomorrow,
> Creeps in this petty pace from day to day,
> To the last syllable of recorded time;
> And all our yesterdays have lighted fools
> The way to dusty death. Out, out, brief candle!
> Life's but a walking shadow; a poor player,
> That struts and frets his hour upon the stage,
> And then is heard no more: it is a tale
> Told by an idiot, full of sound and fury,
> Signifying nothing.[12]

is great poetry at once fitting and transcending its dramatic moment. To grope towards such an explanation we have to sound our consciousness for the confluent effects of image-patterns (time, movement, speech, light, theatre), evocative tricks of sound ('struts and frets'), rhetorical speech (composed statement broken by obsessive repetition and exclamatory imperative) and other contributory currents; which is not to say that it is our consciousness that we should end by talking about, or that we should be unaware that interpretation of this sensitive kind alludes implicitly to mental events which are not provable.

Thirdly, the version of the objective approach which purports to elucidate the author's intentions and thought-processes or to re-create the knowledge and expectations of a contemporary audience or readership is liable to be unsatisfactory even in its own terms if it is not informed by a lively subjective sensibility. One likely intention of an author, one likely expectation of a contemporary reader or audience, may precisely have been that the work should arouse responses. It is more probable that *Beowulf* was composed to stir the heart than to reveal a transitional stage in Anglo-Saxon religious beliefs. If we are debarred from discussing the success or failure of a work in arousing emotional responses, and the nature of the responses aroused (inevitably using our own responses as data, however guardedly we view the relation between them and the responses the author or original audience might have entertained), we can often present only a very inadequate account of the work, even considered simply as a historical event. Literary-historical or cultural-historical scholarship, while it serves the important functions of counteracting anachronistic misreading and making good necessary background knowledge which a latter-day reader might lack, tends inevitably to focus attention on matters which the author, just because he and his readers could assume them, did not see fit to include in his text. These may be essential supplements to the text, and immensely interesting in themselves, but they do not constitute the work; we should avoid confusing a necessary condition for an adequate latter-day reading (a knowledge of Thomist theology in the case of Dante, for instance) with that reading itself; or the prerequisites for composition (Lawrence's childhood and youth) with the product of the composition (*Sons and Lovers*).

Finally, the repudiation of a subjective element in criticism effectively restricts the person who calls himself (or herself) a

'literary critic' to summarising and drawing inferences from the
findings of specialists in literary biography, literary history, social
history, sociology, psychology, linguistics, semiotics and so forth;
or alternatively, compels him to become such a specialist himself,
to commit himself (choosing by personal disposition or conviction)
to one or other of the various disciplines which include literary
works among their sources of evidence. This denial of a specific
originative function to the 'literary critic' might be welcomed,
particularly by dedicated specialists, as the closing-off of a feckless
dilettante option. But should we not want to discuss – as none of
these specialisms can do – the transaction between the composition and the reader, the reader who has (*qua* reader, whatever his
additional interests may be) no specialised discipline to practise?
Study of the author, his contemporary readers and their society
catches the work at certain moments of its being; but a work also,
and perhaps primarily, has being when a reader reads it today or
tomorrow. The critic is such a reader, and can approach a work in
this aspect of its being with a directness and confidence (humanly
speaking) which he can never achieve in discussing its gestation or
its contemporary impact. A work of literature can be considered
from a multitude of points of view: historical, cultural, biographical, psycho-analytical, linguistic, and so on. Each of these
perspectives has its own academic specialists, and their business is
simply to ensure that the literary material is appropriately used
according to the methodological principles of their disciplines.
(This is not to be confused with the use of historical, psychological
or other ideas by literary critics (who may or may not be competent
to handle and evaluate them).) But there are two points of view,
those of the writer and the reader, which will largely go by default
as far as intelligent public articulation is concerned if the person
who calls himself a literary critic (rather than a historian, social
scientist, linguist, or whatever) refuses to take responsibility for
them. And while all points of view may be of equal value for the
total intellectual and spiritual life of mankind, these are the
supremely important ones for literature. A work is a thing
conceived and composed, and a thing perceived and experienced,
and these aspects, or rather events, are so intimately connected
that in describing works we habitually fuse them, forget to ask
ourselves whether in talking about 'the rhyme-scheme ABBA',
'the tragic dénouement', 'the exquisite description of returning
Spring' (or 'the new, more vigorous theme in D' or 'the sculptured

severity of the portrait'), we are referring to something composed
or something perceived, to a conception or an experience. (Even
the human roles may be seen as overlapping: the composer can
plainly be said to 'perceive' the work progressively as he brings it
into being, and the perceiver to 'compose' it in that in order to
apprehend it properly his mind must project into view, so to
speak, a version of its components in due sequence or pattern.)
The various specialised disciplines may *serve* the reader to some
extent, by offering a multitude of vantage points from which the
work and its relations to the rest of the universe can be observed
and found interesting: they do this best, perhaps, when a humane
and versatile man of letters (an Edmund Wilson, say) is able to
draw upon, or practise, several of them and present their findings
with reasonable authority. No doubt they serve the writer
sometimes too. But what they cannot and do not aspire to do is
place in the foreground of our scrutiny this transaction between
the writer and the reader – or (less question-beggingly) between
the composition and the experience – of which the text is the
correlative object. For that purpose another special discipline is
needed, that of the literary critic who seeks to explain and (where
appropriate) justify the work by finding the rationale of composition in the form and quality of our experience.

We are thrown back yet again, therefore, on the necessity of
practising an affect-conscious criticism in spite of the variability of
affects. The problem should not be overstated. A recognised
impossibility of attaining Euclidean standards of conclusive demonstration is acceptable and normal in humane discourse about
humane activities; and the scope of consensus is, after all,
considerable. Everyone agrees that *Jude the Obscure* is a depressing
novel, and a working majority could probably be found even for so
specialised an opinion as that in Donne's 'Hymn to God the
Father' the puns *Donne-done* and *sun-son* are uncannily poignant.
The analytical question 'Why?' can therefore safely be asked in
both cases. In practice plenty of quite detailed critical analysis
alludes explicitly or implicitly to affects without anyone making a
particular fuss about the fact. (The allusion to affect may, of
course, be concealed within a quasi-objective formula – 'without
palliating these horrors, the author ...' – or embraced within
generalised crypto-affective concepts such as reader 'identification' with a character or group of characters.) Nevertheless, affects
cannot simply be taken for granted: they are at best hearsay

evidence, so to speak. As I have already suggested, therefore, certain provisions need to be made if critical discussion which refers to affects is to be intellectually respectable and analytically productive: first, a prohibition of claims to exceptional sensitivity, or disaparagement of other critics' responsiveness or sincerity; and second, a requirement that relevant evidence, objects correlative to the declared emotion, should be brought forward by anyone who contributes to such a discussion. This second point needs elaborating, for it is crucial to the methodological propriety of citing affects. Simply to indicate the literary material which corresponds to our emotion may often be sufficient to carry our point; but it provides us with no recourse, or rather no basis for conducting a fruitful argument, against the person who, after addressing himself to the same body of material, denies the appropriateness of our declared emotion. Very often, especially when the emotion correlative to a *single* conception is in question, this divergency is unavoidable and we must just agree to differ: the critics of a supposed poem formed by the single word

April

would presumably fall irreconcilably into pro- and anti-April factions. But in analysing a composition of the least complexity – say the first seven lines of *The Waste Land* – we can at any rate proceed in such a way as to transfer the burden of proof from ourselves to our opponents. The essential methodological point is to put forward affects as *explanations*, not as *evidence*. If we say, 'our response to the passage is x, therefore the sense or quality of the passage is p', and our opponent replies that in his view x is not a natural or appropriate response to the passage, then the burden of proof clearly lies upon us, to establish the propriety of x (upon the evidential value of which we have staked our entire argument). This reduces our argument to an assumption of superior sensitivity. If, on the other hand, we say, 'the passage presents the characteristic p (or the pattern $p - q - r$), and the most plausible rationale we can offer for this characteristic is a correspondence to the affect x (or the affective pattern $x - y - z$)', then our opponent, assuming that he accepts our characterisation of the compositional quality or pattern of the passage, is placed under an obligation to challenge our affective rationale with a more satisfying one of his own. An example will amplify my point.

April is the cruellest month, breeding
Lilacs out of the dead land, mixing
Memory and desire, stirring
Dull roots with spring rain.
Winter kept us warm, covering
Earth in forgetful snow, feeding
A little life with dried tubers.[13]

'The passage' (we might say), 'by drawing together images whose emotional charges seem essentially disparate – spring rain a resented disturber, romantic lilacs coarsely "bred" (so that the sentiment of purity associated with vegetable as against animal reproduction is subtly and disagreeably violated), the repellent "dead land" suddenly revealed as the voluptuous temptation of a paradoxically snow-warm winter – brings to the surface ambivalences in our emotional attitude to spring, indeed to human vitality itself, which our ordinary notions repress or overlook; the repetitive present participles, obtrusively placed before the line-break pauses, enact aurally the ominous, nagging quality of spring's irresistible approach, and suggest semantically a condition characterised by multiform, temporally indefinite, and consequently anxiety-engendering, change.' The opponent who denies all or some of this because of a subjective difference of affect must establish that this difference does not arise from an inadequate reading by offering an at least equally satisfactory explanation of why the generation of lilacs should be instanced as an act of cruelty, why the participles appear where they do, and so on – always retaining, of course, the option of declaring the passage or part of it, a compositional failure. Whether it is his account or ours which finally appears the more persuasive (to ourselves or to third parties), the critical discussion is likely to be analytically productive, since each party is striving to provide a rationale which shall adequately account for all the compositional characteristics of the passage, or at least leave fewer unexplained than the other's rationale.

Thus my argument arrives at a version – oddly enough, a slightly more austere version – of an assertion, already quoted (p. 136) in the anti-affectivist polemic of Wimsatt and Beardsley: 'the more specific the account of the emotion induced by a poem, the more nearly it will be an account of the reasons for emotion, the poem itself.'

More generally, it invokes a traditional precondition of hypotheses in empirical science: that what is disputable (in this case, the affect) must be offered as a working *explanation*, always open to displacement by fuller and subtler explanations, of what is, relatively and humanly speaking, not disputable (the text and its publicly demonstrable meanings and suggestions construed within the ruling conventions of imaginative literature); it cannot rank as *evidence*, as a publicly acceptable *datum*, in its own right. In reflecting privately upon a work, we may, as a matter of preliminary behind-the-scenes exploration, start from our feelings and look for their origins in the work; but in contributing to the public discussion about it, we must start from the work and ask whether our feelings can illuminate and justify its composition, the nature and deployment of its constituent conceptions.

6

Recapitulation and Analysis

As I noted in the *Preface*, the argument conducted in this book has both a positive and a negative aspect, which are nevertheless logically related to one another. On the one hand, I have put forward, and in the last four chapters have attempted to defend against certain anticipated objections, a general theory about literature, using fiction as a test case. On the other hand, I have set out to refute a series of what I take to be theoretical and methodological misconceptions inimical to the understanding of literature, again drawing largely upon fiction and fiction criticism for examples. The two processes are logically related in that the misconceptions I hope to have exposed are identical with, or closely derived from, the theoretical positions, and associated attitudes and prejudices, which I have considered as presenting the most powerful objections to my own main thesis. Defending the general theory has entailed repudiating the misconceptions; and conversely, repudiating the misconceptions (many of which I felt to be such long before the inception of this book) has entailed formulating and expounding the positive thesis which asserts what they deny or ignore.

This combination, or rather convergence, of positive and negative strategies has its implications for critical practice. If my main thesis is correct, then an awareness of it should have a significant influence upon critical method; not by providing an omnicompetent analytical technique – a general proposition about class of variable objects cannot in itself furnish descriptions of individuals – but by justifying the primary critical enterprise of 'finding the rationale of composition in the form and quality of our experience', the form and quality of experience being taken as specially characterised, in the case of literature, by affects of desire and relationships among such affects. Meanwhile, the methodological *exclusions* which are the negative corollary of the positive argument should, if they are correct, disencumber critical practice of a number of unhelpful and inappropriate expectations and formulations. And these positive and negative consequences for critical practice are intimately connected. To disencumber is, precisely, to facilitate, or at least to release time and energy for progress in an appropriate direction. Accordingly, the forthcoming analysis of *Wuthering Heights* will have to fulfil two requirements if it is to play the part assigned to it in the structure of my argument: that of exemplifying, and provisionally vindicating, the kind of critical practice implied and endorsed by the theoretical discussion. Firstly, it should be seen to be *critically constructive*, to advance discussion of the novel in one or more areas; and these advances should, of course, be clearly indebted to my central theory and its subsidiary, methodological elaborations. A consonance between theoretical argument and practical analysis will, I hope, be apparent throughout; but one section in particular – the third, which considers the function of the character and career of Heathcliff, makes an especially ambitious attempt to derive a resolution of a strenuously debated critical issue. Secondly, the analysis should be seen to be *competent and thorough*; it should not appear, by reason of its methodological exclusions, to constrict or distort the novel, but should sustain the point that within the critical terms of reference I have proposed the compositional, imaginative and affective complexity of a work can be firmly indicated and freely explored. (I should perhaps repeat here that certain perspectives upon literature are in my view the legitimate province of disciplines other than literary criticism; there will therefore be no treatment in the analysis of *Wuthering Heights* as a source of evidence about north-country dialect (linguistics), nineteenth-century landscape perception (geography), the emotional development of Emily Brontë (literary biography), or the decline of the yeoman farmer (social or economic history). Nor, on this occasion, will comparisons be drawn with other works, except incidentally; I am fully aware that analysis of the individual and analysis of the class are interdependent activities, and that the intelligibility of a single work depends in part upon a familiarity with certain basic genre-conventions, but I shall assume that for any person likely to read the analysis these conventions do not need to be spelt out before the *haecceitas* of Emily Brontë's novel can begin to be explored.) The reader will, I hope, feel finally that the analysis as a whole demonstrates the co-operative functioning of different parts of the novel, and of different levels of conception within it; and that a clear sense is conveyed of *Wuthering Heights* both as a composition (an object assembled in accordance with certain ends) and as an emotional and aesthetic experience.

In a fairly unsystematic way, the progress of the analysis will correspond to that of the theoretical argument of Chapters 1 to 4 (Chapter 5 providing a methodological justification for the analysis as a whole). I shall therefore briefly review the theoretical content of those chapters, and indicate some points of connection with the analysis.

In Chapter 1 I argued that the emotions induced by literature and the other arts are incomplete and unsatisfying; that they are the emotions of desire and aversion appropriate to a fantasy, rather than the (at least potentially) satisfying or completive emotions induced by equivalent actual experience. By 'desire' I do not simply mean basic or general drives and impulses such as love, fear, regret or acquisitiveness. I maintain that because signs and images, including those of language, prompt our minds to consider the things they represent, without allowing us to attain them (so long as we continue to concern ourselves with the signs and images), the act of reading literature always entails the arousal and non-satisfaction of appetencies, at however low a level of intensity. Indeed – to borrow a refinement from Chapter 5 – this is true of all reading; the special characteristic of imaginative literature is that it gives *priority* to this aspect of the reading experience, and organises its structures in such a way as to elaborate and bring into relationship with one another the desires which its component linguistic units, or rather the conceptions collaboratively engendered by them, arouse. It is by this clarifying and structuring effect upon desires, from which the reader derives a temporary sense of intellectual and spiritual mastery over them, that imaginative literature compensates him for the psychological unrest it provokes. Section I of my analysis of *Wuthering Heights* will offer a panoramic account of this process, reviewing the progress of the story from beginning to end and noting the broader qualities which engage the reader's sympathies and anxieties and the end-directed structures which maintain and intensify them.

In Chapter 2, answering potential objections to my theory from the standpoint of historical realism, I argued that literature cannot, properly speaking, augment our knowledge or understanding of primary reality (except of our own psyches), and that critical expectations and judgements based on the assumption that it can

do so are likely to produce distortion. I suggested, on the other
hand, that the imaginative conceptions of literature can *remind* us
of the real world to a greater or lesser degree, and that such
mimetic realism serves purposes consistent with my theory – to
facilitate immediate recognition of, and consequent response to,
the conceptions; to evoke, and engage sympathy with, those
human concerns which are most typically manifest in familiar
social situations; and, in respect of the work as a whole, to
minimise the reader's expenditure of energy on comprehending
(comparative) incidentals of context in order to free energy for
responses to more highly charged materials (crises of plot,
significant qualities of character, intensities of perception). In
section II of the analysis I shall consider some interesting
specialised uses of mimetic realism in *Wuthering Heights*.

In Chapter 3 I argued that, while moral preferences enter into
our response to literature, other, non-moral preferences legitimately do so as well – legitimately, that is, unless literary evaluation is
seen as absolutely contingent upon moral evaluation. The appeal
to approval or indignation, to the sense of what is morally to be
desired or held in aversion, is a particular form of the engagement
of desire, not its universal or sole appropriate form. Accordingly,
there is no systematic correspondence between moral and literary
quality (though there may *tend* to be an *association* between them,
owing to the compositional subtlety and discipline required to
engage desires which are complex and long-term and thus by
inference higher than simple instinctual drives); and a critical
theory which requires the meaning and quality of a satisfactory
work to be exhaustively explained in terms of moral judging and
valuing is likely to be gravely inadequate. *Wuthering Heights*,
through the ambivalent, and critically disputed, moral status of
Heathcliff, raises in a particularly problematic fashion the question
of the relationship between moral and other kinds of response to
fiction; section III of my analysis will attempt to explore and resolve
this problem.

In Chapter 4 I attacked the view that the necessary starting-
point for the criticism of literature is the analysis of 'style' or
'language' (meaning small-scale verbal configurations); and maintained that the affective function of literature – the quickening of
desire and its implication in an intelligible literary structure which
orders and clarifies it – can be demonstrated at the level of small-
scale conceptions ('language') as well as at the level of large-scale

conceptions ('plot', 'theme', and so on), in so far as these are separable from each other. In section IV of the analysis I shall look at small-scale conceptions in *Wuthering Heights* – principally at imagery, but also at some conceptionally functional effects of rhythm and timbre, and at the use of time-references – and shall discuss some of the ways in which they interact with larger-scale conceptions of character, locale and so forth to engender and enrich affective tensions and structures.

In Chapter 5 I discussed some of the methodological problems posed by criticism which refers to affects, and ·conceded the impropriety of substituting the analysis of responses for the analysis of features of the work itself. I suggested that affects might properly be brought into the critical discussion, not in the guise of *evidence* about the work, but to aid a provisional *explanation* (freely offered to the judgement and sensitivity of other readers, and always open to supersession or qualification by more plausible and comprehensive explanations) of the work's local and overall features. The analysis of *Wuthering Heights* will respect this principle; affective functions will be offered as rationales for aspects of the novel's texture and structure.

The choice of any single case to illustrate a critical theory of purportedly general applicability is bound to seem somewhat arbitrary. No single instance – indeed no series of instances – observed to conform with a theory can demonstrate the impossibility of counter-instances. But logical proof of this kind is hardly in question. The purpose of the present chapter is not so much to 'prove' finally the validity of the theory as to defend it from the suspicion of analytical sterility. In earlier chapters I have attempted to relate my arguments to critical practice; in discussing critical treatments of works by Tolstoy, Dickens and George Eliot, in an extended analysis of a passage by Henry James, and in a number of brief analyses of extracts. For the following analysis (which taken together with the earlier analytical sections roughly evens the balance between theory and practice in the book), I have chosen a novel of undisputed, or almost undisputed, greatness, whose nature and portent remain the subject of energetic critical debate. Neither unquestionably a work of social realism (though claimed as such by some realistic critics), nor unquestionably a work in the morally normative 'great tradition' of English fiction (though given the qualified approval of the Leavises), a novel of powerful 'gross and overall effects', yet subtly and purposefully articulated at the level of verbal detail, *Wuthering Heights* has attracted various and often competitive critical attention. I wish to take advantage of this open (if crowded) field, not to adjudicate among competing critical approaches, still less to offer a mono-thematic approach of my own, but, through an exploration of the novel's complexity and coherence, to suggest something of the variety and fertility of the analytical possibilities endorsed by my theoretical argument.

ANALYSIS: WUTHERING HEIGHTS

I

'The story rushes onwards with impetuous force ...' observed an anonymous contemporary reviewer of *Wuthering Heights*.[1] The observation can be taken to mean more than that incidents in the novel follow one another with great rapidity – indeed, as I shall show later, the progress of the tale is by no means single-paced. Rather it registers, in the form of an intuitive response, an imaginative intensity in the work which inheres, not merely in individual episodes, but in a dynamic structure which secures an unbroken, if varying, momentum. The intuitive assertion that *Wuthering Heights* is the opposite of a relaxed or leisurely novel can be crudely justified by pointing to the nature of its action, the extent and complexity of its plot in proportion to its length, the rarity and brevity of reflective passages, and so on. But close analysis should and can yield a far subtler and more elaborate, and far more extensively justified, version of the anonymous re-viewer's uncontroversial but impressionistic description.

The imaginative intensity of *Wuthering Heights* derives, I sug-gest, from the collaborative force of a variety of demonstrable qualities, a number of which I shall examine in later sections of the analysis. It derives from a high degree of mimetic conviction, sustained, in spite of the extraordinary and even supernatural character of some of the action, by a number of authenticating techniques. These techniques, and the mimetic realism of the novel in general, will form the subject of section II of the analysis. It derives from a continuous, disturbing tension between values embodied in (or quickened to consciousness by the conception of)

Heathcliff's character and career, and other values implicit in the story. This tension, unmistakable though it is, has proved remarkably resistant to critical consensus, and the examination of this issue in section III represents perhaps the boldest attempt in the analysis to intervene in specific and recent critical debate. The intensity of the novel derives, further, from its exhaustively-composed nature: that coherence of small-scale with large-scale conception, verbal detail with broad design, which minimises the dilution and dispersal of imagination and feeling. Section IV of the analysis will suggest some aspects of this coherence. But the present section will examine *in extenso* the narrative 'onrush' itself, exploring the dynamic (end-directed) structures which secure and maintain imaginative and affective engagement. In view of the surprising tendency of one's memory to fillet and re-order any complex plot, a certain amount of uninspiring summary will be a necessary part of this process.

Wuthering Heights describes, not always in chronological order, events at two neighbouring houses in Yorkshire, Wuthering Heights and Thrushcross Grange, over a period of thirty-one years from 1771 to 1802. The narrator is an effete southern gentleman, Mr Lockwood, the (largely absentee) tenant of Thrushcross Grange during the last of these years, 1801–2. Most of his narrative is a verbatim report of a second narrative – the recollections of Nelly Dean, nurse and housekeeper at one house or the other throughout the period – which is delivered at his request after his curiosity has been aroused by a couple of bewildering visits to the Heights. Nelly Dean's narration, which is interrupted by Lockwood at several points, and by an eight-month interval towards the end of the novel, largely observes chronological sequence, and includes, within inverted commas, a number of narrative speeches by other characters.

This narrative method, so described, sounds both leisurely and complicated: as if the author's principal concern has been to reproduce the authentic flavour of chimney-corner storytelling, even at some cost in directness and economy. Such is indeed one of its purposes, and references in the text to Mrs Dean's bringing in Lockwood's supper (Chapter 4, Penguin edition, p. 74),[2] or pressing medicine upon him (*10*, 130), confirm the effect. But the narrative is at the same time vitally energised, not simply by the intrinsic interest of the conceived events, but by three cumulatively powerful and end-directed structures, patterns of tension, expectation and resolution which draw the reader's interest onward. The first, embracing the entire narrative, is a repeated *AB* pattern, where *A* may be called 'Lockwood's bewilderment' and *B* 'Lockwood's enlightenment'; the second is the organisation of Nelly Dean's main narration into graded crescendi or accumulations of tension; and the third is a relationship, analogous to that between discord and related concord, between the (chronologically close but narratively distant) opening and closing sections of the tale. I shall consider each in turn.

1. The most basic of dynamic structures in fiction is the structure *mystification-explanation*. Chapters 1 to 3 of the novel, in which Lockwood twice visits his landlord at Wuthering Heights, subject him (and the reader) to an onslaught of mystifying data, which he relentlessly misinterprets.

'Mr. Heathcliff?' I said.
A nod was the answer.
'Mr. Lockwood, your new tenant, sir. I do myself the honour of calling as soon as possible, after my arrival, to express the hope that I have not inconvenienced you by my perseverance in soliciting the occupation of Thrushcross Grange: I heard, yesterday, you had had some thoughts—'
'Thrushcross Grange is my own, sir,' he interrupted, wincing, 'I should not allow any one to inconvenience me, if I could hinder it – walk in!'
The 'walk in' was uttered with closed teeth, and expressed the sentiment, 'Go to the Deuce': even the gate over which he leant manifested no sympathising movement to the words; and I think that circumstance determined me to accept the invitation: I felt interested in a man who seemed more exaggeratedly reserved than myself. (1)

Lockwood's initial impression, on entering the house, of unexceptional domesticity quickly vanishes as the inhabitants respond with physical and verbal hostility to his most tentative advances. Heathcliff, whom Lockwood takes at first for a gentlemanly introvert with 'an aversion to showy displays of feeling' (1, 47), soon reveals himself 'an unmannerly wretch' (2, 58), and is subsequently to be heard tearfully imploring a feminine ghost to enter the house through a bedroom window. Heathcliff's ménage, apart from the servants Joseph and Zillah, consists of two snappish juveniles – not his wife, and a third servant (Lockwood's first conjectures), nor yet his son and daughter-in-law (Lockwood's second try), but his daughter-in-law through an unmentioned son, and a person of entirely unexplained status who nevertheless bears the same name, Hareton Earnshaw, as the original sixteenth-century owner of the house, identified in an inscription over the front door. All these morose and unsympathetic characters appear to detest one another. When the weather obliges Lockwood to stay overnight his curiosity is further provoked by the diary of one Catherine Earnshaw, which he finds by his bed. The diarist proves to be a childhood companion of Heathcliff's, an ally against the persecution of the sanctimonious Joseph and his master Hindley, an unidentified tyrant who fills the role of a recently deceased father. Her name, along with 'Catherine Heathcliff' and 'Catherine Linton', has been scratched repeatedly on the window-ledge, justifying a presumption that all three names refer to the same person. Lockwood's subsequent sleep is disturbed by two dreams, in the second of which the girlish spectre of 'Catherine Linton' begs admission through the window, declaring that it has been a waif for twenty years. Lockwood cries out in terror, rousing Heathcliff; his account of the dream occasions the emotional outburst by Heathcliff mentioned above.

This, then, is *A*: arriving at Wuthering Heights in a complaisant, and complacent, frame of mind, Lockwood is assailed by hostilities and confusions which finally penetrate his unconscious and reduce him to panic; his physical trials – being attacked by dogs, bleeding at the nose, and on his return 'sinking up to the neck in snow, a predicament which only those who have experienced it can appreciate' (3, 73) dramatise this process. His consequent illness is both the outward expression of his bewilderment and the opportunity for its removal. It has become obvious that only the history of the household at Wuthering Heights can explain its present state; and this history is given to the convalescent Lockwood in *B*, Nelly Dean's main narration, which extends from Chapters 4 to 30 and to which Chapter 31, in which Lockwood, recovered and enlightened, pays a farewell visit to the Heights, is an inconclusive epilogue, a sort of false bottom to the novel. The last three chapters, the true conclusion, present the same *AB* pattern, with very much the same proportions though on a smaller scale. Lockwood returns, to find both households puzzlingly trans-

formed, and Heathcliff dead (32, 336–40); Nelly delivers her
second explanatory narration (32–34, 340–66); and Lockwood
again adds a brief and this time final epilogue (34, 366–7).

Thus the story (in this aspect, which is not the whole story)
develops by presenting a mystery and then unravelling it; rather as
in the detective story, except that in that genre the proportions of *A*
and *B* tend to be the opposite of those in *Wuthering Heights*. (The
typical detective-story structure is designed to intensify, by delay
and frustration, the intellectual relief of an explanation which, in
general, is encumbered with only the simplest of emotive
accompaniments: the discomfiture of the wrongdoer, the acquittal
of the unjustly accused, the applause resounding in the detective's
unsusceptible ears. In *Wuthering Heights*, by contrast, the explanation contains its own complex progressions of tension and
resolution, which are the emotive centre of the work; the *AB*
pattern is only a part of the total dynamic structure.) The density
and compression of Chapters 1 to 3, like the density and
compression of a flattened spring, impart to the story – or rather to
our engagement with it – an initial impetus of a kind exceptional,
perhaps unique, in English nineteenth-century fiction, where more
leisurely openings, entailing other compositional risks, predominate. The capture of the reader's interest by an episodic memoir-
novel, such as Charlotte Brontë's *Jane Eyre* or *Villette*, or Dickens's
David Copperfield, depends heavily upon the swift establishment of
a lively sympathy for the central character, and upon the intrinsic
interest of successive episodes, at least until the emergence,
generally some way into the book, of one or more suspense-themes
(such as whether Lucy Snowe will win the heart of Paul Emanuel).
Other, more complex structures (*Vanity Fair* or *Middlemarch* or *Our
Mutual Friend* or *Little Dorrit*) introduce a variety of characters and
gradually draw them into relationship with one another; here a
common compositional procedure is to maintain a fair degree of
continuity at the beginning, as Thackeray does with the early
divagations of Becky Sharp, and insinuate other characters and
other material from time to time in digestible doses. In both types,[3]
our involvement characteristically intensifies as the threads of the
tale begin to be pulled together, but risks being dissipated, or at
any rate sorely tested, in the preludial or expository opening
chapters. In the case of *Wuthering Heights* the danger is a slightly
different one: that the complex and fragmentary material of
Chapters 1 to 3 might provoke irritation and rejection, instead of a

wish for further, elucidatory, information. That for most readers it does not do so can be attributed largely to the mediating consciousness of Lockwood, whose easy-flowing discourse, so measured and with so strongly characteristic a combination of ostentatious aplomb and elegant self-irony, provides an important continuity of tone and perspective.

'It is strange', I began in the interval of swallowing one cup of tea and receiving another, 'it is strange how custom can mould our tastes and ideas: many could not imagine the existence of happiness in a life of such complete exile from the world as you spend, Mr. Heathcliff; yet, I'll venture to say, that, surrounded by your family, and with your amiable lady as the presiding genius over your home and heart—'

'My amiable lady!' he interrupted, with an almost diabolical sneer on his face. 'Where is she – my amiable lady?'

'Mrs. Heathcliff, your wife, I mean.'

'Well, yes – Oh! you would intimate that her spirit has taken the post of ministering angel, and guards the fortunes of Wuthering Heights, even when her body is gone. Is that it?'

Perceiving myself in a blunder, I attempted to correct it. I might have seen that there was too great a disparity between the ages of the parties to make it likely that they were man and wife. One was about forty; a period of mental vigour at which men seldom cherish the delusion of being married for love, by girls: that dream is reserved for the solace of our declining years. The other did not look seventeen. (2)

Lockwood's opening remark is an eighteenth-century platitude; his joke near the end of the extract has an air of Byron, but the sensible, anti-Romantic Byron of *Don Juan*. One does not, however, need to be aware of these resemblances to register Lockwood's temperamental remoteness from the world of the Heights, a remoteness which within the substance of the novel represents, or corresponds to, the reader's possible difficulty in imaginative commitment: Lockwood's bemused reactions convert what might, on the part of the reader, be a bewilderment *about* the story into a bewilderment which co-operates with the story, which becomes part of the dynamic of his imaginative and emotional engagement.

2. A second end-directed structure is the progression of the long central narrative which follows and answers to this opening section. Nelly Dean's narration is neither simply one thing after another, nor an impetuous uninterrupted *presto*, but a well-paced melody with points of comparative relaxation as well as crises of highly-wrought tension. Like a melody, it is divisible into phrases, or phases, which are separately discernible as well as being subservient parts of the whole. There are, I believe, three outstanding crises – at Chapters 8–9, Chapters 15–17, and Chapters 27–8 – each of which brings to an end a period of tension and suspense, and is followed by a comparative lull. They fall, it will be noted, at approximately the quarter-, the mid-, and the three-quarter-points of the novel; the third actually falls somewhat later than this symmetrical scheme suggests, and partly for that reason – the preceding suspense having been so painfully drawn out – has a particularly heart-sinking finality about it which makes us feel it as a true conclusion to the narrative, though not to the novel. I shall summarise and discuss the three main phases separately.

Summary: Chapters 4 to 9

At the beginning of Nelly's narration the year is 1771. The master of Wuthering Heights is Mr Earnshaw; he has two children, Hindley and Catherine, aged fourteen and six respectively. Earnshaw brings home from a trip to Liverpool a 'dirty, ragged, black-haired child' (4, 77) whom he has found starving in the streets. The boy is christened Heathcliff, and proves a taciturn, self-reliant child. He displaces Hindley, who treats him cruelly, in his father's favour, and exploits this advantage in order to blackmail Hindley into surrendering to him the nimbler of two colts. He becomes, too, the inseparable ally of the mischievous Catherine; and even wins the respect of an initially hostile Nelly by his patience during a bout of illness.

When Hindley becomes master after his father's death, he relegates Heathcliff to the status of a servant; Heathcliff and Catherine become virtually ungovernable, however, and take to running away to the moors, unwashed and unkempt, for entire days. During one of these expeditions they peer through a window at Thrushcross Grange, the home of the well-bred Linton family, whose two children, Edgar and Isabella, they observe quarrelling over a puppy. The timid Lintons cry out in terror when they hear noises at the window, and the intruders are captured. Catherine is treated kindly, and remains at the Grange for five weeks recovering from the attentions of the house bull-dog; Heathcliff is mocked as a gipsy, rebuked for his blasphemous language, and shown the door.

From this point, estrangement between Heathcliff and Catherine looms. When Catherine returns she has been trans-formed from a 'wild, hatless little savage' (7, 93) into an elegantly-dressed young lady with insecure ringlets; and has attracted the attention of Edgar Linton, who begins to pay visits. The abashed Heathcliff screws up the courage to ask Nelly to make him 'decent', and she encourages him to present a clean and amiable appearance when the Lintons call for dinner; but Hindley chases him out of the room, and Edgar inadvertently insults him, provoking Heathcliff to throw a tureen of hot apple sauce in his face. With the option of competing with Edgar thus closed, by his own pride and by Hindley's persecution, Heathcliff sinks into 'an almost idiotic excess of unsociable moroseness' (8, 108), and broods on thoughts of revenge against Hindley. Catherine retains an unwavering affection for him, but spends many evenings with the Lintons.

At the beginning of Chapter 8 Hindley's delicate wife gives birth to a son, Hareton, and dies the following winter. Hindley's grief drives him to dissipation, and it is against the background of his drunken violence and blasphemous rages that this phase draws to an end. Chapter 8 ends with a lovers' tiff between Catherine and Edgar which seals their attachment. In the next chapter we learn that she has accepted his proposal of marriage. In a famous dialogue with Nelly she declares, 'It would degrade me to marry Heathcliff, now'; but goes on to affirm a deep sense of identity with him.

> My love for Linton is like the foliage in the woods. Time will change it, I'm well aware, as winter changes the trees. My love for Heathcliff resembles the eternal rocks beneath – a source of little visible delight, but necessary. Nelly, I *am* Heathcliff – he's always, always in my mind – not as a pleasure, any more than I am always a pleasure to myself – but as my own being .... (9)

Heathcliff, however, overhears only her first declaration, and slips away into the evening. Catherine waits up for him, and is drenched when a violent thunderstorm breaks at midnight. The following day Heathcliff still does not return, and Catherine falls into a delirium. The chapter ends with her recovery, the deaths of Mr and Mrs Linton, and, after an interval of three years which is lightly passed over, her marriage to Edgar, now the master of Thrushcross Grange.

Here Nelly suspends her narration.

The first phase of B establishes an immediate response to A by clarifying and elaborating the fragment of Catherine's diary quoted in Chapter 3: a single sentence in the latter – 'He [Hindley] has been blaming our father (how dare he?) for treating H. too liberally; and swears he will reduce him to his right place' (3, 64) – adumbrates the whole complex of affections and hostilities which are shown developing in Chapters 4 to 6. At the same time the phase develops a momentum of its own. The household of Wuthering Heights is seething with animosities and infantile rivalries whose working-out will plainly constitute a large part of the coming action. Structurally, the pivotal character is Hindley, and much of the tension, particularly in the earlier chapters, springs from the continuing contest of wills between Hindley and a variety of opponents – a contest which is not to be resolved in this phase – not, indeed, until a still more powerful tension takes over its dynamic role – and is kept alive with some subtlety on the author's part. At first Hindley is ranged against Mr Earnshaw, Catherine and Heathcliff, with only the servants maintaining a rough neutrality. He himself has initiated hostilities by evincing hatred for Heathcliff, but this results from a not unjustified sense of personal deprivation (the fiddle Mr Earnshaw promised to bring him back from Liverpool has been crushed during the laborious journey with Heathcliff). From the first, then, and still more after the episode with the colts, in which he appears at once victimised and vindictive, it is natural to feel both sympathy and dislike for Hindley. Indeed the emotional intensity of these chapters seems to me to spring, not only from the conflicts among the principal characters, but from just this kind of painful (and life-like) ambivalence in their personalities. Each has attractive qualities vitiated, in greater or lesser degree, by faults which can poison the human atmosphere of the household. Mr Earnshaw is compassionate to Heathcliff, and can be tender, though not patient, with Catherine; but his failure in paternal even-handedness alienates Hindley from the rest of the family and ensures subsequent discord. Catherine is lively, and kind-hearted – 'for when once she made you cry in good earnest, it seldom happened that she would not keep you company' (5, 83) – but her misbehaviour wounds and exhausts her father in his physical decline. Heathcliff is a special case: more of him in III below. The cumulative impression – as has so often been noted – puts one in mind of the domestic fatalities of Greek tragedy: the characters are not so much wicked as cursed with passions and blindnesses which transparently indicate eventual disaster.

As the story progresses the alliance against Hindley is broken apart. Mr Earnshaw's death deprives it of its most powerful member and elevates Hindley to a position of authority. His revenge against Heathcliff is not at first completely effectual, partly because of the continuing rebellious solidarity between Heathcliff and Catherine and partly because his own uxorious devotion to his wife preoccupies him. But the acquaintanceship of the Lintons subverts the relationship between Heathcliff and Catherine and gives Hindley an excuse to drive Heathcliff into the position of a virtual outcast. Heathcliff's progressive isolation, the rebuffing of his brief attempt to be 'decent', and the unattractiveness at this stage of the callow over-mothered Edgar, combine to impart a sad and ominous quality to the closing chapters of this part of the narration: sad because of the dissolution of trust between Heathcliff and Catherine (a dissolution rendered all the more poignant by Catherine's continued gestures of devotion, in the face of ever-increasing disparity of interests), and ominous because of Heathcliff's simmering resentment and the obvious inequality of force of personality between Catherine and Edgar. Meanwhile, just as Hindley appears to have completed his crushing of Heathcliff's aspirations, he himself is devastated, and rendered semi-sympathetically vulnerable again, by the death of his wife. The contest is re-opened: Heathcliff narrowly misses taking a powerful revenge by ensuring the death of the baby Hareton, when Hindley, drunk, wielding a carving knife, and ranting of damnation, carelessly lets him fall over a banister. This climactic episode of grim, if unacted, violence runs on directly into the 'I *am* Heathcliff' conversation, Heathcliff's flight, and a thunderstorm which demolishes part of a chimney-stack. Then calm descends suddenly – as so often in *Wuthering Heights* – with physical collapse: the illness of Catherine and the subsequent deaths of the elder Lintons.

By the beginning of Chapter 10, then, the story has reached an obviously temporary equilibrium. Heathcliff and Hindley are out of each other's way. Catherine and Edgar are contentedly married, but Catherine's expressed identification with Heathcliff is fresh in our minds; and we learn from Nelly that her illness after Heathcliff's departure has rendered still more acute her impatience with contradiction and her proneness to fits and rages. The equilibrium is in both respects dependent, therefore, on Heathcliff's absence; and from the obscure and romantic circumstances of his flight, from his prominence in the portion of the book we have read so far, and of course from what we already know of a much later period from Chapters 1 to 3, it is easy to infer that he will not be absent for long.

Summary: Chapters 10 to 17

Heathcliff reappears five months after Catherine's marriage, having grown rich by unknown means and developed a mature and manly aspect. He uses his wealth to ingratiate himself with Hindley and obtain permission to stay at Wuthering Heights. When he calls at Thrushcross Grange, it is clear that Catherine has missed him deeply; Edgar is irritated by the couple's open expressions of devotion, but contains himself with an effort.

Isabella Linton falls in love with Heathcliff, despite attempts by both Catherine and Nelly to convince her of his malevolent character. Heathcliff mocks her at first, but after reflecting that she is Edgar's heir makes advances to her during a visit to the Grange. Catherine reproaches him: he replies that, since she is torturing him to death (by being married to Edgar), he proposes to take indirect revenge upon Isabella. Nelly repeats the conversation to Edgar, who rushes to eject Heathcliff. Catherine joins Heathcliff in goading Edgar, defaming him as a petulant coward; Edgar strikes Heathcliff a disabling blow in the throat, and goes to fetch reinforcements to expel him. Catherine persuades Heathcliff to leave, and then asks Nelly to help her simulate illness in order to frighten Edgar into renewed submission to her will. Nelly refuses, and when Catherine secludes and starves herself takes the matter lightly at first. But Catherine falls into genuine delirium; her thoughts revert to her childhood ventures with Heathcliff, and it becomes clear that she is inwardly repenting her adult commitment to Edgar and repudiating her life as civilised lady at the Grange.

> 'Look!' she cried eagerly, 'that's my room, with the candle in it, and trees swaying before it ... and the other candle is in Joseph's garrett ... Joseph sits up late, doesn't he? He's waiting till I come home that he may lock the gate. Well, he'll wait a while yet. It's a rough journey, and a sad heart to travel it; and we must pass by Gimmerton Kirk, to go that journey! We've braved its ghosts often together, and dared each other to stand among the graves and ask them to come ... But Heathcliff, if I dare you now, will you venture? If you do, I'll keep you. I'll not lie there by myself: they may bury me twelve feet, and throw the church down over me; but I won't rest till you are with me ... I never will!' (12)

Edgar is horrified to discover Catherine's wasted condition, and unfairly rebukes Nelly for keeping him in ignorance of it. Meanwhile Heathcliff has eloped with the foolish Isabella. He begets a child on their wedding night, or thereabouts,[4] but on returning to the Heights excludes Isabella from his room, and makes her life a misery.

Catherine partially recovers from her fever, but is weakened and predicts her own death within a year. In Chapter 15 Heathcliff pays a clandestine visit to the Grange. A passionate scene, in which Heathcliff embraces Catherine and reproaches her furiously for deserting him – first for Edgar and now for death – culminates in her final collapse, and the re-entry of Edgar. Catherine dies without recovering consciousness, after giving birth prematurely to a daughter. Edgar is prostrated by grief while Heathcliff, exiled to the garden, beats his head frantically against an ash-tree and implores Catherine to haunt him. At last he returns to Wuthering Heights, where he survives a murderous attack by Hindley. Isabella – who reports this last episode with vengeful intensity – flees to the Grange, and thence to the South, where she eventually gives birth to a son. Hindley drinks himself to death (perhaps with a helping hand from Heathcliff); he has, we learn, mortgaged his land to

Heathcliff in order to pay gambling debts, and consequently the true Earnshaw heir, Hareton, is effectively disinherited.

There follows the longest and most placid time-interval in the novel: the twelve years in which the Lintons' daughter, Cathy, grows up. (I propose to follow the practice of Edgar Linton in referring to his wife as 'Catherine' and his daughter as 'Cathy'. There is no consistency on this point in the novel.)

In this phase we watch with fascinated horror as Heathcliff lays siege to Thrushcross Grange, and at the same time progressively establishes himself as master of Wuthering Heights. I shall discuss later the nature of our equivocal response to Heathcliff; suffice for the moment to note that, whether it is the fascination or the horror that dominates our response, Heathcliff's aggression against the Linton household, and its approaching consequences – foreshadowed by Nelly's comparison of Catherine's state of mind to unexploded gunpowder (10, 131) – provide the main affective impetus of the earlier chapters of this phase. Around the middle of Chapter 12, as Catherine's illness begins to seem more genuine than not, and her delirium throws up images of graveyards, this gives way to the more particular apprehension that she may die. Her death is not, of course, intended by Heathcliff, though it may be the inevitable consequence of his actions; having set our anxiety in motion, so to speak, Heathcliff now steps into the frame of suffering, and merits, or at least demands with unexampled vehemence, a share of our compassion. (In the last of these chapters we find him weeping when Isabella correctly observes that, but for him, Catherine would still be alive.) The pathos of Catherine's death momentarily eclipses the antagonism between Heathcliff and Edgar – or at any rate our awareness of it – and a curious equipoise prevails as both men mourn: Heathcliff out of doors, raging with undiminished energy, Edgar indoors, sinking into 'the hush of exhausted anguish' (16, 201), like symbolical extremes of grief.

If this fatal siege by Heathcliff were the sole theme of the central phase of Nelly's narrative, one might feel the story to have come, by Chapter 16, to a dead stop. Other developments, however, maintain our awareness that Heathcliff's energies are not restricted to the pursuit of Catherine and need not therefore be extinguished by her death. The last chapter of this phase, 17, brings to conclusion the struggle between Heathcliff and Hindley, with the latter's death and the former's appropriation of his property. It rounds off, too, with the relief of Isabella's escape from the Heights, the theme of Heathcliff's seduction and persecution of her, which has run alongside the major theme of his disruption of the Lintons' contentment, intensifying our impression of his resourcefulness, and the general atmosphere of anxiety. Two details of the Isabella material point forward to the tensions of the next phase. One is that Heathcliff, increasingly dominant at Wuthering Heights, can lure and imprison, as well as assail; the other is that his retributive intentions extend to the next generation. Both are emphasised by the episode at the end of Chapter 17, in which Heathcliff secures the guardianship of Hareton Earnshaw by threatening that he will otherwise take steps to reclaim his own son from Isabella.

Summary: Chapters 18 to 30

Cathy reaches the age of thirteen without going outside the grounds of Thrushcross Grange except under Edgar's supervision, and without learning of the existence of Wuthering Heights. At length, while Edgar is visiting Isabella, who is dying and wishes to entrust the boy Linton to his care, she breaks bounds and discovers the Heights. Nelly pursues her there. Heathcliff is absent, but Cathy innocently gives away the news, which is subsequently reported to him, that his son will soon be coming to the Grange. Hareton is evidently attracted by Cathy; he is hurt and resentful, however, when she speaks to him as a servant and refuses to acknowledge him as her cousin.

Linton is brought to Thrushcross Grange, and proves to be a weakling. Cathy pets him, but at Heathcliff's insistence he is whisked away to the Heights the following morning. Heathcliff expresses contempt for the 'puling chicken' (20, 242); he declares, however, that he will treat him well as he wishes to see his son survive to inherit the Grange. (Linton is Edgar's heir through Isabella, unless Edgar himself has a son.) Soon Heathcliff concocts the scheme of marrying Linton to Cathy, so as to secure the latter's personal fortune, as well as the estate, into his own power in the event of Edgar's death. He waylays Cathy while she is out bird's-nesting, and lures her to Wuthering Heights, where she meets Linton again. The pair of them make fun of Hareton, who has been denied education by Heathcliff and cannot read his own name over the door. Cathy becomes sentimentally devoted to Linton, despite his peevish temperament, and corresponds secretly with him until Nelly finds out and forces her to stop.

A few months later Heathcliff again waylays Cathy and Nelly, by the gate of Edgar's grounds. He tells Cathy that Linton has fallen ill and is pining for her kindness. Nelly authorises a single visit, but warns that they must not be continued: Cathy, however, slips away repeatedly to the Heights while Nelly is confined to bed with a cold.

During one of these visits, Hareton naively boasts to Cathy that he has learned to read the lintel inscription. He gets the name right, but cannot manage the date (1500); Cathy ridicules him, provoking him to a violent outburst of mortified pride and jealousy which causes Linton to fall down in a fit. In due course Nelly again discovers Cathy's truancy; this time she informs Edgar, who prohibits further trips to the Heights.

From about this point, Edgar and Linton both begin to decline rapidly in health. Heathcliff, eager to procure the marriage in the near future, lest Linton die and spoil his chance of seizing Cathy's fortune, forces his son to write supplicatory letters to Cathy. Eventually she wins Edgar's permission to meet Linton regularly on the moors. Terrorised by Heathcliff, Linton professes to be gaining strength, but is evidently dying. In Chapter 27, with Edgar and Linton near to death, Heathcliff at last resorts to force; intimidating Cathy and Nelly into entering the Heights again, he locks them in, and compels Cathy to consent to the marriage on pain of indefinite detention. Linton gloats over his acquisition of Cathy's property; Heathcliff helps him to wrest her locket from her, and himself tramples upon the portrait of Edgar that it contains.

Nelly is released after 5 days and advises Edgar of the situation. He proposes to alter his will in order to divert Cathy's personal property into the hands of trustees (and away from Heathcliff's); but the lawyer has been suborned by Heathcliff and does not answer the summons until Edgar is already dead. Cathy escapes in time to console her dying father by pretending that she is happy with Linton.

At the beginning of Chapter 29 Heathcliff enters Thrushcross Grange as its master. He reminisces at length to Nelly about his love for Catherine, and reveals that he has twice opened her grave; he professes to a belief in ghosts, and looks forward to being literally mingled with Catherine's remains when he too is dead. Having established his authority at the Grange, he takes Cathy back with him to live at Wuthering Heights. After Linton's death, which follows within weeks, we are left with the household that Lockwood finds in Chapter 1.

If the second phase presents Heathcliff, based at the Heights, laying siege to the Grange, the third can be seen as reversing the direction of movement. Heathcliff is now a Klingsor-like wizard, drawing victims from the Grange to his domain: first Linton, and then, with great resourcefulness, Cathy. We are by now sufficiently conscious of Edgar's very modest powers of controlling others to anticipate that the sprightly Cathy, with her 'perverse will' (*18*, 224), must inevitably break free of his protective restraints. The process is a long one, however, and the tension is built up remorselessly, with respites (Nelly's and Edgar's interventions at the ends of the twenty-first and twenty-fourth chapters) that only intensify one's anxiety, by holding out hopes of salvation which allure momentarily but against which one can feel the whole logic of the developing situation irresistibly working. (The dynamic *structure* here remains the same even if we choose to say that with part of our minds we rejoice in, or identify with, Heathcliff's pursuit of revenge.) This three-phase progression towards postponable but inevitable disaster repeats, of course, the 'melodic' shape of the entire central narration; so that Heathcliff's victory is felt as the culmination both of the campaign he has been waging around the embattled Cathy, and of a sequence of events, no less inexorable, initiated in the lifetime of Mr Earnshaw; it is a double 'arrival'. Other developments in this last phase of the narration confirm the painful, almost tragic, effect. The repeated failure of Hareton's fundamentally sympathetic efforts to impress Cathy reinforces our sense that every humane hope is destined to disappointment; and a pathetic contrast to Heathcliff's ruthless energy is presented by Edgar's slow decline and death – a contrast which attains its greatest intensity in Chapters 27–8, when Heathcliff crushes Edgar's portrait, and rejoices to think of the anguish which Cathy's apparent desertion will cause her dying father.

When Heathcliff strides into the Grange to take possession, at the beginning of Chapter 29, we anticipate energetic expression of

triumph. But with Heathcliff's long speech to Nelly, the novel
modulates suddenly into a kind of post-climactic resignation and
morbidity which reveals this third crisis to have been no more
truly final than its predecessors. We realise that the completeness
of Heathcliff's revenge by acquisition has done little to soothe or
compensate for his agonising obsession with Catherine; it has
been essentially a side issue, a secondary outlet for his will. In the
household to which he returns, he will be as dissatisfied as either
of his victims, Hareton and Cathy.

3. It has already been noted that the closing chapters, 32 to 34,
repeat the dynamic *AB* pattern of Chapters 1 to 30. The third end-
directed structure I wish to indicate is the relationship, at once of
symmetry and of dynamic contrast, between these last three
chapters and the first three. At the conclusion of Nelly's first and
longest narration, with Heathcliff's vengeance having reached
apparently its greatest possible fulfilment, the novel's tensions
threaten to expire without being resolved: this aesthetically and
emotionally incoherent outcome is represented by Chapter 31, in
which Lockwood pays a parting visit to the Heights, and finds the
relationship of the principal characters little changed from those
presented in Chapters 1 to 3. (Hareton has been making further
efforts to improve his mind; but Cathy's sneers provoke him to
throw his books into the fire.) In the next chapter, however, Emily
Brontë revives the tension at once; firstly by thrusting Lockwood
again, on his return in September 1802, into bewildering circumstances which require elucidation (his own quarters at the Grange
are cold and deserted, and Nelly has decamped to Wuthering
Heights); and secondly, with a backward loop which binds
together our whole perception of the novel, by presenting in
Nelly's second narration the same Heathcliff-Hareton-Cathy
ménage we met in the first section, undergoing now transformations which raise (and finally fulfil) hopes of a once-improbable
happy ending.

Nelly takes up the tale a fortnight after Lockwood's departure,
with her own move to Wuthering Heights: Heathcliff has
summoned her to be a companion for Cathy and keep her out of
his sight as much as possible. Nelly brings over some of Cathy's
books from the Grange, and these provide an opportunity for the
repentant girl, encouraged by Nelly, to conciliate Hareton. A
critical passage will perhaps bear quotation.

Catherine employed herself in wrapping a handsome book neatly in white paper; and having tied it with a bit of ribband, and addressed it to 'Mr. Hareton Earnshaw', she desired me to be her ambassadress, and convey the present to its destined recipient.

'And tell him, if he'll take it, I'll come and teach him to read it right,' she said, 'and, if he refuse it, I'll go upstairs, and never tease him again.'

I carried it, and repeated the message, anxiously watched by my employer. Hareton would not open his fingers, so I laid it on his knee. He did not strike it off either. I returned to my work: Catherine leaned her head and arms on the table, till she heard the slight rustle of the cover being removed; then she stole away and quietly seated herself beside her cousin. He trembled, and his face glowed – all his rudeness, and all his surly harshness had deserted him – he could not summon courage, at first, to utter a syllable, in reply to her questioning look, and her murmured petition.

'Say you forgive me, Hareton, do! You can make me so happy, by speaking that little word.'

He muttered something inaudible.

'And you'll be my friend?' added Catherine interrogatively.

'Nay! you'll be ashamed of me every day of your life', he answered. 'And the more, the more you know me, and I cannot bide it.'

'So, you won't be my friend?' she said, smiling as sweet as honey, and creeping close up.

I overheard no further distinguishable talk; but on looking round again, I perceived two such radiant countenances bent over the page of the accepted book, that I did not doubt the treaty had been ratified, on both sides, and the enemies were, thenceforth, sworn allies. (32)

The harmony between the young couple astounds Joseph and Heathcliff. But the latter, after a momentary rage when they jointly denounce him for disinheriting them, is unmanned by the tormenting resemblance between their eyes and those of the dead Catherine, and becomes incapable of taking food. Finally he dies. Hareton and Cathy are able to recover their inheritances, marry, and move to the Grange.

The effect here is, of course, partly one of joyful rebuttal of the pessimistic implications of Chapter 31: the closing chapters represent a sudden and final upturn in the mood of the novel. The true epilogue – the last page of the novel, with the lovers together in the moonlight, and a soft wind breathing over the triple grave – is a refutation of the false epilogue, Chapter 31, with Lockwood taking leave of an embittered household. But this closing section also refutes, both in its emotional tone and in the clarity with which Lockwood (and the reader) can now interpret and evaluate the situation, the confused and distressing experience of Chapters 1 to 3. The intellectual discords sounded by Lockwood's opening narrative have been progressively resolved by Nelly; in this conclusion, its emotional discords are also resolved: by betrothal, by death (for the 'frightful, lifelike gaze of exultation' (34, 365) in the dead Heathcliff's eyes testifies to the final appeasement of his passion), and, not least, by a transformation in the ambient universe, the snowstorm of Lockwood's overnight stay at the Heights being replaced by the sweet warm spring, 'the grass as green as showers and sun could make it, and the two dwarf apple trees, near the southern wall, in full bloom' (34, 356) described by Nelly in the final chapter. On the imagery of the novel's closing chapters, and its relation to other elements of dynamic structure, more will be said in section IV below.

II

Our involvement in a work of fiction, from the level of the smallest-scale conceptions upwards (and downwards again), depends upon the presentation to the imagination of things we recognise, in contexts we recognise or have been induced to conceive, and to which we can therefore render a ready minimal response: a minimal response which can then be built, by further structures of interconnection and reinforcement, into a complex and sustained commitment of feeling. In this very wide and quite uncontroversial sense, every fictional work is 'realistic'. Works depicting non-mimetic worlds or societies are no exception, since to be intelligible at all their most detailed conceptions must be of things recognisable by a reader, however grotesque their recombination; we may not be familiar with hobbits or Houynhnhms, but we are familiar with all the separate attributes out of which their physical and social natures are imaginatively constructed. Such works, certainly, pose specialised compositional problems: if Emily Brontë had set her novel in Gondal, a far greater labour of description and background narration would have been necessary to give the reader's imagination as secure a footing in the non-mimetic world as it enjoys in the essentially mimetic one of the actual work. But *Wuthering Heights*, though taking over a little material from what we know of the Gondal tales, is firmly fixed in a geographically, socially and culturally mimetic setting. Its attention to realism (in this, still very wide, sense) serves the obvious enough purpose of engaging feelings which have to do with the familiar problems of living in a particular society and culture – how to make a viable marriage, how to keep one's property out of undesirable hands, and other concerns which a George Eliot or a Trollope novel might equally well treat. I shall have comparatively little to say in connection with this realistic dimension. But certain mimetic elements in the novel also serve a further purpose, specific to a work which trespasses far outside temperate Trollopian zones of feeling and experience: that of mediating between the reader's commonsense assumptions (apparently reaffirmed by the realistic setting) and the extraordinariness, the high drama and extra-naturalistic references, of much of the plot and dialogue. The commonplace urbanity of Lockwood – a refugee from a thoroughly 'realist' novel, who would serve admirably as a minor character in *Vanity Fair* or *Middlemarch* – is, for the first section of the novel, the indispensable instrument of this mediation.

1801 – I have just returned from a visit to my landlord – the solitary neighbour that I shall be troubled with. This is certainly, a beautiful country! In all England, I do not believe that I could have fixed on a situation so completely removed from the stir of society. A perfect misanthropist's Heaven – and Mr. Heathcliff and I are such a suitable pair to divide the desolation between us. A capital fellow! He little imagined how my heart warmed towards him when I beheld his black eyes withdraw so suspiciously under their brows, as I rode up, and when his fingers sheltered themselves, with a jealous resolution, still further in his waistcoat, as I announced my name . . ..

Possibly, some people might suspect him of a degree of underbred pride – I have a sympathetic chord within that tells me it is nothing of the sort; I know, by instinct, his reserve springs from an aversion to showy displays of feeling – to manifestations of mutual kindliness. He'll love and hate equally under cover, and esteem it a species of impertinence, to be loved or hated again – No, I'm running on too fast – I bestow my own attributes over liberally on him .... (1)

Here Lockwood's trite received *ideas* about misanthropic reserve – ideas which are in themselves the unremarkable cultural property of an unremarkable social type – provide a stepping stone to the decidedly remarkable *reality* of Heathcliff's feelings which is to be fleetingly exposed in Chapter 3. The conception describable as *Mr Heathcliff: abnormal repressed feeling* is at first insinuated into our consciousness within, as it were, a reassuring box of social realism (Lockwood's civilised speculation); it is only after we have become accustomed to it in this guise that the further step of revealing it as high romantic passion is ventured. And at that point Lockwood's speculation beats an explicit retreat:

He got on to the bed, and wrenched open the lattice, bursting, as he pulled at it, into an uncontrollable passion of tears.
    'Come in! come in!' he sobbed. 'Cathy, do come. Oh do – *once* more! Oh! my heart's darling! hear me *this* time – Catherine, at last!'
    The spectre showed a spectre's ordinary caprice; it gave no sign of being; but the snow and wind whirled wildly through, even reaching my station, and blowing out the light.
    There was such anguish in the gush of grief that accompanied this raving, that my compassion made me overlook its folly, and I drew off, half angry to have listened at all, and vexed at having related my ridiculous nightmare, since it produced that agony; though *why*, was beyond my comprehension. (3)

Lockwood's embarrassed sense of the disproportion between his 'ridiculous nightmare' and Heathcliff's consequent agony deflects any puzzlement or embarrassment we ourselves might feel at that disproportion; Lockwood as emotionally uncommitted narrator expresses for us *within* the novel a temporary dissatisfaction which we might otherwise feel as a dissatisfaction *about* the novel. His puzzled observations reassure us that continued engagement with the story is not dependent upon regarding Heathcliff's passion as proportionate, and as already sufficiently accounted for – that we are responding appropriately in finding it, for the moment, inexplicably excessive, and may read on in the expectation that its intensity will be intelligible when the total pattern is clear. Lockwood's dreams, too, perform a mediating role between the ordinary and the extraordinary – indeed between the natural and the supernatural. Dreaming is at once an entirely natural and familiar process, and so a property of realism, and a context in which extra-natural and emotionally highly-charged images can be introduced. The second of Lockwood's dreams takes us directly into the strangest conception in the novel, the haunting of Heathcliff by Catherine's spirit, and as if in compensation or reassurance the representation of the mechanism of dreaming itself is exceptionally realistic. The derivation of the cudgel-fight and Branderham's pulpit-hammering from the rapping of fir-cones against the window is a fairly obvious example. Equally well-observed are, in the first dream, the characteristic abrupt shift of purpose (unexplained and admitting no need for explanation) from breaking into Thrushcross Grange to visiting the chapel; and in the second, the ingenuity with which a certain kind of nightmare imitates the outward trappings and the 'feel' of waking experience:

> This time, I remembered I was lying in the oak closet, and I heard distinctly the gusty wind, and the driving of the snow; I heard, also, the fir-bough repeat its teasing sound, and ascribed it to the right cause; but it annoyed me so much, that I resolved to silence it, if possible; and, I thought, I rose and endeavoured to unhasp the casement. The hook was soldered into the staple, a circumstance observed by me when awake, but forgotten.
> 'I must stop it, nevertheless!' I muttered, knocking my knuckles through the glass, and stretching an arm out to seize the importunate branch: instead of which, my fingers closed on the fingers of a little, ice-cold hand! (3)

The superimposition of the dream upon the actual place and moment helps to blur the edges of 'reality', and prepares the reader's imagination for the supernatural suggestion which is to come. The figure Lockwood now discerns through the window is, in some ways, a naturalistic derivation from his reading of Catherine's diary – a faceless waif, with no characteristics specific to the actual Catherine; but it significantly uses Catherine's adult surname 'Linton' instead of the more familiar 'Earnshaw'. The inference is, or may be, that a true haunting is in progress; and yet this daring stroke is doubly shielded against the reader's scepticism, since, in the first place, the choice of name *might* be simply an accident of Lockwood's subconscious fancy – similarly, the spectre's 'I've been a waif for twenty years' (3, 67) is just vague enough (seventeen years would be the true period) to be dismissed as a fortuitous near-miss by the dreamer; and in the second place, its significance is entirely lost on us at this point and only becomes clear when we have read much further and unravelled the entangled family histories. By that stage our engagement with the story should be assured.

If, then, our engagement is maintained to the end of Chapter 3, we have in practice accepted the most we shall be required to accept in the way of emotional extremity and alleged supernatural happenings. The long narration of Nelly Dean that follows enjoys in consequence, from the very beginning, the benefit of an established latitude in the reader's tolerance of departures from the familiar. (It does not matter if we refer to this latitude as the novel's 'credibility', for brevity's sake and by analogy with the grounds of our acceptance of truth-telling discourse when it departs from the familiar, as long as we remember that we are using the term metaphorically, and that not belief but engaged interest, dependent upon the imaginative assimilation of conceptions, is in question.) The air of authenticity generated by the opening section is sustained by a variety of means. The multiplication of narratives itself subtly guides our awareness away from the fact that an author is responsible for every word we read: the novel not only simulates description of real objects and events, but also simulates the kinds of medium through which information about objects and events really comes to us: memoirs, letters, first-, second-, or third-hand reminiscences. Playing the game of pretending that events x and y happened, we play too the subsidiary game of supposing that the truth of x and y is more firmly established the more people (Messrs p, q, r, and so on) are implicated in asserting them. The trick only works, of course, because Lockwood and Nelly and the lesser narrators are all plausible characters, clearly distinguished in their manner of speech and habits of thought from one another and *a fortiori* from any authorial voice we might (as sometimes happens with Charlotte Brontë) feel we can overhear seizing an opportunity of confession. Another, related, authenticating quality is the generally understated tone of the narration, for narrative histrionics, even when fathered (non-ironically) on a narrating character, tend to distract attention from the subject-matter of the narration, and to strike the reader either as an attempt to force a response from him which the tale does not naturally engender, or, again, as an outlet for untransformed authorial feelings and obsessions. Both principal narrators in *Wuthering Heights* hold back, for convincing reasons, from a fully expressed emotional response to what they hear and witness – Lockwood because of the defensive urbanity already noted, Nelly through a combination of occupational deference and self-effacement, unpretending commonsense, and comfortable undogmatic faith:

> To be sure, one might have doubted, after the wayward and impatient existence [Catherine] had led, whether she merited a haven of peace at last. One might doubt in seasons of cold reflection, but not then, in the presence of her corpse. It asserted its own tranquillity, which seemed a pledge of equal quiet to its former inhabitant.
>
> Do you believe such people *are* happy in the other world, sir? I'd give a great deal to know.
>
> I declined answering Mrs. Dean's question, which struck me as something heterodox. *(16)*

Neither evinces exaggerated (or even, we may occasionally think, normal) horror or surprise at the violent and macabre episodes, except when personally caught up in them. Their discourse is always measured, often wry (see their comments on Joseph, *passim*, particularly Lockwood's final sarcasm, off-setting the seriousness of the closing paragraphs, or Nelly's 'the wearisomest, self-righteous pharisee that ever ransacked a Bible to rake the promises to himself, and fling the curses on his neighbours' (5, 82–3)). Their analysis of other characters, whether accurate or not, is typically detached and laconic:

> An indefinite alteration had come over [Linton's] whole person and manner. The pettishness that might be caressed into fondness, had yielded to a listless apathy: there was less of the peevish temper of a child which frets and teases on purpose to be soothed, and more of the self-absorbed moroseness of a confirmed invalid, repelling consolation, and ready to regard the good-humoured mirth of others, as an insult. *(26)*

One might compare such authenticating narrative techniques with those of the classical ghost story of Sheridan LeFanu and M. R. James, in which the typical narrator – often a scholar, clergyman or scientist – exhibits a similar dry intelligence that implies unimpressionableness, fends off any suspicion of delusion, and allows the supernatural occurrences to appear all the more terrifying by their juxtaposition, in the medium of an even-toned narrative, to familiar things. Very often, again as in *Wuthering Heights*, the principal narrative of the ghost story incorporates secondary narratives – diaries found in dusty drawers, the private papers of learned physicians, and the like. (Not that *Wuthering Heights* explicitly imitates documentary status: if it did so, such questions as the plausibility of Nelly's possessing total recall would be felt to be pertinent. The novel prudently stops short of this degree of realism and rests upon the convention – as old as Homer – which allows any character to be a born *raconteur* unless positively disqualified by some incompatible quality.) Often, too, in the ghost story secondary narrators of non-intellectual character (rustics, servants, children) are used to corroborate the hauntings with testimony whose deliberate ramblingness and imprecision is at once naturalistically convincing and calculated to disguise the contriving hand of the author; again *Wuthering Heights* employs a toned-down version of this technique, with Nelly's occasional, never irrelevant digressions reminding us of her autonomy as a witness, preventing her narration from seeming simply a transparent wrapping for authorial omniscience.

One further use of realism for smoothing the path to high drama may repay discussion. This is the continuity between naturalistic speech and poetic rhetoric in the dialogue, particularly that of Heathcliff and Catherine. The need for mimetic naturalism in fictional dialogue should not be overstated, for our expectation of life-like speech is to some extent modified by the fictional convention. Characters in novels do not – unless like Miss Bates it is precisely their character to do so – speak quite so repetitively, falteringly or imprecisely as most of us do in reality; and the convention is a necessary one, if only because prose cannot reproduce the nuances of intonation which in life often make clear the sense of imperfectly phrased statements. But some degree of naturalisation is evidently needed if, for example, Catherine's famous declaration, already partially quoted, so stately in rhythm, so daring in thought, so inspired in its central metaphor (and so similar to a stanza in one of Emily Brontë's poems), is not to seem impossibly exalted for an impulsive truant-playing adolescent.

'What were the use of my creation if I were entirely contained here? My great miseries in this world have been Heathcliff's miseries, and I watched and felt each from the beginning; my great thought in living is himself. If all else perished, and he remained, I should still continue to be; and if all else remained, and he were annihilated, the universe would turn to a mighty stranger. I should not seem part of it. My love for Linton is like the foliage in the woods. Time will change it, I'm well aware, as winter changes the trees. My love for Heathcliff resembles the eternal rocks beneath – a source of little visible delight, but necessary. Nelly, I *am* Heathcliff....' (9)

Passages of eloquence such as this are naturalised, I suggest, by three principal methods. The first is exemplified by the sequel to the extract above:

'he's always, always in my mind – not as a pleasure, any more than I am always a pleasure to myself – but as my own being – so, don't talk of our separation again – it is impracticable; and –' She paused, and hid her face in the folds of my gown.... (9)

Poetic intensity, in other words, is varied in climactic passages of dialogue with asides, questions, imperatives, ejaculations, stumblings and repetitions, which remind us of the presence of other characters (thus avoiding the impression that a miniature prose poem has broken free from the fictional situation) and prevent the rhetorical utterance from seeming too immaculately 'composed'. In Wagnerian fashion, rhapsodic expressiveness and functional narration and interlocution flow into one another; there are no free-standing arias in the stilted Gothic manner.[5] Even the most hysterical speech in *Wuthering Heights*, the one which Heathcliff concludes by beating his head against the ash-tree in the garden at Thrushcross Grange, takes off from (and gains effect from contrast with) an entirely characteristic remark of Nelly's.

'Her senses never returned – she recognised nobody from the time you left her', I said. 'She lies with a sweet smile on her face; and her latest ideas wandered back to pleasant early days. Her life closed in a gentle dream – may she wake as kindly in the other world.'

'May she wake in torment!' he cried, with frightful vehemence, stamping his foot, and groaning in a sudden paroxysm of ungovernable passion. 'Why, she's a liar to the end! Where is she? Not *there* – not in heaven – not perished – where? Oh, you said you cared nothing for my sufferings! And I pray one prayer – I repeat it till my tongue stiffens – Catherine Earnshaw, may you not rest, as long as I am living! You said I killed you – haunt me then!' (16)

The last two imprecations here illustrate a second naturalising quality, a retention of colloquial diction and syntax even at moments of great intensity. The content and context of the sentences are extraordinary, but their syntactical and semantic patterns are entirely commonplace – first the minatory imperative sentence beginning with the full name of the person addressed;[6] then the short two-part sentence in which the second part responds with sledgehammer 'logic' to an attributed statement in the first. Compare, with a little updating of diction,

Catherine Earnshaw, get that washing-up done before you go out!

You said you wanted your freedom – get out then!

The syntactical colloquialism of the following speech needs little commentary.

'Do you suppose I'm going with that blow burning in my gullet?' he thundered. 'By hell, no! I'll crush his ribs in like a rotten hazelnut, before I cross the threshold! If I don't floor him now, I shall murder him some time, so as you value his existence, let me get at him!' (11)

The rotten hazel-nut is an inventive, superbly disdainful image, but it sounds in context just sufficiently like the kind of cliché we fall back on in heedless moments (cf. *crush like a fly, make mincemeat of*) to disarm any suspicion of over-composition.

It is true that Heathcliff's speeches, always as vigorous as his personality, sometimes ascend above the colloquial level and attain an oratorical dignity and breadth of design. This is particularly so in his last long conversation with Nelly, in which he talks about the apathy which is at last overtaking him; the vigour is still present, but exhibited as it were in a slower tempo, in a forcefulness of syntactical design rather than in the pungency of short individual phrases.

'Five minutes ago, Hareton seemed a personification of my youth, not a human being – I felt to him in such a variety of ways, that it would have been impossible to have accosted him rationally.

'In the first place, his startling likeness to Catherine connected him fearfully with her – That however which you may suppose the most potent to arrest my imagination, is actually the least – for what is not connected with her to me? and what does not recall her? I cannot look down to this floor, but her features are shaped on the flags! In every cloud, in every tree – filling the air by night, and caught by glimpses in every object by day, I am surrounded by her image! The most ordinary faces of men and women – my own features mock me with a resemblance. The entire world is a dreadful collection of memoranda that she did exist, and that I have lost her!

'Well, Hareton's aspect was the ghost of my immortal love, of my wild endeavours to hold my right, my degradation, my pride, my happiness, and my anguish –' . . . . (33)

This (generally) splendid prose comes, to be sure, more plausibly from Heathcliff than it would from any other character in the novel, given the powerful intelligence he exhibits, in action as well as in speech, and the impression he gives of undisclosed psychological resources – an impression initially derived from his childhood taciturnity, and reinforced by the mysterious three-year absence which transforms him into a gentleman. One cannot exactly picture him reading Johnson or Gibbon, but on the other hand one cannot quite put it past him either – it is precisely his quality that one does not know what one can put past him. (Occasionally the author's invention fails to live up to the standard of expressive force created for Heathcliff: one feels rather ashamed for him at the trite 'immortal love' and 'wild endeavours' of the last sentence quoted, and the limp generalities that follow.) But perhaps the main consideration which induces us to accept this degree of eloquence – and here I come to my third naturalising quality – is our sense, generated by the plot, that this speech is the product of prior, perhaps long and repeated, meditation; though it has a specific occasion, its substance is an *idée fixe* whose obsessive recurrences can readily be enumerated to Nelly because Heathcliff has repeatedly enumerated them to himself. This effect of partial premeditation is typical of Heathcliff's discourse; temperamentally and by the exigencies of his outcast status a reticent character, he only unfolds his deepest thoughts, memories and feelings on privileged occasions; to Nelly, a mere sounding-board, when it is tactically safe to unburden himself (he waits seventeen years before relating, presumably for the first time, the story of his disinterment of the newly-buried Catherine); and, of course, to Catherine herself. But from Catherine he is separated, during the critical period of their relations, by her marriage to Edgar, so that his later speeches to her, too, are largely outbreaks of suppressed feeling – of premeditated reproach and appeal. Utterances such as the following have, accordingly, a definite air of partial rehearsal about them which is not at all incompatible with genuine passion.

> 'And as to you, Catherine, I have a mind to speak a few words now, while we are at it – I want you to be aware that I *know* you have treated me infernally – infernally!' (11)
> 'You are welcome to torture me to death for your amusement, only, allow me to amuse myself a little in the same style....' (11)
> 'You loved me – then what *right* had you to leave me? What right – answer me – for the poor fancy you felt for Linton? Because misery, and degradation, and death, and nothing that God or satan could inflict would have parted us, *you*, of your own will, did it. I have not broken your heart – *you* have broken it – and in breaking it, you have broken mine. So much the worse for me that I am strong. Do I want to live? What kind of living will it be when you – oh, God! Would you like to live with your soul in the grave?' (15)

That latter part of this last extract must be to some extent unpremeditated, since it is only at the beginning of this episode that Heathcliff realises that Catherine is dying, but in effect it only adapts to a grimmer context Heathcliff's contention that by her marriage Catherine has destroyed the true grounds of her happiness, and consequently of his. Viewed in isolation the speech may look a little mannered, but in the novel we accept it because its substance is borne out by the plot and because, though it is probably not how we *would* put the case if we were in Heathcliff's position, it is just how we would *want* to put it, just the kind of thing we meditate saying to people, though a justified fear of sounding silly always prevents us on the day. But if we can in principle imagine ourselves saying it, and feeling an associated emotion, then we can imagine Heathcliff saying it, and feel an emotion associated with his doing so; the essential point is not that we should be able to turn premeditation into action, but that we should wish to do so – or, which is equally effective for emotional engagement, fear to do so, or wish or fear that another should do so.

With Catherine premeditation is much less in character, and on the whole it is other considerations which authenticate her flights of eloquence. The visionary speeches of her delirium (12) illustrate both the first and the second of the naturalising features discussed above: their mellifluous poetic line is appropriately deflected at times both by ejaculatory outbursts and inconsequentialities ('Did he shoot my lapwings, Nelly?'; 'Oh, I'm burning!') and by turns of colloquial – or more specifically infantile – idiom and syntax ('This bed is the fairy cave under Penistone Crag...'; 'I won't rest till you are with me ... I never will!'). What remains of poetic inspiration in these speeches – the rhapsody on feathers, Nelly as a witch gathering elf-bolts, the haunting vision of the Heights (quoted above, p. 173), with Joseph's candle still burning as he awaits her return – is rendered acceptable by the fact, or convention, of heightened imagination in the delirious. The 'I *am* Heathcliff' speech is a special case, however; its profoundly contemplative central pronouncement is inconceivable without some degree of premeditation, and the speech is preceded by a long dialogue with Nelly in which we do indeed have the impression of damned-up thoughts pressing towards an outlet, thoughts so private and problematical as to elude Catherine's usual reckless impulsiveness of expression. The speech is her thirty-second of the dialogue, and most of its predecessors are notably tentative and brief: the first four, each separated from the next by several lines of narration, being the following:

'Are you alone, Nelly?'

'Where's Heathcliff?'

'Oh, dear! ... I'm very unhappy!'

'Nelly, will you keep a secret for me?'

The fifth reveals that Edgar has proposed marriage, and been accepted; there follows the 'catechism' in which Nelly explores and condemns Catherine's motives for accepting. Then we have two false starts.

'Nelly, do you never dream queer dreams?' she said, suddenly, after some minutes' reflection....

'If I were in heaven, Nelly, I should be extremely miserable.' (9)

In each case Nelly declines the unwholesome gambit, and tries to change the subject or arrest the conversation. The effect of all this delay is to prepare the reader for (and indeed work up his impatience for) some deeply meditated disclosure far removed from Catherine's normal level of discourse. Then, for the second time in the novel, an account of a dream provides the occasion for a stepping-up of imaginative and emotional intensity. Catherine overrides Nelly's resistance, and in her longest speech of the dialogue before 'I *am* Heathcliff' relates her dream of feeling miserable in heaven, and rejoicing when the angels cast her down 'into the middle of the heath'. The speech ends with a pair of quasi-commonplace similes:

'Whatever our souls are made of, [Heathcliff's] and mine are the same, and Linton's is as different as a moonbeam from lightning, or frost from fire.' (9)

This speech, therefore, anticipates – though in a less rhetorically powerful fashion – the two principal themes of the 'I *am* Heathcliff' speech: her renunciation of an orthodox spiritual relation to the universe in favour of total identification with Heathcliff (for the 'heath' in the earlier speech stands both verbally and figuratively as an abbreviation for Heathcliff and all that he represents to her); and the assertion, in metaphoric form, that her association with Heathcliff by its very nature transcends or undercuts that with Edgar. When we arrive at the later speech, its eloquence of expression is consequently set off in our minds against a certain expectedness of content, derived from this earlier formulation; if both content and expression were produced without apparent premeditation, our general awareness that Catherine is tapping deeper levels of thought than usual would probably not suffice to prevent a certain sense of incongruity between the utterance and her known character. As it is, any resistance we might feel against her producing the crucial sentences is counteracted both by our quickened impatience (which provides a motive – an expectation of something especially interesting – for swallowing the speech whole), and by the consideration (which we need not consciously˙ articulate to ourselves) that this is at least her second shot at expressing this complex of ideas, that she has had time to struggle towards an adequate phrasing of them.

In the above discussion I have concentrated, for the sake of saying something comparatively new and technically specific, upon problematical zones in the novel in which an observant realism is used to naturalise the extraordinary, to preserve continuity between melodramatic speech and incident on the one hand, and a firmly naturalistic setting on the other. But I do not at all wish to reduce the realism of *Wuthering Heights* to a collection of compositional problem-solving techniques. On the contrary, the effectiveness of all such devices rests upon a consistent substructure of plausibility in the imagined world, an essential affinity between what we are prompted to imagine by the text and our stored-up perceptions of actual people, places and events. The unusual mimetic accuracy of *Wuthering Heights*, both in external authenticity and in psychological insight, has been extensively celebrated by critics.[7] I will merely note three points which have not, to my knowledge, received a great deal of attention. One is the three-dimensionality, the sudden Tolstoyan surprisingness, of even some of the relatively minor characters: Joseph's uncommonly sympathetic aspect as he tries to prevent the infant Catherine and Heathcliff from discovering that Mr Earnshaw is dead in his chair (5); Linton Heathcliff's one speech of painful self-knowledge and genuine affection for Cathy (24, 285); Nelly's occasional, confessed, misdeeds, such as her early maltreatment of Heathcliff (4), which strengthen the quality of maturity and acquired moral shrewdness in her retrospective narration. Another astutely observed detail is the way in which Catherine's tactical display of hysteria shades gradually into true delirium; a less perceptive writer would have felt obliged to indicate a point of demarcation, at which 'pretence' is replaced by 'reality', and thus have falsified the fluidity between conscious and subconscious, and between bodily states and mental states, to which this novel is so alert. And a third point of realism is the surprising, if unostentatious, frankness about sex, as displayed by Zillah's anxiety that Hareton and Cathy should not be left together in the house unsupervised ('Hareton, with all his bashfulness, isn't a model of nice behaviour' (30, 326)), and in the series of allusions which make it clear that Heathcliff shows sexual brutality towards Isabella on their wedding night, begets Linton then or thereabouts, and suspends conjugal relations soon afterwards.[8] All three of these points demonstrate Emily Brontë's possession of a 'realism' which has little to do with sharing in nineteenth-century ideologies or epistemologies, and much to do with independent-minded observation of human beings; all three are beyond the scope of most of her contemporaries, and those who might have accomplished them (George Eliot, for example) would have been inclined to labour what Emily Brontë almost takes for granted.

III

The name 'Heathcliff' is both the first and the last in the text of *Wuthering Heights*. Heathcliff's arrival in the Earnshaw household is the first significant event in Nelly Dean's narration; and he is a participant – usually, indeed, the moving force – in every crisis thereafter, unless we except the final reconciliation between Hareton and Cathy. So thoroughly is the novel structured around the conflict between Heathcliff and a series of antagonists that it is at once important and unimportant to explore the nature of our engagement with his character and career: unimportant because, as I hinted in section I, the affective *tension* aroused by Heathcliff's antagonisms is felt whether we sympathise with him or with his opponents; important because it is strange and interesting that this should be so, or appear to be so. One might dismiss the problem by suggesting that the novel's ambivalence or openendedness in this respect is precisely one of its virtues: a reader can make of it what he likes. But few critics have been content to say this, and one can understand their reluctance; much of the action of the novel is of a kind which naturally gives rise to strong and unequivocal feelings and judgements. I wish to suggest that the marked diversity in evaluations of Heathcliff, from Charlotte Brontë's outright condemnation in her 'Editor's Preface'[9] to the favourable or at least exculpatory comments of some modern critics,[10] corresponds to a genuine tension within every attentive reader's response – a tension which in turn owes its origin, not to any sense of a radical moral ambiguity in the novel, but to a strenuous conflict between moral and extra-moral aspirations simultaneously quickened by the work.

Let us be in no doubt, first, about the grounds for moral revulsion at Heathcliff's behaviour. He is vindictive, cruel and cunning. His vengefulness, even before Catherine's rejection of him, is literally bloody-minded ('I'd not exchange, for a thousand lives, my condition here, for Edgar Linton's at Thrushcross Grange – not if I might have the privilege of flinging Joseph off the highest gable, and painting the housefront with Hindley's blood!' (6)); and this is no mere adolescent bluster, but a preview of later violence. Even if we discount Joseph's suspicion that he hastens Hindley's death (17, 222), Heathcliff certainly comes close to unlawful killing in the earlier episode in the same chapter in which, after breaking into the Heights through the window, he dashes the head of the already 'senseless' Hindley 'repeatedly against the flags' (213). His cruelty is frequently indulged for its own sake, beyond any motive of securing an object or even exacting direct revenge against a persecutor. After imprisoning Cathy in order to compel her marriage to Linton, he mutters (as an aside, not a terrorising ploy):

'It's odd what a savage feeling I have to anything that seems afraid of me! Had I been born where laws are less strict, and tastes less dainty, I should treat myself to a slow vivisection of those two as an evening's amusement.' (27)

When Cathy tries to seize the key from him he threatens to knock her down, and when she persists administers 'a shower of terrific slaps on both sides of the head, each sufficient to have fulfilled his threat, had she been able to fall' (27, 302). He is capable too of inflicting, and deriving pleasure from inflicting, acute mental distress. He confesses to Nelly his tormenting of Isabella ('I've sometimes relented, from pure lack of invention, in my experiments on what she could endure, and still creep shamefully cringing back' (*14*, 188); and, as we have noted, rejoices at the separation of Cathy from Edgar during the latter's mortal illness:

> 'Miss Linton, I shall enjoy myself remarkably in thinking your father will be miserable: I shall not sleep for satisfaction.... He'll think you are tired of waiting on him, and run off, for a little amusement....' (*27*)

This episode exemplifies Heathcliff's readiness to take revenge on one person through another: on Hindley through Hareton, when he regrets the missed opportunity of causing the baby's death and allowing Hindley to suppose himself responsible (*9*) – another instance of his alertness to the possibility of inflicting psychological distress; and on Edgar through Isabella as well as Cathy. The hanging of Isabella's springer, Fanny, takes this tendency to grotesque lengths. But Heathcliff's cruelty extends to those not even tangentially associated with his own sufferings. He is reputedly 'a cruel hard landlord to his tenants' (*18*, 232); and Linton, himself of a sadistic temperament, remarks, 'I wink to see my father strike a dog, or a horse, he does it so hard' (*28*, 313). This is by way of comparison with Heathcliff's treatment of Cathy, when he tramples on her father's portrait and strikes her so violently that her mouth fills with blood. Lastly, Heathcliff ruthlessly exploits others' weaknesses and misfortunes for his own purposes: Isabella's infatuation with himself, Hindley's gambling and general dissipation (the product of a grief at bereavement for which Heathcliff, who will later suffer a similar anguish, characteristically shows no sympathy), and Linton's fatal sickness and timidity, which he works up with threats to a pitch of terror in order to pressurise Cathy into crossing his threshold:

> With streaming face and an expression of agony, Linton had thrown his nerveless frame along the ground: he seemed convulsed with exquisite terror.
> 'Oh!' he sobbed, 'I cannot bear it! Catherine, Catherine, I'm a traitor too, and I dare not tell you! But leave me and I shall be killed! *Dear* Catherine, my life is in your hands ... I can never re-enter that house ... I'm *not* to re-enter it without you!' (*27*)

On the other hand, if Heathcliff's sins are manifold, he does not quite, as Charlotte's 'Preface' alleges, 'stand unredeemed'. He has several qualities – some, admittedly, only lightly indicated – which should, without any great recourse to moral casuistry, command sympathy and approval. One is his courage and patience under duress, noted by Nelly when she nurses him through measles (4). A second is his honesty as a child: 'he said precious little, and that generally the truth' (4, 79). This persists into maturity in the form of plain speaking and a lack of concern to palliate his own motives – though he is not above falsehood, or at least sophistry and distortion, in his efforts to ensnare the young Cathy (21–2, 25, 27). A third (not, perhaps, strictly a moral virtue) is his intellectual vitality, which extends to a certain sarcastic but not unattractive sense of humour, best seen in his early fencing with Lockwood (especially the exchanges about the 'beneficent fairy' (2)), and in his unflappable response to Joseph's complaint about his currant trees (33, 349). Fourth is his loyalty to Catherine: even if his adult love for her is 'a sentiment fierce and inhuman', as Charlotte would have it, his boyish resolution to break the windows of Thrushcross Grange, if necessary, in order to rescue her from the clutches of Mr and Mrs Linton (6) is appealing. And fifth and sixth come the two virtues Charlotte does concede: his 'half-implied esteem for Nelly Dean'; and his 'rudely confessed regard for Hareton Earnshaw' – a regard strenuously expressed at a point at which the reader is particularly likely to welcome it, when Linton and Cathy have been mocking Hareton for his illiteracy and 'frightful Yorkshire pronunciation' (21, 254).

I shall account later for this seemingly random assortment of creditable qualities. But the usual case for the defence of Heathcliff rests, of course, less on these than on the contention that his injurious actions are a response to being injured himself – first 'degraded' by Hindley from equal status within the Earnshaw family, then robbed of the undivided attention of his soul-mate by Catherine's marriage to Edgar. These afflictions, however, though they may extenuate Heathcliff's behaviour to some extent, are far from accounting for it, since his essentially ruthless and selfish disposition predates them. The episode of the two colts, in the very first chapter of Nelly's narration, makes this perfectly clear, and I quote it at length.

I wondered often what my master saw to admire so much in the sullen boy who never, to my recollection, repaid his indulgence by any sign of gratitude. He was not insolent to his benefactor;

he was simply insensible, though knowing perfectly the hold he had on his heart, and conscious he had only to speak and all the house would be obliged to bend to his wishes.

As an instance, I remember Mr. Earnshaw once brought a couple of colts at the parish fair, and gave the lads each one. Heathcliff took the handsomest, but it soon fell lame, and when he discovered it, he said to Hindley,

'You must exchange horses with me; I don't like mine, and if you won't I shall tell your father of the three thrashings you've given me this week, and show him my arm, which is black to the shoulder.'

Hindley put out his tongue, and cuffed him over the ears.

'You'd better do it at once,' he persisted, escaping to the porch (they were in the stable); you will have to, and if I speak of these blows, you'll get them again with interest.'

'Off, dog!' cried Hindley, threatening him with an iron weight, used for weighing potatoes and hay.

'Throw it,' he replied, standing still, 'and then I'll tell how you boasted that you would turn me out of doors as soon as he died, and see whether he will not turn you out directly.'

Hindley threw it, hitting him on the breast, and down he fell, but staggered up immediately, breathless and white, and had not I prevented it, he would have gone just so to the master, and got full revenge by letting his condition plead for him, intimating who had caused it.

'Take my colt, gipsy, then!' said young Earnshaw, 'And I pray that he may break your neck; take him, and be damned, you beggarly interloper! and wheedle my father out of all he has, only, afterwards, show him what you are, imp of Satan – And take that, I hope he'll kick out your brains!'

Heathcliff had gone to loose the beast, and shift it to his own stall – He was passing behind it, when Hindley finished his speech by knocking him under its feet, and without stopping to examine whether his hopes were fulfilled, ran away as fast as he could.

I was surprised to witness how coolly the child gathered himself up, and went on with his intention, exchanging saddles and all; and then sitting down on a bundle of hay to overcome the qualm which the violent blow occasioned, before he entered the house. (4)

Suppose this episode omitted, and Heathcliff might plausibly be called a robust, mischievous, but essentially harmless child corrupted into malignity by ill-treatment. Its presence demonstrates that his calculating acquisitiveness and unrelenting determination to get his own way are there from the first. Hindley, of course, cuts no more admirable a figure in this incident than Heathcliff does. But this, let it be remembered, is the period at which 'the young master had learned to regard his father as an oppressor rather than a friend' (4, 79), at which, with Nelly's warming to Heathcliff after the measles episode, 'Hindley [had] lost his last ally' (4, 79); the passage quoted, indeed, makes the helplessness of his situation obvious. Heathcliff is not merely standing up for himself: he is exploiting an unjust advantage; and the lack of scruple and (even more striking) the single-minded efficiency with which he does so prove to be precedents for his subsequent career.

The central affliction, and obsession, of the adult Heathcliff, the main justification or mitigation of his conduct, is the severance of his bond with Catherine. But just how reasonable, in fact, *is* his grievance against Catherine's marriage? The question is more open than many of Heathcliff's defenders suppose. Catherine's reasons for marrying are as rational as most girls', and, what is perhaps more to the point, reveal in their naive adulation of Edgar genuine and straightforward sexual attraction.

'... because he is handsome, and pleasant to be with ... because he is young and cheerful ... because he loves me ....
And he will be rich, and I shall like to be the greatest woman of the neighbourhood, and I shall be proud of having such a husband.

'I love the ground under his feet, and the air over his head, and everything he touches, and every word he says – I love all his looks, and all his actions, and him entirely, and altogether.'
(9)

Catherine, to be sure, is no Elizabeth Bennet, and leaves the worth of Edgar's character unexplored. But Edgar does, in fact, prove a trustworthy and devoted husband. Nelly asserts that in the years of Heathcliff's absence Edgar and Catherine 'were really in possession of a deep and growing happiness' (10, 132). Catherine, it is clear, requires forbearance during her 'seasons of gloom and silence' (131), but then Edgar is just the man to provide it. It is commonly argued that by marrying him Catherine offends against her profound affinity with Heathcliff, and is bound in consequence to incur disaster. One might equally well observe that if only Heathcliff had been considerate enough to stay away, Catherine and Edgar would probably have muddled through like any other couple: the gunpowder would continue, in Nelly's phrase, to lie 'harmless as sand' (131), gunpowder though it be. (That this would have made for a disappointing novel has no bearing on the *moral* issue at present under discussion.) Of course, as Nelly's critical response to Catherine's list of her motives implicitly predicts, there is still something crucially absent from her marital feelings for Edgar: a deep and unequivocal commitment. But this is not to say that she would have been better off with Heathcliff. Does not the relationship between Heathcliff and Catherine, movingly though it is evoked, suggest the kind of achingly intense infantile attachment (to parent, sibling, teddy-bear or Proustian hawthorn-bush) which may seem, and in a sense be, spiritually fundamental, since it is rooted in the earliest remembered experiences, but nevertheless needs to be put in proportion if we are to set up adult relationships? There is little or nothing in it to indicate any likelihood of the kind of adult sexual union of which her love for Edgar shows Catherine to be capable. Indeed, for reasons which will be explored below, great care is devoted to suppressing any suggestion of an erotic content in the relationship. In her long conversation with Nelly, Catherine does, it is true, allude seriously to the possibility of marrying Heathcliff (9, 121), but this allusion (necessary to procure, by its instant rejection as a 'degrading' option, Heathcliff's departure) is noticeably unprepared – as it could easily have been prepared – by hints of adolescent romance: shared daydreams about the future, and so on. No-one in the Earnshaw household, howver hostile to Heathcliff and Catherine, suggests or suspects amorous feeling between them (compare Zillah's anxiety about Hareton and Cathy, noted above); and it is significant that Heathcliff's subsequent marriage to Isabella engenders nothing describable as sexual jealousy on Catherine's part, and that Heathcliff does not appear to expect that it will. It is perhaps significant too that when Heathcliff, overhearing Catherine's conversation with Nelly, steals out in presumed distress, he does so immediately before

Catherine's remark, 'he shall never know how I love him; and that, not because he's handsome, Nelly, but because he's more myself than I am' (9, 121). This leaves conveniently unexplored the possibility that Heathcliff might have been sufficiently mollified by this reassurance of fundamental affection for the eventual catastrophe to have been avoided; why, otherwise, should so emphatic a point be made (at the cost of some momentary implausibility – he has to pass fully out of earshot in the space of a semi-colon) of his not hearing it? The emotional necessity – indeed the emotional feasibility – of a marriage between Heathcliff and Catherine is left unestablished; and this consideration weakens whatever justification there may be for Heathcliff's disruption of the actual marriage.

Another, rather different and to my mind even weaker, moral extenuation of Heathcliff's actions is sometimes offered. This defence rests upon the view that the Linton ethos, the genteel world of Thrushcross Grange, is decisively repudiated by the novel, and that Heathcliff's deeds are in part mitigated by being either (a) an expression of true warmth and spontaneity of feeling, in contrast with Linton tepidity and formality, or (b) an ironic turning against the Linton world of its own legal and economic weapons, a kind of expropriation of the expropriators. (These versions correspond roughly to the views of Q. D. Leavis and Tom Winnifrith on the one hand, and Terry Eagleton on the other.[11]) Now it is true that the Lintons sometimes appear in a rather unsympathetic light; if this were not so, the antagonism between them and Heathcliff would assume a moral polarisation more appropriate to a fairy-tale than to this psychologically naturalistic novel. But the novel offers no grounds for a general repudiation of the Linton world. That its deficiencies are clearly signalled – above all the ways in which its social defensiveness sets limits to human sympathy, as in the elder Lintons' contemptuous treatment of the boy Heathcliff, or Edgar's cold and prim disowning of Isabella after her marriage – does not mean that it is condemned outright. There are qualities limiting human sympathy at Wuthering Heights too: the mean-spirited guarding of self-interest (' "And who is to look after the horses, then?" ') that prompts Heathcliff to refuse Lockwood a guide – it is the Grange-bred Cathy who protests here (2, 58–9); the killjoy evangelical gloom radiated by Joseph; the unwillingness, encountered both by Lockwood and by Isabella on her first evening at the house, to adapt domestic routine, or suspend internal quarrels, in order to show courtesy to a newcomer. Both sets of limitations are the natural products of particular economic and social situations: a leisured affluence, gentle-mannered but sheltered and self-protective; and a hardy self-sufficiency which values the protestant virtues of hard work and serious-mindedness but is intolerant of physical and emotional weakness. Their parity, as well as their separate inadequacy, is reflected in the final union between Hareton and Cathy, who cannot fully realise their potential generosity of feeling until each has broken down the other's conditioned defensiveness. Supposedly symbolical details, cited to show the inferiority of the Grange world, are often of questionable purport. Tom Winnifrith observes the contrast between the cheerful roaring fires repeatedly described at Wuthering Heights and the cooler atmosphere of Thrushcross Grange.[12] But this is a difference naturalistically grounded in their respective topographical positions. Not being exposed to 'atmospheric tumult', Thrushcross Grange does not much need blazing fires. When appropriate we do in fact hear of fires being lit there: during Catherine's convalescence, for example (*13*, 172). Conversely, Isabella is compelled to share the warmth of the kitchen at Wuthering Heights with Joseph and Hareton because the alternative is to 'starve among the damp, uninhabited chambers' (*17*, 210). The truth is that the powerful fires of Wuthering Heights are part of a cluster of images associated with the house (tempest, blizzard, irascible dogs, 'villainous old guns, and ... horse-pistols' (*2*, 47)) which together create an effect of emotional vehemence – not necessarily either a more or a less desirable quality than the emotional temperateness of Thrushcross Grange. Still more unconvincing is Terry Eagleton's exposure of 'the genteel culture of the Lintons, surviving as it does on the basis of material conditions it simultaneously conceals.'[13] Eagleton makes much of the biting of Catherine's ankle (*6*) as an index of the concealed violence underlying Linton prosperity:

> As the children spy on the Linton family, that concealed brutality is unleashed in the shape of bulldogs brought to the defence of civility.[14]

Actually, there is only one bulldog. Eagleton's (presumably generalising) plural protects his remark from bathos, but prompts an unfortunate cross-reference in the reader's mind to that earlier episode (2) in which Heathcliff's *two* dogs fly at the throat of the misbehaving Lockwood and bear him down. Eagleton's conclusion,

> Culture draws a veil over such brute force but also sharpens it: the more property you have, the more ruthlessly you need to defend it[15]

does not seem to be borne out. (And incidentally, wouldn't 'the *less* property you have, the more ruthlessly you need to defend it' sound equally irrefutable?) Certainly Heathcliff is himself a landlord by the time his dogs attack Lockwood; but this only serves to undermine Eagleton's point in another way, for Heathcliff is no representative of genteel 'culture', and his brutality, being unconcealed, needs no vicarious exposure. A commonsense conclusion would seem to be that anyone in eighteenth-century rural Yorkshire who could afford a guard-dog would naturally have one – the Earnshaw household certainly keep dogs (6, 87; 7, 93) – and that if the Grange's Skulker is fractionally fiercer than the Heights' Gnasher and Wolf, that is largely because the Lintons are less capable than Heathcliff and his housemates of doing their own terrorising. The fact is that *Wuthering Heights* is not socially partisan at any important level. Though *we* may know that the wealth of families such as the Lintons rested upon economic exploitation, this is not a matter to which the novel devotes any great attention, as it would have been appropriate, and perfectly possible, to do if Heathcliff's acquisitive aggression were to be conceived as in any sense an ironic retribution. (I take it that a single reference to Mr Linton's rent-day (6, 90) does not in itself constitute a thematically significant tendency.) In the characters of Edgar and Isabella, a certain personal fecklessness, associated with a life without labour, is exposed; but the emphasis is on the personality defect itself rather than on its socio-economic origin – an emphasis reflected in the terms of Heathcliff's denunciations of them, which (apart from a passing reference to Edgar's 'magisterial heart' (14, 188)) are notably free from specifically social resentment. That no reductive social determinism is implied is demonstrated by the parallel case of Hindley Earnshaw, whose weakness of character goes much deeper than Edgar's – compare, as Nelly does, their responses to widowerhood – and is clearly the product of personal, not social, factors: inborn temperament or parental rejection. Enough, too, is made of the notion of Hareton as the 'rightful' heir to Wuthering Heights[16] to dispel any idea that Heathcliff's acquisitive activities are conceived simply as the pitting of one kind of economic force against another, that no moral distinction is to be drawn between the improper sequestration of property and its legitimate possession. For Heathcliff's acquisition of the entire Linton property certainly *is* improper – indeed (though he gets away with it) illegal. It is brought about by bribery, unlawful detention, and a forced marriage; and as C. P. Sanger showed in his celebrated essay,[17] Heathcliff's possession of the Thrushcross Grange estate is in any case legally baseless or at least extremely questionable. To refer to these methods as (in Terry Eagleton's words, but my italics) 'property *deals*' and '*arranged* marriages',[18] with the implication that Heathcliff is just beating the Lintons at their own legalistic game, is to obscure a plain moral contrast between Heathcliff's chicanery, backed by *force majeure*, and the straightforward trust in legal propriety shown by other characters: by Edgar when he attempts to alter his will to protect Cathy's interests, or by Nelly when she insists that Edgar's direction to bury him beside his wife should be carried out.

The burden of my argument so far, then, is that Charlotte Brontë is essentially right, and the pro-Heathcliff faction among critics essentially wrong: our attitude to Heathcliff, if we read the novel attentively, ought naturally to be one of slightly-qualified hostility. In his favour, from a moral point of view, are only an arbitrary-seeming handful of virtues, and some far from sufficient provocation. Yet it will almost certainly be felt that this misrepresents our response: something essential about Heathcliff has been left out. Or to put it another way, and scrupulously sidestep the affective fallacy, there is an untidiness about my account so far which one hesitates to father on a novel so authoritatively constructed. Can one be content to say that Heathcliff is a formidable villain, trailing loose ends of virtue and mitigation?

The inadequacy both of my analysis and of the others mentioned above results, I suggest, from three closely related – in fact ultimately identical – errors: a methodological error, an error about affect, and an error about the way the novel – one might venture to add, any novel – functions. The methodological error is to approach the matter of Heathcliff and his career solely from the point of view of his choices as a free (or, alternatively, conditioned) agent, and their morally attributable consequences: to ask whether this or that act is approvable or pardonable or deplorable, and draw up a balance-sheet on his character. The error about affect is to assume that feeling positive involvement with Heathcliff as we read must entail a positive *moral* judgement on his deeds. And the error about the functioning of the novel is to suppose that, because from a Heathcliff's-eye view the situations the character is placed in are anterior to the actions he performs in confronting them, so in the novel itself – an artefact of language acting upon our imaginations – the situations must be experientially prior to the subsequent actions of the character. This last and fundamental error confuses the imaginary lived experiences of the characters, in which as in real life one can only modify what is to come, not what has been, with the reader's experience of the fiction, in which every conception present to the imagination potentially modifies (or rather helps to realise) every other conception irrespective of chronological or causal sequence. In the novel as we apprehend it, everything is equally 'given', and actions are no more (and no less) contingent upon the situations that precede them than situations are contingent upon the actions that succeed them; just as the shadow cast by a figure in a Rembrandt painting is no more contingent upon the position of the figure than the position is contingent upon the shadow, whatever may be the case in the real world which is being imitated. Certainly we find Heathcliff choosing to do things in response to particular situations; from this point of view the situations are anterior to the actions, and we respond to the actions in the knowledge that they 'could have been' different – with alarm, disapproval, and other reactions appropriate to free, temporal acts. But from another point of view, Heathcliff's character is anterior to the situations which allow it to be displayed in action, just as an idea in a poem is in a sense anterior to the imagery used to express or elaborate it: the imagery is coined to make the idea manifest, and likewise the situations are coined to make the character manifest. From this point of view such responses as alarm or disapproval are out of the question, since we are responding not to something which *happens* or *acts*, but to something which *is*: Heathcliff's manifest character. The first type of response to Heathcliff might be compared to observing, with appropriate emotions, that one's friend is driving too fast and without due care and attention; the second to sharing vicariously the sensation of reckless speeding. These two types of response are likely to conflict disturbingly. The first has already been treated at length; I shall now discuss the second – or rather its sources in the novel – before returning, finally, to the question of conflict between them.

The primary quality of Heathcliff's manifest character – visible as early as the episode of the colts, and indeed implicit in the first descriptions of him given by both Lockwood and Nelly – is an indestructible force and resolution of will: we can call it *wilfulness* provided that we discount the word's secondary suggestion of mere juvenile perversity. The manifestation of this quality entails certain fundamental compositional choices by the author.[19] Firstly, wilfulness cannot be effectively exhibited at its highest intensity in a character whose will is directed towards easily accessible ends and who usually has little difficulty getting his own way. Consequently Heathcliff is given difficult and extensive aspirations, and his path is strewn with obstacles which he overcomes only to become aware of new ones. And secondly, only certain kinds of end can be attained in any meaningful form without tractability and compromise: a happy marriage cannot, for example. And therefore Heathcliff is restricted to pursuing ends which by their nature require the refusal of compromise: uncontested power, comprehensive acquisition, revenge, and a transcendent love for which the world is well lost. To a large extent, as I shall now show with a considerable amount of necessary simplification, the development of the plot is dictated by these two connected imperatives.

Heathcliff's brief period of immunity as Mr Earnshaw's favourite serves, as we have seen, to impress his energetically wilful disposition on the reader. Once this point is made, things begin to go wrong for him. Mr Earnshaw promptly dies, and his authority passes to Hindley, who treats Heathcliff tyrannically. This persecution provides an opportunity for him to rant vigorously and brood on bloody revenge, but it has only a short-term value in exhibiting his wilfulness, since the conflict with Hindley could too obviously be resolved in a year or two by Heathcliff's leaving the Heights: as a farm labourer or a soldier (say) Heathcliff could hardly be worse off than under Hindley's yoke. If this anti-Earnshaw struggle is to continue, therefore, without the consideration just mentioned arising in the reader's mind, Heathcliff must acquire some convincing motive for staying in the area – or better still, for going away (thus pre-empting any puzzlement at his voluntarily remaining under oppression in Hindley's house) and then returning in an independent, but still hostile, relation to the Earnshaw household. This motive is, of course, the breaking of his early alliance with Catherine by the advent of the Lintons, the painful estrangement made inevitable by her eventual, doubt-ridden betrothal to Edgar, and his consequent sense of an inferiority which he cannot redress while he remains a virtual servant at the Heights, but might redress elsewhere. Note how important this precise state of affairs, including Catherine's divided attitude, is if the expression of Heathcliff's will is to continue. For if Catherine and Heathcliff stayed together, Heath-cliff would be content. On the other hand, if Heathcliff lost Catherine because she did not much like him, his persistence in pursuing her would tend to make him a comic, or merely tiresome and disgusting, character; and little plot-mileage, unless at the level of crude melodrama, could be got out of his passion once the marriage had taken place, since without Catherine's sympathy he could not gain legitimate access to Thrushcross Grange at all. Therefore Catherine must marry Edgar, and yet remain attached to Heathcliff; and to make this plausible (and not mere coquetry), the nature of the two attachments must differ. This is why her devotion to Heathcliff finds its defining limit at the point at which her involvement with Edgar begins: at the pubertal dividing-line between infantile fixation and socialised sexuality. In the end the devotion to Heathcliff must prove stronger, since if the marital bond did so, Heathcliff's strivings would expire in disappointment, or at least become rather monotonous. But if Heathcliff actually regained Catherine, his will would be satisfied. And if Catherine went on vacillating for too long, she would appear fickle and ridiculous, both attachments would be brought into contempt, and the story would peter out.

The only way out of this further *impasse* is for the attachment to Heathcliff to prove potent, wreck Catherine's emotional stability, and bring about her death. One might suppose that this would destroy Heathcliff's main purpose in life, and so leave his wilfulness at a loss for expression; but in fact, given certain elements in his character which have already been forcefully conveyed to us, it provides opportunities for the exhibition of his will even more bounteous than before. He can rave in the garden and strike his head against the ash-tree; he can dig up Catherine's grave, twice; he can long for reunion in death and beg Catherine's spirit to haunt him; all these extremities are consistent with the passionate and superstitious Heathcliff revealed during Lockwood's overnight stay at the Heights. Meanwhile, thanks to his vindictive temperament – established for us, as I have already pointed out, well before Catherine's defection – Heathcliff can find secondary, if ultimately unsatisfying, outlets in the aggregation of Earnshaw and Linton property and the wreaking of revenge on his past persecutors. (His sadism may be seen as an extension of this vindictiveness into a general aggression against the sensate universe: a returning of pain for pain; or as a diversion of sexual energy whose normal erotic expression is blocked by the obsession with Catherine. However one may wish to rationalise it, it serves the important purpose of emphasising that Heathcliff's specific revenges are self-expressive, acts that manifest his inner being, not acts decided upon, prudentially (for routine financial gain, for example) or for want of something better to do.) These pursuits, conducted with great resource against physical and moral opposition on all sides, occupy most of the later half of the novel, and culminate in complete success. But Heathcliff's victory is not the final satisfaction for him, nor the final exhaustion of the novel's central impulse, that it may momentarily seem to be. On the contrary, that impulse – the pressure of Heathcliff's will – is felt till the end. All world-directed willing has been used up – this is eloquently displayed in Heathcliff's eventual inability to bother with food and drink[20] – but the longing for reunion with Catherine remains. At last, by sheer force of will, as it seems, Heathcliff breaks through to an exultant death: his satisfaction and the cessation of his temporal being are simultaneous. Even this is not quite conclusive. The allusions near the end to the superstition that he 'walks' maintain the awareness that his quality is to strive (so that if he *does* live after death, his existence will be an active and assertive one, of consorting with his soul-mate on stormy evenings, and frightening little boys), and preserve to the last page a sense of the threat he represents to the humane hopes represented by Hareton and Cathy – a threat, however, finally dispelled.

'No, Mr. Lockwood,' said Nelly, shaking her head. 'I believe the dead are at peace, but it is not right to speak of them with levity.'
    At that moment the garden gate swung to; the ramblers were returning.
    '*They* are afraid of nothing,' I grumbled, watching their

approach through the window. 'Together they would brave satan and all his legions.' (34)

Heathcliff's career, then, is a sustained and elaborately designed fictional embodiment of wilfulness. I do not mean that Heathcliff is 'a symbol' for the will: we do not need to perform any act of interpretation in order to arrive at any subterranean meaning. It is simply that in the tension between Heathcliff's inexorable purposes and the external world which seeks, or happens, to oppose them, the force of willing and striving is dramatised at great intensity; and the story is so contrived as to keep this tension perpetually before us and avoid any circumstance which might dissipate it.

If we turn back now to the virtues we detected in Heathcliff, we find that they are largely contingent upon this chief imperative. Two – his courage and patience under stress, and his intellectual vitality – are necessary attributes of a purposefully striving will; without them, Heathcliff could not plausibly accomplish what he does. A third, his honesty, particularly about his own motives, is also essential to the purity of his wilfulness, since to resort to dissimulation is to concede that an obstacle cannot be overridden by main force, and thus to reveal a lack of confidence in the direct effectiveness of one's will. Heathcliff's plain speaking has, moreover, the functional value of allowing him to declare his purposes openly: his intention of marrying Linton to Cathy, for example, is announced at a remarkably early stage (21, 249). His loyalty to Catherine, which has an altruistic element in it, is an inevitable corollary of her being the chief object of his willing, and provides grounds for the reciprocation on her part which, as we have seen, is necessary if this central strand of the plot is to be plausibly extended. The two remaining virtues – Heathcliff's not disrespectful attitudes towards Nelly Dean, and his 'rudely confessed regard' for Hareton – might seem clear exceptions to the rule that in Heathcliff all else is subordinated to the assertion of will. But the first of these has the important functional value of smoothing the transmission of Heathcliff's thoughts and reminiscences to the reader; it is sufficiently authenticated by the confidence in Nelly created by the measles episode. Moreover, for his own purposes Heathcliff generally has nothing to lose and much to gain from conciliating Nelly; and when the crisis comes he is not too respectful to lock her up for several nights at Wuthering Heights.

As for Hareton, he is the only character in whom Heathcliff recognises an analogy to himself; in siding with him (verbally, not practically) against the baiting of Linton and Cathy he is re-articulating, in diminution as it were, his own past frustrations. Significantly, too, he does not praise Hareton for the qualities the reader is likely to find attractive, such as his comparative kindness (save when sorely provoked) to Linton, or his naive eagerness to learn his letters, but vaguely commends his 'first-rate qualities' in contrast to the 'poor stuff' that is his own son (21, 253) – a comparison which implicitly fixes upon and celebrates those qualities, of manly strength and tenacity of purpose, which are Heathcliff's own.

The existence of these morally approvable or unexceptionable qualities emphasises the point that the essence of Heathcliff is not to be a villain (though in his relations with other characters he typically acts villainously and excites our horror and indignation) but to embody wilfulness. Our obscurely-grounded but unmistakable engagement with him, the counterpoise to our revulsion at the injuries he inflicts, arises from the fact that he does what – with part of our minds – we would all like to do, namely assert our will without the least hesitation or remorse or failing of energy. Heathcliff's painful striving against obstacles to his will elicits feelings of complicity from us because such strain – generally, of course, at a less heroic level of intensity – is ever-present in our consciousness. The universal conflict between the desire to impose what we will upon a recalcitrant world and the desire, arising from sympathetic aversion to the sufferings of others, to act altruistically, is evoked by the central conflict in the novel between Heathcliff's relentless force of will and the wishes and welfare of a series of other characters. Thus the internal affective tension in the novel is not between an attractive good and a repulsive evil (as both pro- and anti-Heathcliff partisans would imply, though distributing the sides differently) but between a good which is attractive and an amoral drive which is also attractive in a completely different way. Since the latter is a perpetual threat to the former, the two are irreconcilable, and our minds are partitioned between them, or sway to and fro: in so far as we perceive Heathcliff as a free, or at least temporal, agent, and look at the consequences of his deeds, we regret or condemn; in so far as we experience him as he intrinsically *is* (no freer to be otherwise than a major chord is free to be a minor chord or the imperious expression of Michelangelo's Moses to be not imperious), we sympathise, even rejoice, for a fundamental urge of our psyches is being quickened. The genuinely disturbing nature of this tension (in comparison with which an opposition of pleasant good and unpleasant evil is hardly a tension at all) perhaps accounts for some of the sophistries coined in Heathcliff's defence. His career so powerfully evokes in us the urgency of willing that wherever our prejudices (as rejected lovers, foes of the bourgeoisie, or self-identifiers with the passionate outsider) give us the slightest encouragement, we hasten to construct ethical defences of his actions, and so to resolve the tension between altruistic and wilful desires by convincing ourselves that they are not really in tension at all. But the true resolution, in the aesthetic experience of the novel, is that brought about by Heathcliff's death, as complete a blessing for himself as it is for the ethically positive Hareton and Cathy whom it liberates. In the real world, of course, the tension has no reliable or permanent resolution: that humane considerations may conflict with our most powerfully energised drives is a state of affairs we are stuck with. The affective force of *Wuthering Heights* lies largely in the fact that it acknowledges and extensively dramatises this conflict and the suffering it produces, while working with dynamic logic towards a consoling – if somewhat grave and stoical – final vision. A little more will be said on this last point at the very end of the analysis.

IV

It was argued in Chapter 4 that the small-scale conceptions of a fiction – the conceptions immediately associated with detailed 'verbal configurations', in Lodge's phrase – are interdependent with the large-scale conceptions we refer to as 'plot', 'locale', 'character' and so on. The eye-catching verbal *leitmotiven* of certain novels – 'darkness' in *Heart of Darkness*, 'whelp' in *Hard Times* – have only such value as their uses and contexts confer; the pointing Roman of *Bleak House* derives his 'deadly meaning' from the fact that it is Tulkinghorn, finally, that he is pointing at. But these are, at any rate, novels in which from time to time our attention is forcibly directed towards highly-charged *minutiae*. In *Wuthering Heights*, by contrast, the smaller-scale conceptions are, as it were, self-effacing; the novel does not yield recurrent phrases or images that alert us to a meaning, or insist upon an emphasis, which we could not readily infer from the rest of the work. Rather a variety of connected images helps to build up an impression of a place or character or situation, and it is that place or character or situation that we are immediately conscious of. The novel, in other words, is essentially realistic rather than symbolic, if by 'symbolism' we understand (as I propose to do) imagery which requires to be *interpreted into a meaning*, not merely experienced in its overt imaginative content and emotive force, if it is to register its proper effect. It is true that certain classes of image are particularly common in *Wuthering Heights*. But the fact that much of the novel's figurative language appears in direct speech – the whole work, of course, is in the first person – means that recurrent metaphors can usually, perhaps always, be given a naturalistic explanation, without recourse to esoteric symbolic value. That Heathcliff is frequently likened to the devil does not (without further supporting evidence) mean that he is a 'satan figure' and that consequently an entire interpretation of the novel as a religious allegory is in order; all it means for certain is that most of the characters see his behaviour as quite exceptionally vicious and call upon diabolic metaphors in order to say so – as well they might in an eighteenth-century rural society permeated by Methodism. In the same way, the extensive use of animal imagery, which helps to give such vigour to the dialogue, follows naturalistically from the setting: what metaphorical resource would rural characters be more likely to employ in describing or addressing one another, tenderly, pityingly, contemptuously, or fearfully? The imagery has none of the schematisation necessary to a coherent use of symbolism – Nelly calls Cathy a lamb, a fox and a mouse within the space of two pages in Chapter 18 (228–9) – but is rather adapted to the expressive needs of particular characters at particular moments. Thus Edgar, unable to depart after a row with Catherine, is likened by Nelly to a cat who cannot leave a mouse half-killed (8, 112); later, in the three-way confrontation with Heathcliff at Thrushcross Grange, Catherine stigmatises him as mouse-like ('Heathcliff would as soon lift a finger against you as the king would march his army against a colony of mice' (11, 154)). Hindley is to Nelly a 'wild beast' when drunkenly fondling Hareton (9, 114) and a 'stray sheep' when abandoned to the cunning of Heathcliff (10, 146): and so on. The imagery of *Wuthering Heights*, metaphorical and otherwise, is, in short, a flexible servant of the story. This is essentially true even of the most schematic deployment of imagery in the novel, the comparison of imagined heavens by Linton and Cathy.

'He said the pleasantest manner of spending a hot July day was lying from morning till evening on a bank of heath in the middle of the moors, with the bees humming dreamily about among the bloom, and the larks singing high up over head, and the blue sky and bright sun shining steadily and cloudlessly. That was his most perfect idea of heaven's happiness – mine was rocking in a rustling green tree, with a west wind blowing, and bright, white clouds flitting rapidly above; and not only larks, but throstles, and blackbirds, and linnets, and cuckoos pouring out music on every side, and the moors seen at a distance, broken into cool dusky dells; but close by great swells of long grass undulating in waves to the breeze; and the woods and sounding water, and the whole world awake and wild with joy. He wanted all to lie in an ecstacy of peace; I wanted all to sparkle, and dance in a glorious jubilee.

'I said his heaven would be only half alive, and he said mine would be drunk; I said I should fall asleep in his, and he said he could not breathe in mine, and began to grow very snappish. At last we agreed to try both as soon as the right weather came; and then we kissed each other and were friends.' (24)

There is symbolism here, if you will, but it is the characters, not the novel, who are being symbolic; Cathy and Linton *know* that they are describing their 'most perfect idea of heaven's happiness', and thereby, implicitly, the difference between their personalities. This is not a case like, for example, the association of Gerald Crich in *Women in Love* with images of snow, ice and so on: an esoteric symbolism which helps to interpret him for the reader, all unbeknown to himself. The contrasting heavens of Linton and Cathy add little to our understanding of the pair, for we already know perfectly well that Linton is languid and self-cossetting, while Cathy is impetuous and vital; their function is to present objective correlatives for emotions – to quicken by imagery and rhetorical suggestiveness our participation in the characters' feelings (or, since the characters are themselves imaginative mediums through which our engagement is solicited, simply to quicken our feelings). The evocative beauty of the images speaks for itself, but some reinforcing verbal subtleties deserve comment: the droning *m*s of Linton's ideal, as against the breathy *w*s of Cathy's; the discreet, interlaced alliteration of Linton's ('blue sky and bright sun') as against Cathy's impulsive couplets ('west wind', 'dusky dells', 'world awake and wild'); the regular syntactical pattern of Linton's –

> the bees humming ...
> the larks singing ...
> the blue sky and bright sun shining ...

– against the long enthusiastic flow of clauses, sustained by hasty *ands* and *buts*, its rhythmical energy renewed by those emphatic trochaic bird-names in the middle ('throstles, and blackbirds, and linnets, and cuckoos') with which Cathy recalls her own vision. These qualities of imagery and aural suggestion act as direct emotional stimuli, without requiring to be translated into 'meaning'; and the responses they produce are co-ordinate with those produced by the associated conceptions of character and incident. Co-ordinate, not identical; the desire stimulated by the conception engendered by 'rocking in a rustling green tree' is not the same as the desire stimulated by the conception describable as *the adolescent vitality of Cathy Linton*, for there are (in my sense of the term) as many different desires as there are stimuli. But they are sufficiently similar, the one falling within the wider affective zone marked out by the other (which is what we mean when we say that an image or other verbal detail is appropriate to its dramatic or narrative context[21]), to reinforce each other within the work's total affective structure.

Small-scale conceptions, then, support and enrich large-scale conceptions. A prime example of this collaboration – in citing which I lay no claim to originality, and which I have indeed already touched upon – is the richly developed contrast in general character between Thrushcross Grange and Wuthering Heights. Both reflect, in their ambience and physique, the psychological character of their inhabitants (who are, of course, themselves influenced by their locale). The emotional temperateness native to the Lintons is supported by a complex of image-types whose common features are stillness, sensual beauty, and an absence of hard edges.

On a mellow evening in September, I was coming from the garden with a heavy basket of apples which I had been gathering. It had got dusk, and the moon looked over the high wall of the court, causing undefined shadows to lurk in the corners of the numerous projecting portions of the building. I set my burden on the house steps by the kitchen door, and lingered to rest, and drew in a few more breaths of the soft, sweet air; my eyes were on the moon .... (10)

Gimmerton chapel bells were still ringing; and the full, mellow flow of the beck in the valley came soothingly on the ear. It was a sweet substitute for the yet absent murmur of the summer foliage, which drowned that music about the Grange, when the trees were in leaf. (15)

'Mellow', 'sweet' and 'soothing' are the characteristic epithets, trees in leaf, plentiful fruit, gentle light and mellifluous sounds the characteristic natural images. The element of ominous expectancy in the former passage (for Heathcliff is about to make his reappearance) is expressed through nothing more physically forceful than the lurking 'undefined shadows'.

Glass, too, with its implication of clear, calm perception, and its fragility which is more practicable in an emotionally temperate household, is a dominant image at Thrushcross Grange. Shortly after the first passage above we find Heathcliff looking up at 'the windows which reflected a score of glittering moons' (10, 133); 'a shower of glass drops' hangs from the ceiling of the drawing-room into which Catherine and Heathcliff peer on their first visit (6, 89); Cathy keeps a lock of Linton's hair in 'a little glass box' (19, 234). Glass at Wuthering Heights, in contrast, generally gets broken: Heathcliff breaks into the house through the window on the night of his fight with Hindley (17), while the window of the haunted chamber is shattered, at least in imagination, during Lockwood's nightmare (3). More cool and disembodied still is the moon image, so prominent in the episode of Heathcliff's first intrusion, and reiterated elsewhere in connection with the Grange – notably when Heathcliff takes possession of it:

It was the same room into which he had been ushered as a guest, eighteen years before: the same moon shone through the window; the same autumn landscape lay outside. (29)

The serene ambience in both episodes brings home the fact that Heathcliff is invading a spiritual world, not merely a physical building. The moonbeam/lightning contrast, used by Catherine to express the difference between her character and Edgar's, might be said to epitomise the contrast in prevailing imagery between Grange and Heights. Wuthering Heights is, eponymously, stormy:

> Wuthering Heights is the name of Mr. Heathcliff's dwelling. 'Wuthering' being a significant provincial adjective, descriptive of the atmospheric tumult to which its station is exposed in stormy weather. Pure, bracing ventilation they must have up there at all times, indeed: one may guess the power of the north wind, blowing over the edge, by the excessive slant of a few stunted firs at the end of the house; and by the range of gaunt thorns all stretching their limbs one way, as if craving alms of the sun. (1)

This last anthropomorphism alerts the reader (not necessarily at a fully conscious level) to the association, partially causative, which is being established between climatic and domestic states. A slightly later passage confirms the association, internalising the tempest in a literal as well as a figurative sense. Lockwood is assailed by Heathcliff's dogs.

> Mr. Heathcliff and his man climbed the cellar steps with vexatious phlegm. I don't think they moved one second faster than usual, though the hearth was an absolute tempest of worrying and yelping.
>
> Happily, an inhabitant of the kitchen made more dispatch; a lusty dame, with tucked-up gown, bare arms, and fire-flushed cheeks, rushed into the midst of us flourishing a frying-pan; and used that weapon, and her tongue, to such purpose, that the storm subsided magically, and she only remained, heaving like a sea after a high wind, when her master entered on the scene. (1)

Tempests rage around Wuthering Heights at critical moments: just before the death of Mr Earnshaw, Nelly tells us, 'a high wind blustered round the house, and roared in the chimney' (5, 84); and after the flight of Heathcliff, a thunderstorm breaks, demolishing part of the chimney-stack and 'sending a clatter of stones and soot into the kitchen fire' (9, 125). (Weather bulletins, in fact, often confirm fluctuations in the mood of the story; Catherine's death and burial are followed by a sudden failing of summer (17, 206).) Apart from storm, the prevailing climatic phenomenon at Wuthering Heights is snow, which is, of course, cold and warm at the same time – like the house itself with its blazing fires and its dismal uninhabited chambers, and like its inhabitants as Lockwood first encounters them: outwardly cold (in that they lack the surface geniality of the Lintons or of Lockwood himself), but inwardly burning with hidden rage and longing.

The distinction in imaginative ambience between the two houses is tellingly modified at the end of the novel, as the story moves towards its calm and positive conclusion. In the final section, it will be remembered, Lockwood returns to Thrushcross Grange after several months' absence to find Nelly has deserted it for the Heights.

> I would have asked why Mrs. Dean had deserted the Grange; but it was impossible to delay [the women engaged in laying the fire for him] at such a crisis, so I turned away and made my exit, rambling leisurely along, with the glow of a sinking sun behind, and the mild glory of a rising moon in front; one fading, and the other brightening, as I quitted the park, and climbed the stony by-road branching off to Mr. Heathcliff's dwelling.
>
> Before I arrived in sight of it, all that remained of day was a beamless amber light along the west; but I could see every pebble on the path, and every blade of grass, by that splendid moon.
>
> I had neither to climb the gate, nor to knock – it yielded to my hand.
>
> That is an improvement! I thought. And I noticed another, by the aid of my nostrils; a fragrance of stocks and wall flowers, wafted on the air, from amongst the homely fruit trees. (32)

The emphatic restatement of the moon image, hitherto associated with Thrushcross Grange, prepares the reader – all the more effectively if the preparation is unconscious – for the softened and lightened quality of what is now to be narrated: we have not approached Wuthering Heights in this light before. The scent of flowers is the first of the images of natural sweetness and warmth which (as remarked at the end of section I above) dominate the closing episodes at the Heights, and stand in such eloquent contrast to the image-types hitherto associated with the house. (The period of the episodes Nelly narrates conveniently happens to be the spring. But the planting of flowers by Cathy and Hareton in Chapter 33 – indicative, to certain critics, of the triumph of the capitalist over the yeoman – deftly obscures this fortuitousness, establishing a causal link between the prominence of idyllic natural imagery and the genial transformation in the human situation which it emotively reinforces.) As Nelly narrates the closing days of Heathcliff's life, we find the expiration of his power of will – or rather its diversion from the terrestrial world – reflected in a proliferation of Grange-like images against which his person stands ever more isolated. Fire gives way to ashes, the sound and fury of the storm to mildness, stillness and gentle murmurs:

> He was leaning against the ledge of an open lattice, but not looking out; his face was turned to the interior gloom. The fire had smouldered to ashes; the room was filled with the damp, mild air of the cloudy evening, and so still, that not only the murmur of the beck down Gimmerton was distinguishable, but its ripples and its gurgling over the pebbles, or through the large stones which it could not cover. (34)

The moon image returns almost at the end of the novel to confirm the liberation of Cathy and Hareton, who, returning from an evening stroll, pause 'to take a last look at the moon, or, more correctly, at each other, by her light' (34, 367). But the three closing paragraphs that follow look back across the full span of the story:

> My walk home was lengthened by a diversion in the direction of the kirk. When beneath its walls, I perceived decay had made progress, even in seven months – many a window showed black gaps deprives of glass; and slates jutted off, here and there, beyond the right line of the roof, to be gradually worked off in coming autumn storms.
>
> I sought, and soon discovered, the three head-stones on the slope next the moor – the middle one, grey, and half buried in heath – Edgar Linton's only harmonised by the turf and moss, creeping up its foot – Heathcliff's still bare.
>
> I lingered round them, under that benign sky; watched the moths fluttering among the heath and hare-bells; listened to the

soft wind breathing through the grass; and wondered how any one could ever imagine unquiet slumbers, for the sleepers in that quiet earth. *(34)*

The description of the decaying state of the church, which might at a glance seem a mere casual observation on Lockwood's part, in fact serves a number of important purposes. Firstly, the broken windows, the autumn storms, and the general sense of destruction refer back to the 'wuthering' category of images and remind us that the dénouement has been a kind of triumph for Heathcliff's striving (a triumph in the form of extinction) as well as for the humane hopes represented by Hareton and Cathy. At the same time, if we add to the images just mentioned the bare headstone of Heathcliff, and the repeated 'heath', we find in the passage an equilibrium between the austere and forceful images associated with Heathcliff and the gentler ones ('harmonized', 'benign sky', 'soft wind breathing through the grass', 'quiet earth' and so on) associated with his opponents and victims; so that the close of the novel is a true conclusion, incorporating its thematic tensions in miniature. In the action of Chapters 32 to 34, the central tension is brought to an end by a total divergence of the competing forces, as Heathcliff withdraws from all terrestrial concerns and relationships; in this three-paragraph epilogue, with the dead Edgar substituted for Hareton and Cathy as representative of the humane forces in the novel, the tension is resolved into a genuine harmony. The resolving, or dissolving, factor is death; and this is seen in retrospect to have been inevitable. From the moment Edgar and Catherine form their attachment, the aspirations of Heathcliff and those of Edgar are irreconcilable – parallel lines that can only meet in eternity. They cannot both possess Catherine. After she dies, both come to see their own ultimate purpose in death.

'Ellen, I've been very happy with my little Cathy. Through winter nights and summer days she was a living hope at my side – but I've been as happy musing by myself among these stones, under that old church – lying, through the long June evenings, on the green mound of her mother's grave, and wishing, yearning for the time when I might lie beneath it.' *(25)*

'Disturbed her? No, she has disturbed me, night and day, through eighteen years – incessantly – remorselessly – till

yesternight – and yesternight, I was tranquil. I dreamt I was
sleeping the last sleep, by that sleeper, with my heart stopped,
and my cheek frozen against hers.' (29)

It is noticeable that both passages emphasise, first, union with
Catherine, but second, extinction and rest, rather than any
optimistically conceived eternal relationship. Though it is essential
to Edgar's untormentedly humane temper that he should believe
Catherine in a 'better world' (17, 219), and to Heathcliff's
invincible energy of willing that he should see union with
Catherine, on other occasions, in positive and active terms, the
keynote of both these utterances is release from suffering; and at
this level the longings of the two men are compatible and the
tension between them is capable of final resolution. They cannot
both, objectively speaking, be 'at one' with Catherine in the
exclusive sense they wish; but this problem loses its meaning
outside life. Subjectively, the death they yearn for is a true
salvation from the pain of separation from Catherine; it puts a
certain end both to the pain and (in a sufficiently consoling sense)
to the separation.

The death of Heathcliff appears as a great relief both for himself
and (indirectly, in that its approach puts an end to his malevolent
interference in their affairs) for other characters. Indeed, the
deaths of Catherine and Edgar too, though at the time they cause
distress, in which the reader sympathetically participates, appear
in retrospect as solutions to incurable pains: in Catherine's case,
the irreconcilable division in her feelings; in Edgar's, the loss of
Catherine. Hindley and Isabella also depart emotionally ship-
wrecked lives. The transience of human life thus appears,
unusually, as a welcome safety-net, rather than as a blight to
happiness or a price one has to pay for living. This could seem
morbid, or gratuitously and querulously pessimistic, like the
hangings in *Jude the Obscure*. Yet here the effect is essentially
different. In most novels, even in many whose action covers a
considerable time-span, life is the implicit norm and death an
exception; we are presented with a world of living, in a sense
immortal, beings, from which occasionally, and with exceptional
dramatic effect, one drops out. In *Wuthering Heights* death is the
norm, not, of course, in the sense that characters are dying at
every moment, but in the sense that the story is pervaded by
reminders of the relentless flight of time, and frequently invokes a

time-scale beyond that of a single human life. The transience of Heathcliff's and Catherine's generation is subsumed under a general law of transience. The narrative sequence, with its initial leap into the past, its slow unrolling of the intervening years, and its final advance into a period unforeseen at the beginning, draws attention to the elapse of time precisely by disrupting its normal, even and linear, progress. The late introduction and extended treatment of the second generation, so contrary to generally plausible canons of novelistic unity, so boldly risking a long-drawn anti-climax, emphasises the cyclic change and renewal of human life, the inevitable yielding of the fathers to the children. And in detail, the novel is exceptionally explicit about temporal sequence. It begins with a date – '1801'; and the coda, chronologically subsequent to the delivery of the main narrative, begins with '1802' (32). An actual majority of chapters, in fact, begin with a reference to a time-interval.

Summer drew to an end, and early autumn ... (22)

The rainy night had ushered in a misty morning ... (23)

At the close of three weeks ... (24)

'These things happened last winter, sir ...' (25)

Summer was already past its prime ... (26)

Seven days glided away ... (27)

On the fifth morning, or rather afternoon ... (28)

The adolescent Heathcliff puts crosses on an almanac to record the evenings when Catherine deserts him for the Lintons (8, 109). The infant Cathy, eager to be old enough to visit Penistone Crags, measures 'her age by months' (18, 225). Nelly repeatedly casts her mind back to the infancy of her charges, Heathcliff, Catherine and Hareton, and her 'playmate', Hindley (notably in the hallucination episode at the beginning of Chapter 11); and shortly after Heathcliff's death, her musings, like a speeded-up, imperfect film, run through his career from his origins to his as yet unaccomplished funeral.

'Is he a ghoul, or a vampire?' I mused. I had read of such hideous incarnate demons. And then, I set myself to reflect,

how I had tended him in infancy; and watched him grow to
youth; and followed him almost through his whole course; and
what absurd nonsense it was to yield to that sense of horror.

'But, where did he come from, the little dark thing, harboured
by a good man to his bane?' muttered superstition, as I dozed
into unconsciousness. And I began, half dreaming, to weary
myself with imaging some fit parentage for him; and repeating
my waking meditations, I tracked his existence over again, with
grim variations; at last, picturing his death and funeral; of
which, all I can remember is, being exceedingly vexed at having
the task of dictating an inscription for his monument, and
consulting the sexton about it; and, as he had no surname, and
we could not tell his age, we were obliged to content ourselves
with the single word 'Heathcliff'. That came true; we were. If
you enter the kirkyard, you'll read on his headstone, only that,
and the date of his death. (34)

But the law of transience for the individual is also, conversely, a
law of comparative permanence for the family, the house, the
ambient world. Many references to time centre upon the two
houses themselves; and the three-hundred-year continuation of
'the ancient Earnshaw stock' (8, 104) is several times recalled to
our minds. Before first crossing the threshold of Wuthering
Heights in Chapter 1, Lockwood notices the legends '1500' and
'Hareton Earnshaw' carved over the front door – an inscription
with which the Hareton of the novel is to be preoccupied. His
announcement of the identical name a few pages later – 'My name
is Hareton Earnshaw ... and I'd counsel you to respect it!' (2, 56) –
is all the more striking for the absence of any comment on it by
Lockwood. Shortly afterwards, Cathy, reproving Heathcliff and
Hareton for their willingness to let Lockwood depart into the night
unaccompanied, exclaims to Hareton, 'Then, I hope his ghost will
haunt you; and I hope Mr. Heathcliff will never get another
tenant, *till the Grange is a ruin*' (2, 59 – my italics). Thus the
Aeschylean history of the generations in the novel is from the
beginning set within and against a much wider history, in which
stone houses rise and fall, and family names and birthrights
persist for centuries; and behind this history is the true permanence of the natural world which is so strongly present in the
novel: the earth with which the characters are so intimately
involved that its fluctuating moods sympathise with their own

fortunes, and to which, with such remarkable literalness, they see themselves as finally returning. The awareness, at once grievous and paradoxically consoling, that we are only passing visitors to a long-enduring world, is always at least implicit in *Wuthering Heights*. And so the desirability of extinction for Heathcliff, and for other characters, is not a morbid outgrowth, in inimical relation to a world in which survival is the norm and the acquisition of earthly joys the supreme end, but rather appears as a resignation, if a sadly premature one, to a state of affairs which cannot be averted and perhaps should not be mourned too deeply. The swiftly progressing decay of the kirk signals the sudden and emphatic pastness of the story we have heard; but Hareton and Cathy are to marry, with the novel's single, unobjectionable stroke of symbolism, 'on New Year's day' (34, 366).

Appendix
The Justification of
Criticism

I

With the conclusion of the specimen analysis, my argument and its vindications are in intention complete: at any rate, further elaboration (or refutation) must be conducted elsewhere. In this speculative *Appendix*, I wish to say a little more about the implications of my argument for the profession of criticism, and for an understanding of the relationship between literature and literary criticism (including the academic study of literature) and the community in which these activities are practised. Much of the discussion will trespass into areas of philosophical, political and educational debate which, I am well aware, justify far more exhaustive exploration than I have space for here; nevertheless, my incursions will be vindicated if they give rise, as I intend they shall, to an intuitively appealing and provisionally defensible account of the function of literature and its ancillary activities within our collective life. A corollary of that account will be a justification, in social and ethical terms, of the ancillary activity called 'criticism'.

The need for such a justification may be felt all the more pressingly in view of the argument expounded in the preceding chapters, which might be taken to understate the social value both of criticism and of literature itself. It may well seem to be making a very modest claim for literature to assert that it quickens and orders desire, especially when this claim is accompanied by a refutation of other, ostensibly bolder, claims commonly made for it: that it can tell truths (including social truths), impart moral guidance, or induce psychological equilibrium; and if this argument tends to depreciate literature, it must tend correspondingly to depreciate the secondary pursuit, criticism. I remarked in Chapter 2 that a modest sustainable claim is preferable to a lofty implausible one.[1] But our intuition that literature is a collective good, not merely a private and instrumental good like a square meal or a comfortable bed, that the possession of a flourishing

224

literature enriches a human community, does require acknow-
ledgement and explanation. I have argued that for the individual
reader the quickened desire engendered by a work of art,
combined with the sense of possible psychological governance
over desire consequent on the aesthetic cohesion of the work, is for
all its element of painfulness a personal good: 'desire is to lack of
desire as life is to death'.[2] One might add to this that for all its
privacy the experience of literature turns the mind outwards
towards the world, the more effectively the more catholic that
experience is allowed and encouraged to be. The enjoyment of
novels and poems may be solitary, but it is rarely solipsistic. The
range and variety of our literature, of our art in general,
corresponds, though always of course imperfectly and incomplete-
ly, to the range and variety of imaginable objects of appetite in the
world, from the most simple to the most complex; to the reader of
literature, when he reads, the world is an interesting place, and to
feel that this is so is an important personal good. (The tension
which might arise between this heightened apprehension of the
world and a humdrum life of limited satisfactions is a consequence
I would not dismiss as trivial – it is, in fact, the painfulness of the
individual aesthetic experience writ large – but, as with the
individual experience, most readers seem to find the price worth
paying.) This correspondence of art to imaginable objects of desire
is, incidentally, a guarantee both of the potential durability of
works produced in the past (because few such objects cease to be
imaginable, though they may cease to be real or common if they
have ever been either of these things) and of the need for the
production of new works (because new objects of desire, especially
complex ones such as modes of living, are continually becoming
imaginable). To point out the imaginative extroversion of literary
experience does not, however, take us very far in establishing the
value of literature for the community at large. One might dismiss
this as an unreal issue by contending that a community is no more
than a gathering of individuals, bound together by ties of a
pragmatic kind (economic interdependence and so forth) with
which literature need have no special concern. But I would not
wish to maintain this view in an unqualified form – important
though it is to insist that individual enrichment needs no 'social'
justification – since it implicitly severs the experience of literature
from that aspect of our individuality which is fulfilled in an
awareness of and relation to others, including not only family and

friends but known and unknown, living, dead and unborn fellow citizens and fellow human beings. At the end of the *Appendix* I will return to this question of literature as the possession of a community. For the moment I will content myself with suggesting that if literature provides the individual benefit I have described, it also, and consequently, provides a collective benefit. By maintaining, diffused through the community, a varied and complex awareness of the goods (and evils) conceivable by its members, by illuminating to individuals, who are also citizens, the multifariousness of their own desires, literature and the arts (in the broadest definition, which for our society would include cinema, broadcasting and popular song) serve a function which can reasonably be called political, though it is subversive of any ideological orthodoxy crudely articulated. This function is to counter reductive notions as to ends. Our political discourse is, at its most characteristic, sophisticated in its treatment of means (law, social policy, economic management) but simplistic, and not unjustifiably so, in its treatment of ends. The ultimate aim of political arrangements is presumably to create or facilitate happiness,[3] but the nature and grounds of happiness, inevitably in view of their obscurity and their apparently wide variation from person to person, receive no very subtle exploration at the hands of most political writers. Both practising politicians and political theorists naturally argue with reference, explicit or implicit, to a fairly small number of primary values (liberty, equality, self-respect, security, economic prosperity or whatever) and leave their finer discriminations as to ends, when these are called for, to those intuitions about happiness which we all variously possess, and which may include the intuition that there are considerations making for happiness which political means can do little to influence. But these intuitions, or delicate discriminations, which are so important to the humane conduct of the political process, are themselves developed, maintained and enriched by our entire culture, including our literature and other arts. The arts work with – or more precisely, are perpetually generating, preserving and revising for us – an incomparably richer universe of values than the political philosopher's: a universe which is partially, differently and overlappingly perceivable by each of us. This is not to say that art is more important than politics, or that the primary political values, however simply defined, are not absolutely real and indeed perhaps prior to any others. But if the effect of the contribution of the arts to our collective life is in part to engender a sense of the variety, elusiveness and unpredictability of happiness, and so to set limits to the plausibility of political projects founded on a speciously exact and exhaustive utilitarian calculus of pleasure and pain (or on vague and unexamined assumptions notionally verifiable by such a calculus), that is neither surprising nor undesirable. This sense may indeed be acknowledged and incorporated within political theory. Ronald Dworkin notes 'the liberal attitude which insists that government must not force a conception of the good life upon its citizens',[4] and this attitude, familiar to us from Mill, is certainly coherent with the view just expressed – though the liberal would no doubt ground his argument against the governmental enforcement of modes of living upon a theory of the moral autonomy of the individual, as well as upon the fallibility of any calculus of goods. (I would not disagree with him, but the issue here is too extensive to pursue.) Dworkin's subsequent remarks, which identify a need to reconcile the liberal attitude with a recognition of man's social nature and with a positive valuation of culture, harmonise still more closely with the present argument.

This fundamental liberal attitude must now be defended against two attacks from non-liberals of the left and right – one theoretical and one practical. The theoretical attack argues that liberalism rests on a nihilistic or otherwise unattractive or impoverished view of human nature .... These opposing views take the position that man is social. Of course, the liberal doesn't deny that, but the argument is that liberalism is committed to what's often called a Humean, or Benthamite, or atomistic conception of human nature. It is absolutely necessary for liberals now to demonstrate that this is not true .... The practical problem is this: there are certain things we all want government to do. We want government, for example, to select methods of education, to sponsor culture, and to do much else that looks, on the surface, like endorsing one set of personal values against another and therefore contradicting liberalism. It is very important for liberals to develop a theory that would make a distinction here between enriching the choices available to people and enforcing a choice upon people. The crucial idea, it seems to me, is the idea of imagination. The liberal is concerned to expand imagination without imposing any particular choice upon imagination.[5]

Dworkin's comments imply an ideal conception of the arts, as politically untrammelled yet politically endorsed, as tending to expand individual imagination yet leaving our sense of community unimpaired, which may look paradoxical for a moment but which loses its paradoxical appearance if we admit that – as my own argument implies – the variability of human beings is precisely one of the qualities which, once recognised, binds them together. (As Auden aphoristically puts it in 'New Year Letter', 'All real unity commences/In consciousness of differences.') The individual psyche is itself a kind of 'community' of latent interests and appetencies, variously quickened both by primary experience and, with a particular kind of lucidity and coherence, by art; to acknowledge this variability in oneself is a long step towards acknowledging and respecting it among others. The arts serve both to reveal the variety, the innumerable special and contingent efflorescences, of human sensibility, and, by reason of their public nature and the high value the community places on them, to reinforce our mutual respect and our sense of social being, of kinship-and-difference: properly perceived and valued, they aid our liberation from the unhappy choice between imposed and impoverished conceptions of the good life.

II

Few readers of this book will, I imagine, be disposed to deny that literature and other arts have some sort of value for our individual and collective life. Whether this valuation can justifiably be extended to the parasitic activities of criticising, teaching and studying literature is a more debatable, and a more frequently debated, question. A succession of books, articles and symposia devoted to the reappraisal of the status and function of criticism – or more parochially, of academic 'English' – has in the last decade or so revealed an outburst of self-questioning, even of bad conscience, among at least an energetic minority of teachers and critics.[6] Particular anxiety has been expressed about the insecurity of the theoretical base of much academic study, its easy-going amateurishness or, worse, its unconfessed prejudices, embodied in an ideologically-restricted 'canon' of literary works held fit to be taught, studied and cherished. But the process of seeking a justification for the study of literature which shall be morally and philosophically sustainable is at least as old as Matthew

Arnold; and since University Schools of English began to flourish (in the sense of attracting enormous numbers of students) academic lettrists have struggled to apologise for their good luck. Historians can legitimately claim that our knowledge of the past is dependent on their work, indeed (more disputably) that 'history' is what historians write; lettrists can claim at most to be adding something – custodianship, advocacy, commentary – to a self-sufficient body of material to which their own productions are almost by definition subordinate and inferior. Philosophers can claim to be refining the very media of thought (language, mathematics, logic), and so ultimately to be enriching every intellectual discipline; lettrists are exposed to the accusation that their work is one of de-refinement, a reduction of objects whose value lies in their uniqueness to comparatively crude analytical and interpretative approximations. It is, I believe, at least partly to this sense of vulnerability that we can attribute the bold but implausible claims made for literature (and by inference for its guardians and interpreters) by a number of the critical theories discussed in earlier chapters. The most successfully canvassed of these claims, for a long period, was, of course, the Leavises' celebration of literature (or at least the works they approved of) and literary criticism (when conducted in conformity with their own practice) as a continuing experience and discipline central and indispensable to our personal and collective moral life – and, at least implicitly, prior in importance to other subjects in the humanities, let alone to the branches of science and technology. Some of the force and attraction of the Leavises' claim perhaps derived from its incorporating elements of the claims I have associated with Lukács and with Richards: the claim that literature imparts historical truths (the truths detected by the Leavises having to do with cultural decline in a technologico-Benthamite society); and the claim that the serious appreciation and study of literature has a lasting psychic value (expressed by the Leavises through such characteristically morally inflected concepts as 'maturity', 'finer awareness' and 'developed coherence of response'[7]). This Leavisite synthesis has now irreparably broken up, though its fading influence is still visible in the teaching of English at every level. If current developments in literary theory seem to promise any new and persuasively synthetic foundation for belief in the importance of studying literature, it is in the promotion of language and its relations to the centre of attention.

The prestige and excitement of the young disciplines of linguistics and semiotics, coupled with a pervasive belief that 'language' in some sense is prior to and formative of all intellectual activity, may in the end leave literary criticism (or something like it) as a sub-section of linguistic or 'communication' studies, much as, for an older academic tradition which emphasised the rigours of scholar-ship at the expense of the pleasures of criticism, literary study was essentially a special form of historical or philosophical study. On this language-based theory, literary works, or rather 'texts' – the distinction is significant and I shall return to it shortly – represent a characteristic part of a spectrum of texts ranging from road signs through advertising copy to the Scriptures (and indeed, in the infra-red as it were, to oral and even non-verbal 'texts'). Since language is fundamental to our entire existence as human beings (the theory goes on), the scrutiny of texts, in their relation to the social determinants of our experience, has a high claim on academic time and energy; the scrutiny of literary texts is then simply a special case of this, broadly sociolinguistic, discipline. This view is congenial not only to professional linguists and literary critics convinced of the priority of 'language' in literary study, but to the heirs of historical and moral realism, to whom it restores the possibility of deriving instruction from literature, not in an unmediated fashion from the discrete work or *oeuvre*, but from the study of 'texts' in their relations, historical, sociological, cultural, ideological. The enterprise of 'deconstruction', the identi-fication and subversion of the ideologically-charged structures and discourses which dominate all texts, is, paradoxically, readily adaptable to a mode of simple moral and historical assertion, or implication, however far this outcome may be from the liberative project of Derrida: the deconstruction of the forms and discourses which embody your (or 'a society's') unexamined assumptions leaves my unexamined assumptions in possession of the field, particularly if it is they which have determined the *modus operandi* of deconstruction. A new, post-Leavisite, synthesis of claims for criticism, paying its respects to linguistics and deconstruction while retaining a moral and historical confidence worthy of the Leavises themselves, can therefore be imagined, perhaps roughly on the lines suggested here by Carole Snee.

I want to argue for a reconstituted Period Study as the basis of a reconstituted discipline, and not merely as an alternative teaching method or approach. The Period Study offers an opportunity to move away from the inevitable élitism of existing approaches to literature. But in order to succeed, it needs to be problem- or topic-centred, and not text-centred, whether the texts be 'literary' or 'non-literary' in nature. If we start from an issue – women's oppression, the family, unemployment, leisure, construction of class, etc. – then any 'texts' studied have an initial common status, they provide an insight into the topic under consideration. Our concern no longer becomes the evaluation of 'good' and 'bad' writing, or explication, but rather the ways in which 'meanings' and understanding of particular issues are constructed. (The 'text', of course, does not have to be a book, it can be a newspaper report, a song, a mass demonstration, a campaign, etc., etc.). It is then possible to examine the effects of different forms and structures; how they construct meaning; how our images and understanding of a period are created; which events and texts reinforce the *status quo*, which subvert it; what different discourses were available; what the competing ideologies were at any given time; to whom they 'belonged'; how they manifested themselves, etc. This approach thus tends to dissolve the sharp distinction between the 'literary' and 'non-literary' text, and to look at the production of meanings and their consumption. *All* texts are concerned with significations of reality, the ordering and representation of aspects of experience, and a proper Period Study would allow us to identify the myriad discourses which constitute our 'world-view', their autonomy and interconnections.[8]

The passage makes clear, with a certain energy and directness, the ease with which the errors against which the present work has been contending can be restated in a new language. To debate with it at length would involve a parallel restatement of much of my own argument, which has been devoted precisely to insisting on the distinction, in purpose and convention, between imaginative literature and other types of discourse, and on the consequent invalidity of criticism which takes the former to involve 'significations of reality.' I will merely note the recurrence of that circularity, observed earlier in Lukács and Mrs Leavis,[9] which purports to extract from the object of study 'insights', on matters of historical, political or moral significance, which will not in fact be recognised as insights (and this in itself is perfectly reasonable) unless they correspond to, or fall within the limits of, the critic's previously determined beliefs. Here the prior determination is most apparent in the blithe identification of 'issues': not so much in the specific issues listed (though, naturally enough, even in such a short list certain ideological assumptions show through) as in the ingenuous confidence that, in a world in which forms and structures construct meaning, and myriads of discourses constitute our world-view, 'issues' can nevertheless be transparently perceived, as if luminously self-evident, and projected across the centuries, to play like searchlight beams upon texts which have the 'initial common status' of being subordinated to them. The Leavisite's unphilosophical certainty in his moral and social judgements, and unhistorical confidence in using them to identify the supposedly crucial characteristics of an earlier period, are here revived in full strength. Where the passage decisively departs from Leavisite or Lukácsian realism is in its insistence that historical issues are inscribed in language itself, the language out of which texts are made, in the 'forms and structures' which 'construct meaning'; so that the process of analysing texts is *ipso facto* a process of taking possession – in some sense, a more complete possession than the authors' own – of a mentality, a cluster of ideas and attitudes, generated or at least circumscribed by the available discourses. For the critic as commentator on another person's composition is substituted the critic as practitioner of a kind of depth analysis; the part played in psychoanalysis by the agencies of the unconscious being played here by determinant discourses. Common sense replies to this proposal that the study of discourses is a different thing from, and a poor substitute for, the study of works; that however a given language may be anatomised, no writer of interest will fail to use it in a fashion which defies such anatomy, the creation of something new being more important to his activity than obedience to an 'available' discourse; that it is precisely in the transformation of language from a determinant of thought and imagination to an instrument of thought and imagination that we distinguish the work of an able writer. (And if this last point is conceded, the 'available discourses', and perhaps the 'competing ideologies', become as 'myriad' as the able writers.) Common sense, however, needs a resolute defence at this point. Behind the language-based justification of the practice of criticism lies a remarkable and curiously widespread belief: the belief that thought, and other mental acts and experiences, are contingent on language, rather than the other way round. From this belief the conclusion is drawn that everything that can be said is contained within the available discourses, indeed everything that can be thought determined by them: the able writer no less than the incompetent is subject to this determination (which is often taken to be social in its ultimate origin, language and its forms being themselves socially determined), and analytical attention is properly directed first, not to the 'composition' conceived as the result of a free act, but to the discourses and the social structures in which they are implicated.

The currency of this theory may be connected with the notion, expressed in the following passage by Terry Eagleton, that it has the support of certain pre-eminent writers about language.

> The hallmark of the 'linguistic revolution' of the twentieth century, from Saussure and Wittgenstein to contemporary literary theory, is the recognition that meaning is not simply something 'expressed' by language: it is actually *produced* by it. It is not as though we have meanings, which we then proceed to cloak with words; we can only have the meanings and experiences in the first place because we have a language to have them in. What this suggests, moreover, is that our experience as individuals is social to its roots: for there can be no such thing as a private language, and to imagine a language is to imagine a whole form of social life.[10]

I will look at some extracts from Saussure and Wittgenstein in a moment. But a conspicuous weakness in the substance of Eagleton's assertions – a weakness characteristic of this kind of argument – calls for immediate comment. This is the brisk sidestep from 'meaning' to 'experience'. The suggestion that *meaning* is 'produced by language' looks fairly plausible, and indeed for some uses of the word 'meaning' it would be tautologically true. We can speak of 'what the word "dog" means', and so forth, and this is to speak of meaning being produced by language. Whether there is a non-tautological sense in which meaning is produced by language is a different matter: I will only point out here that to suppose that the meaning *originates* with the word or the sentence would be a very eccentric supposition – quite contrary, for example, to that insistence on the arbitrary nature of the linguistic sign which we find in Saussure; so that the necessity already suggests itself of looking outside language for an agency which invests words and sentences with a value which enables them to mean. With Eagleton's suggestion, however, that 'we can only have the ... *experiences* in the first place because we have a language to have them in', we step outside the realm of even qualified plausibility. If I walk into a quicksand and exclaim, 'Help! I'm sinking!', it is reasonable enough to say that my meaning is 'produced by language', in the tautologous sense noted above, but it is hardly reasonable to say that my experience is so produced. (I do not need language to know that I have walked into a quicksand – I only need it to know that 'I have walked into a quicksand', 'je me suis enlisé', etc.) If, in this imaginary circumstance, I were the only man on earth, I would not be a user of language, but I would still have walked into a quicksand. It is in the response of our intellect to physiological and psychological experience, in mental activity initially independent of language (though radically modified, indeed transformed, by it) that we can identify the origin of our linguistic practices. To identify the linguistic practices as the starting-point of thought and experience would be, absurdly, to view all our varied faculties of mind and body as secondary to the single faculty of language, a faculty whose elaborate development in the scope, subtlety and expansion of natural languages (though not, we may agree with Chomsky, its existence or its basic structures) is plainly attributable to the complexity of our extra-linguistic experience.

All this is not to deny that thought of any significant extension or intricacy requires the use of language (or some other system of signs such as musical notation); or that linguistic and other semiotic systems can powerfully tend to petrify habits of thought. It is only to deny that thought is absolutely inseparable from or contingent upon language, or finally constrained by it; to insist that thought can make, or rather be, an independent impulse, though that impulse may immediately and necessarily enter into problematic interplay with the linguistic practices of the thinker and his fellow language users. I will venture a mock-Wittgensteinian metaphor to describe this interplay. Imagine the human race as a solitary squash player. The action of striking the ball is thought; the wall is language. But this is an exceptional kind of squash-court: the wall modifies its shape under the impact of a forcefully-struck ball, and this modification in turn influences the subsequent direction of rebound from that section of wall.

Clearly the player is constrained, in playing each stroke, by the present contour of the wall and the angle of the previous stroke. But the game began with the player striking a ball against a contourless wall. And as he approaches each stroke, the player (who has a certain agility, a certain quickness of wit, and a certain knowledge of the contour of the wall) has a moment to think how to play it. In other words, thought is ultimately prior to language, though this priority is only fully apparent in the intermittent, though inexhaustible, process of creation and modification of language. Literary works are particularly likely to exhibit this process, but the tension between the contents of one's thought and experience and the seeming inadequacy of the immediately accessible linguistic expression is felt, and struggled with, however ineffectually, by most or all of us. 'It is impossible to say just what I mean!' exclaims Prufrock, in common with countless others and in contravention of Dr Eagleton's view of 'meaning'. But an individual or a community can construct new linguistic complexes (sentences, metaphors, poems, books), can initiate delicate semantic shifts, in order to come closer to articulating thought and experience.

If we return to the writers Eagleton mentions, we find conceptions of the relationship between thought and language which are at any rate closer to the version just presented than to Eagleton's own. I quote first from Saussure.

Psychologically our thought – apart from its expression in words – is only a shapeless and indistinct mass. Philosophers and linguists have always agreed in recognizing that without the help of signs we would be unable to make a clear-cut, consistent distinction between two ideas. Without language, thought is a vague, uncharted nebula. There are no pre-existing ideas, and nothing is distinct before the appearance of language.

Against the floating realm of thought, would sounds by themselves yield predelimited entities? Not more so than ideas. Phonic substance is neither more fixed nor more rigid than thought; it is not a mold into which thought must of necessity fit but a plastic substance divided in turn into distinct parts to furnish the signifiers needed by thought. The linguistic fact can therefore be pictured in its totality – i.e. language – as a series of continuous subdivisions marked off on both the indefinite plane of jumbled ideas and the equally vague plane of sounds ....

The characteristic role of language with respect to thought is not to create a material phonic means for expressing ideas but to serve as a link between thought and sound, under conditions that of necessity bring about the reciprocal delimitations of units. Thought, chaotic by nature, has to become ordered in the process of its decomposition. Neither are thoughts given material form nor are sounds transformed into mental entities; the somewhat mysterious fact is rather that 'thought-sound' implies division, and that language works out its units while taking shape between two shapeless masses. Visualise the air in contact with a sheet of water; if the atmospheric pressure changes, the surface of the water will be broken up into a series of divisions, waves; the waves resemble the union or coupling of thought with phonic substance . . . .

Language can also be compared with a sheet of paper: thought is the front and sound the back; one cannot cut the front without cutting the back at the same time; likewise in language, one can neither divide sound from thought nor thought from sound; the division could be accomplished only abstractedly, and the result would be either pure psychology or pure phonology.[11]

It is easy to see how a passage like this might be cursorily misinterpreted as suggesting that mental experience is contingent on language. It gives a general impression of downgrading pre-linguistic thought, and of implying that in effect all is darkness until language manifests itself. A closer reading, however, reveals Saussure as repeatedly acknowledging the independent existence of thought. The wave metaphor clearly admits this independence; indeed, the image of atmospheric pressure acting upon the surface of the water would lend itself (though Saussure presumably did not intend this) to expressing an active role for thought, and a passive role for phonic substance, in creating the linguistic 'wave'. As for the paper metaphor, it needs to be read carefully; Saussure does not say that one cannot divide thought from sound, but that *in language* one cannot do so. His purpose is to indicate the collaborative interplay of thought and sound in forming language, not the contingency of the one on the other or of either on their mutual product. Again, Saussure does not say that there is no pre-existing thought, only that there are no pre-existing *ideas* – an assertion which many philosophers would question for certain senses of 'idea', but which can readily be accepted as tautologically true if by 'idea' we understand 'possible proposition', since the notion of a proposition entails the existence of language. (One could go further if one wished and deny the existence of pre-linguistic 'thought' by the simple expedient of using the word 'thought' for what Saussure calls 'ideas': but this would be another pointless tautology.) Though Saussure undoubtedly characterises pre-linguistic thought in unflattering terms – 'a shapeless and indistinct mass'; 'a vague, uncharted nebula'; 'the floating realms of thought'; 'thought, chaotic by nature' – these do not affect the issue of the causal priority of thought to language, and are in any case the most questionable feature of the passage. One is oddly struck by the passivity which these epithets (by contrast with the inadvertent 'atmospheric pressure' image) attribute to pre-linguistic thought, a passivity which is not always apparent in the mental life of creatures which do not possess language. Consider a cat stalking a bird, for example. Clearly the thinking of a cat does not compare too well for complexity or creativity with that of Shakespeare or Spinoza, but it does not seem that it can properly be stigmatised as 'chaotic', 'shapeless' or 'indistinct' – except (yet again) in a tautological sense. Non-linguistic thought is only undifferentiated to this extent, that it cannot make use of those differentiations, or that degree of differentiation, which can only be sustained in consciousness with the aid of linguistic signs.

An observation of Wittgenstein's can usefully be quoted here.

78. Compare *knowing* and *saying*:
how many feet high Mont Blanc is –
how the word 'game' is used –
how a clarinet sounds.

If you are surprised that one can know something and not be able to say it, you are perhaps thinking of a case like the first. Certainly not of one like the third.[12]

One can hardly imagine a clearer or more persuasive assertion of the reality of thought, of distinct and specific mental experience, independent of language. Indeed Wittgenstein's later work is preoccupied with the problematical relationship – so easily conceived in terms of simple correspondence – between experience and language. His well-known and much-contested assertion that there can be no such thing as a private language does not entail (as Eagleton's apparent allusion to it implies) that there can be no such thing as private experience, unsocialised by language. (What it entails is that language is a social activity: Wittgenstein notes that giving oneself a private definition of a word would be like one's right hand giving one's left hand money.[13]) So far from seeing thought as determined by language, Wittgenstein insists that the sense of a linguistic expression is determined by the use we are making of it, that the same utterance can have different senses within different 'language-games'; still more explicitly, that 'language is an instrument',[14] though we should 'make a radical break with the idea that language always functions in one way, always serves the same purpose: to convey thought'.[15] (As for the *Tractatus*, it concerns itself with logical language, not with natural languages. 'The limits of my language mean the limits of my world'[16] is not a catchphrase propounding sociolinguistic determinism.) Moreover, Wittgenstein's perception of the multiplicity of 'language-games' is a telling argument against the practice of discussing literature in terms of 'texts', if by 'texts' we mean open and unclassified linguistic objects, lying in helpless rows like corpses in a mortuary. Literary texts exist, certainly, just as the text

Fire!

exists irrespective of anyone's issuing an instruction to a firing squad, or raising the alarm in a theatre, or demonstrating the meaning of a word to a non-English speaker by pointing at flames, and yet remains no more than the linguistic object correlative to one or more of these verbal acts. The literary text, likewise, is merely the linguistic object correlative to the literary work, which is a composition by a human being apprehended by other human beings in a language-game (the art of literature) governed by certain widely-understood rules or conventions. If the conventions are lifted – and this need require no alteration to the text itself, simply a thought-experiment in which, say, *Lolita* is conceived literally as a memoir – the experience of reading and the appropriate terms of judgement and commentary become quite different.[17] The *work* is literature; the *text* (as I am using the word here) is not. (And the fact that the experience of a literary work may vary from reader to reader, so that one may in a sense speak of the work as a multiple rather than a single object, is not to be confused with the indeterminate nature of a text which one contemplates without recognising it as corresponding to a literary text at all or without understanding what such correspondence implies.) It is because literature consists not of texts but of works that linguistic techniques appropriate to textual analysis can fail so signally to be authoritative or even helpful for literary analysis.[18] The archetype of such unhelpfulness is the Saussurean distinction between *langue* and *parole*, a distinction roughly equivalent to that between the rules of chess (or the system of such rules, habitually implemented by players) and the totality of possible moves. An understanding of chess confined to this neutrally descriptive level would enable a person to identify illegitimate moves (K x K*, or B x P where another piece is on an intervening square*), but not to identify strong or weak moves, or to comment on the strategic purposes underlying a sequence of play, or to assess the elegance or creativity of a player's style, since these are all teleological features of chess which entail selectivity among moves and sequences of moves which are descriptively equivalent. The ability to play effectively or elegantly or creatively does not follow from the ability to state the rules and tabulate all possible moves: the game is not the same as the list of moves. It is precisely the game (or work), however, rather than the list of moves (or text) that the critic, as distinct from the student of language or notation, is appropriately interested in.

We must reject, then, both the general proposition that language is prior to or constitutive of human experience, with its implied promotion of the study of language to a kind of sovereignty or universality among intellectual disciplines, and the attempt, ultimately founded on this proposition, to identify an ethically sustainable status for the study of literature by incorporating it within a broader study of linguistic 'texts' which purportedly offers a privileged mode of access to cultural and historical realities. Our experience is not determined by language, though language is in perpetual interplay with it; our literature is not constituted by 'texts', but by relations of composition to apprehension which require techniques of analysis quite distinct from those of textual analysis in linguistics. With the rejection, then, both of its philosophical and of its methodological components, the language-based synthesis of justifications for the study of literature appears as implausible as the Leavisite synthesis. The study of literature must stand unprotected on its merits as the study of a single, specific and limited, human activity and its products. In the final section I will argue these merits.

III

Literature is one of the arts practised, enjoyed and esteemed in human society. Its products are works: composed by authors, apprehended by readers, they exist in and by reason of their composition and apprehension, the second of these providing the rationale for the first. This relationship is what constitutes the linguistic structure as a literary work, just as the relationship of craftsmanship and design to the human physique is what constitutes a shape of wood (or whatever) as a chair. The fact that different readers of a work, including the author himself, experience it differently, and the fact that in all likelihood no specific experience of a work is precisely foreseen by the author, are matters of interest but no more disprove the interrelationship of composition and apprehension than the varying kinds and degrees of comfort experienced by different physiques presented with the same chair disprove the relationship between craftsmanship and physiological needs. They simply reflect the fact that people vary. The problems posed by this variability need to be acknowledged in the methodology of literary criticism,[19] but they do not prevent rational and productive discussion of literature.

The object of study and criticism, then, is the relationship of composition to apprehension, a relationship to which the literary text is the correlative object. Discussion of a work is to be directed, mediately or immediately, to demonstrating and analysing this relationship as exhibited in structure and detail, in the interaction between structure and detail, and so on: the analysis of *Wuthering Heights* in Chapter 6 was an attempt, no doubt a flawed and incomplete one, to indicate the possible scope of such a discussion. Two consequences for the terms of reference of literary criticism flow from this conclusion, and each relates to an issue at the centre of current (and long-standing) theoretical debate; before offering a justification of criticism, I will briefly indicate these consequences, in order to make clear precisely what I am proposing to justify. The first is that, though the study of literary composition (as of chair design) entails at least implicit acts of evaluation, the notion of a permanent, value-based 'canon' of literary works, to be isolated for study to the exclusion of a multitude of also-rans, must be repudiated. Any work is in principle fit for discussion which is of interest from the point of view of the relationship between composition and apprehension. The reason we are justified in devoting more extensive analytical attention to Jane Austen's novels than to Miss Barbara Cartland's (if we are) must be approximately this: that essentially the same relationships (local and structural) of composition to apprehension can be detected in any of Miss Cartland's novels, or perhaps in any novel in the genre of which her works are typical; whereas Jane Austen's novels, for all their affinities, are compositionally more complex and varied, and, correspondingly, provide more complex and varied experiences; each quickens and orders desire in a distinctive psychological structure by means of a distinctive compositional structure. Judgements of this kind are, of course, provisional and fallible; as in the case of an individual analysis, as for that matter in the case of the theoretical argument conducted in this book, they involve at a certain stage giving expression, however guardedly, to intuitive impressions which may not receive universal assent. It should be clearly noted, too, that such judgements, however generally assented to, do not *preclude* studying the works of Miss Cartland or any other 'formula' writer. The mass-produced article at least justifies the study of its basic model; a student of architecture is unlikely to study many of, say, Raymond Unwin's garden-city houses, but may well study a few representative examples. Some works may, indeed many necessarily will, be excluded from critical attention on the grounds that they simply are not adequately composed, and are experienced as ineffective. But the danger of circularity in such exclusions brings home the necessity of regarding the literary 'canon' as revisable – or better still, of abandoning the notion of a 'canon', in favour of a mere practice of studying works which, from time to time and in varying degrees, we find to be of interest in our engagement with the art of literature. Someone must, in principle, be prepared to devote analytical attention to any work offered by anyone as literature, and though, life being short, the rest of us may be obliged to concur without further inquiry if the judgement is a dismissive one, this should be viewed as a pragmatic rather than a theoretical necessity.

The second consequence of the definition of the object of study as the relationship between composition and apprehension has to do with the relevance to criticism of scholarly activities other than critical analysis itself: the relevance, in particular, of 'contextual' information which is not derived from the work but is thought to have a bearing on it. Biographical, historical and lexicographical information are the most obvious contenders. The provision of such information as an end in itself, or as a contribution to the wider understanding of a personality, a society, an intellectual climate or a phase in the development of a language, is justified by the intrinsic interest of these subjects; to grant this is simply to note, as I have noted above,[20] that the various amicably co-existing disciplines may make use (each for its characteristic purposes) of materials which abut or overlap. The methodological problem arises when 'contextual' information – 'attendant' or 'adjacent' would be less question-begging terms – is offered as a means of illuminating the literary work itself. The definition of the work as the relation of composition to apprehension provides an intrinsic criterion for evaluating the propriety of citing attendant informa- tion in the process of analysis. The information is to be accepted as relevant to analysis if its possession creates a communicative beam which passes through the work, that is to say connects a demonstrable feature of composition to a possible apprehension. Thus, the assertion that in line 186 of *Lycidas*,

> Thus sang the uncouth swain to th' oaks and rills,

'uncouth' carries (at least primarily) the sense of 'unknown' is relevant because it resolves, for the unlearned reader, an appa- rently pointless incongruity between the epithet in its latter-day sense and tone and the style and content of the 'song' which is the poem: the possession of this information discloses to analysis a compositional coherence, a fitness of speaker to speech, which is not without its affective counterpart. The assertion that in lines 100–101

> that fatal and perfidious bark
> Built in the eclipse, and rigged with curses dark

represents the Laudian church is relevant if it can be incorporated (as Christopher Hill, among others, proposes it can)[21] into a coherent apprehension of the poem as a structure of allegorical reference to contemporary religio-political controversy. But the assertion that Milton was not particularly fond of Edward King, the 'learned friend' lamented in the poem, though mildly interesting from a biographical point of view, is without analytical interest. It does nothing to connect composition to apprehension, at the level either of detail or of structure. If the poem is experienced as a moving elegy, Milton's tepid feelings towards King do nothing to abolish this aesthetic event. If the poem is experienced as failing to move (at least in terms of personal bereavement), Milton's feelings are still irrelevant to the literary work as the critic perceives it; they may explain why Milton failed to write a moving poem (a matter for Milton's biographer), but they do not explain why the poem fails to move its readers, if it does. (Not that biographer and critic might not be the same person; or biography and criticism interlaced within the covers of a single book. But the methodological differences between biographical and critical discussion ought to remain apparent.)

It may be protested at this point that the criterion of relevance I am proposing – that the attendant information shall connect 'a demonstrable feature of composition to a possible apprehension' – is simply a long-winded way of saying that the information should illuminate the meaning of the text. But 'the meaning of the text' is, or has become, a hopelessly ambiguous and disputed idea. My less compact formulation is intended to exclude, on the one hand, the restrictive notion of meaning as singular and privileged entailed by the intentional fallacy ('what Milton meant'), and on the other, the permissive notion of meaning (repudiated in the previous section)[22] as whatever constructions a text will bear, irrespective of its corresponding to a literary composition which finds its rationale in the experience of readers. Liberty of interpretation and analysis is to be circumscribed solely by a recognition of the need to provide for the composition an affective rationale as coherent and exhaustive as possible.

(Any normal reader will prefer attendant information to meet the additional, extrinsic criterion of historical correctness, so that anachronistic, or simply false, notions which cannot have formed part of the composition (considered as an act performed by the writer) are excluded. Nevertheless, strange though this may sound, I believe that the intrinsic criterion (in which the composition is considered as apprehended by the reader) is in practice sufficient. An unhistorical reading of a detail will tend not to cohere with the rest of one's apprehension of a work, as the example of 'uncouth' above suggests. It is, to be sure, theoretically possible (though to my mind very unlikely) that an intrinsically coherent and exhaustive analysis of a work might be founded upon major inaccuracies. (Somehow the historically false interpretations of detail would have to cohere with one another and with the larger structures as effectively as historically correct ones.) In this case one would have to admit that an accidentally and comprehensively ambiguous work had been produced. One can imagine, further, a critic of Borgesian ingenuity constructing a thorough, self-consistent and extrinsically quite 'incorrect' analysis of, say, *Lycidas* as an allegory of the Boer War, and challenging his readers to deny that he had demonstrated a relationship of composition to apprehension. Here the eccentricity of the feigned 'apprehension' would isolate the view from critical discourse, but the exploit would be harmless enough. In conceding this much I am not attempting to devalue historical accuracy, simply noting a that it is a *different* virtue from critical judgement: in principle the two are independent).

When these two elaborations have been made, then, the function of literary criticism can be finally restated as follows. The business of the literary critic is the study of the art of literature and the analysis of its products, literary works, defined as relationships of composition to apprehension characterised by the quickening and ordering of desire. It encompasses, in principle, all works offered as literature; and it extends to the assimilation of such attendant information as serves to illuminate the work as defined above. Beyond the boundaries here drawn lie the neighbouring but distinct disciplines: linguistics, history, biography and the rest.

This business of criticism can, in part, be taught; and something not unlike it forms, as we know, a component of the secondary-school and higher-education curriculum. If literary criticism itself, an activity practised professionally by a relatively small number of individuals, requires justification, so *a fortiori* does its expensive dissemination by the academies. The justifications which survive, or in some cases are strengthened by, the argument of this book will now be stated. They rest upon certain assumptions which must be made explicit. I assume that the possession of knowledge, and the development of the intellect and sensibility, are desirable both from the point of view of the person concerned and from the point of view of the community of which that person is a member. I assume that the production of works of literature, and the enjoyment of them, are likewise desirable. Finally, when I come to the comprehensive statement of what I take to be the individual and collective value of the study of literature, I shall assume, as I have already implicitly done in my comments on the social value of literature itself, the aptness of what Rawls describes as 'the idea of social union': 'the notion of the community of humankind the members of which enjoy one another's excellences and individuality elicited by free institutions, and ... recognise the good of each as an element in the complete activity the whole scheme of which is consented to and gives pleasure to all.'[23] These assumptions are unproved, and may not be uncontentious; but their defence would require another and longer book, and I must provisionally rest my case upon a bare statement of them.

Firstly, then, the study of literature promotes knowledge: that is, knowledge of literature, the human activity and its products, not of life or love or history or politics or any of the innumerable human experiences with which literature concerns itself. (Knowledge of these, using the term strictly, cannot be reliably pursued through the intrinsically distorting medium of literature.) I would not for a moment claim that literature is more worth knowing than any other object of knowledge – on utilitarian grounds one might rank the pursuit of medical knowledge, for example, more highly; but if knowledge is in principle good, the burden of proof lies on those who would make an exception to this principle. My final paragraph will suggest that knowledge of literature may in fact be socially beneficent in a modest way. One might add, in defence of the amplitude of most English departments, that, so far as degree-level education is concerned, the direction of students' appetite for knowledge ought in any case to be respected. The teaching of adults requires mutual commitment, both on the ground of the equal citizenship of the teachers and the taught, and because effective learning at an advanced level cannot proceed without it. To this extent, the popularity of English courses is its own justification; though it is true that some of that popularity is attributable to a confusion between an interest in literature and an interest in the things literature is loosely conceived as being 'about', and that the former does not always survive the process of being distinguished from the latter.

The second justification of literary study is the intellectual training, in observation, interpretation, analysis, comparison and judgement, achievable by addressing oneself to objects subtle and varied in their design, wide-ranging in their reference, complex in their relation to human thought and feeling, and problematical – as the existence of debate about the nature of literature demonstrates – in their linguistic, epistemological and aesthetic status. Every worthwhile discipline is exacting in a different way; the analysis of literature (or any other art), with its distinctive requirement that the responses of one's sensibility shall be rationally reconciled with the findings of one's intellectual judgement, and given expression in an acquired but flexible and modifiable technical vocabulary, seems to me, when properly practised, to be as strenuous and as intellectually rewarding as any other, and to be significantly different from all others.

The third and fourth justifications correspond to the two points of view which I suggested in an earlier chapter were the appropriate preoccupation of literary criticism: that of the writer and that of the reader.[24] The contribution which literary study, particularly in the context of academic institutions, can make to the activity of either should, of course, be stated very guardedly. No-one will seriously claim, for example, that it is in the schools of English, any more than in the academies of art and music, that artistic creativity has its principal sources. It remains true, though, that the great majority of literary artists, not excluding such ostensibly *naif* figures as Burns and Clare, have been in some degree learned – in the sense of being intimately acquainted with the work of earlier writers, and with certain systematic techniques such as metrical forms. The study of literature, then, is a form of preparation for composition, though the ultimate effect of studying one's predecessors may be a process of stylistic evolution which leads one away from their practice. Even academic teaching – if it is founded on the recognition of literature as an art rather than as a mode of revelation or a sociological or anthropological phenomenon – may, one dares to hope, provide assistance to a potential writer in achieving a grounding in literary traditions and techniques. I speak of 'assistance' because any developing writer is likely to be exploring literature independently, and the last thing one would expect of such a person is a consistent, evenly-maturing responsiveness to the components of a typical syllabus – one should expect, on the contrary, excessive enthusiasms and aversions, complaints at the omission of X from the booklist, at the failure of Y to display the indispensable virtues of Z, and so forth. Teaching and examination methods should go some way to meet this possibility by facilitating and rewarding wide, even somewhat random, reading outside the formal syllabus.

Not only the developing writer, but the developing reader, requires latitude of this kind. Here again one should beware of overstating the significance of teaching, or of published criticism for that matter, in forming reading 'competence'. It ought to be conceded, indeed, that reading literature does not, in principle, need to be taught at all; for if it did, one would have to consign to a limbo of non-'competence' virtually all readers before the present century, to say nothing of infants as yet unbaptised by secondary-school English literature classes. But every child listening to a bedtime story recognises some of the most essential conventions of imaginative literature – recognises, too, incidentally, that the purpose of the exercise is not, primarily, instruction, but a lifting of the heart. Assuming that the basic intellectual capacity is present, a person provided with a library of literary works, with time and encouragement to read them, and with a normal range of social and cultural experiences, will finally evolve the ability to read literature just as well as you or me. What academic tuition can do is accelerate the process in a number of ways. Firstly, the tutorial or the seminar provides a formalised opportunity for comparing impressions of a work; it liberates the reader from singleness of perspective – which the solitary mind can only overcome gradually, by re-readings which are generally more revealing the wider the time-interval between them – and exerts a pressure towards the more precise description (and therefore the more precise apprehension) of the composition under scrutiny. Secondly, teaching can draw attention to genre conventions which may be imperfectly grasped, or to linguistic shades and subtleties which may be overlooked, by inexperienced readers. (The danger here is of running ahead of the student's developing ability, and leading him to substitute routines of analysis for the necessary prior stage of immediate if tentative response: the dutiful, well-drilled student often needs to be discouraged from symbolic or thematic over-interpretation of works which his unaided judgement would at once have recognised as transparent, literal and direct.) Awareness of compositional strategies, of the interaction of small-scale and large-scale conceptions and structures, becomes progressively internalised – domesticates itself, so to speak – within the mind of the experienced or instructed reader, so that the expenditure of energy required simply to apprehend the subtleties and complexities of literary works is correspondingly reduced. This sophistication of apprehension serves then the same psychological purpose as economy and lucidity of composition: that of sparing the maximum amount of energy for emotional response. Finally, the impetus, even the compulsions, of an institutional course can counteract that conservatism or narrowness of taste which often accompanies genuine literary enthusiasm. Despite the frequency with which a writer we are sure we will never like becomes, five years later, one of our favourites, we all tend to overvalue our current aesthetic love-objects, and to undervalue, in consequence, works which remain merely potential objects of our admiration. Many a student (or teacher, for that matter) owes to the requirements of a syllabus the enrichment of his literary experience by Dickens or Melville or Proust.

These four justifications for the study of literature are commonplace and obvious, and I claim no originality for them. They are also relatively modest; they do not, for example, give the study of literature any political or ethical or educational priority over the study of music or painting.[25] But these modest claims are not contemptible ones; they simply acknowledge the existence of a universe which is not literature, and which cannot be understood, much less reshaped or mastered, through literature, though it provides the materials which the human imagination reconceives, transforms and projects into literature. Inseparable from them is the belief that literature itself has a distinctive value, not only for individual persons but for communities; that it has the power, as I suggested earlier in this chapter,[26] 'to reinforce our mutual respect and sense of social being, of kinship-and difference' by illuminating the richness and variety of human sensibility. But this proposition refers only to the direct impact of works of literature; not to the contemplation of literature as an art, an activity practised by fellow human beings. It is in the encouragement and clarification of this contemplation that the social value of the ancillary activities (teaching and criticism of literature) mainly lies. As Rawls, following Humboldt, argues,[27] one of the satisfactions available to us as members of a society is that of contemplating, appreciating and even fractionally participating in the activity of others who have developed to the full talents which we either do not possess or lack the time to develop. The study of literature – or more broadly, the intelligent appreciation of literature whether academically accelerated or not – is an enrichment of our being, not only in intensifying and subtilising our experience of literary works, but in uniting us with other persons: both with writers, whose acts of composition we complement and justify with acts of apprehension, and with fellow-readers, with whom we share responses and engage in a collective discourse. (And the other persons may be friends or colleagues or fellow-citizens in the here and now, or members of the human community however widely defined in space and time.) 'Social union' in this Rawlsian sense is served also by our contemplation and understanding of other talents, such as those of great athletes or chess players, which we need not depreciate. But these activities are essentially autotelic. If literature and the other arts deserve the pre-eminence among non-utilitarian activities which many societies have accorded them, it is because, though they are specialised activities, practised effectively only by a few, they are nevertheless felt by the many to react upon the whole of our experience, and momentarily to transfigure it in some psychologically significant way. The attempt to explore and account for that significant transfiguration, in the individual work and in the art comprehensively considered, is both the essence of literary criticism and, if it has one, the justification of this book.

Notes and References

PREFACE

1. J. M. Ellis, *The Theory of Literary Criticism: A Logical Analysis* (University of California Press, 1974).
2. J. Rawls, *A Theory of Justice* (Oxford, 1972) p. 20.

1 ART AND DESIRE

1. Gerard Manley Hopkins, *Poems*, fourth edn, ed. W. H. Gardner and N. H. MacKenzie (Oxford, 1967), no. 138.
2. An interesting attempt is made in Leonard B. Meyer, *Emotion and Meaning in Music* (Chicago, 1956).
3. See pp. 135–44.
4. Plato, *The Republic*, tr. H. D. P. Lee (Penguin, 1955).
5. Aristotle, *Poetics*, tr. L. J. Potts (Cambridge, 1953) VI.
6. James Joyce, *A Portrait of the Artist as a Young Man*: ed. C. G. Anderson and R. Ellmann (Cape, 1968) pp. 209–10.
7. See Freud, 'Creative writers and daydreaming', tr. I. F. Grant Duff and J. Strachey, *The Standard Edition of the Complete Psychological Works*, IX (Hogarth Press, 1951) pp. 141–44; *Civilisation and its Discontents*, tr. J. Strachey, *Standard Edition*, XXI, pp. 80–1. See J. Lacan, *Ecrits*, tr. A. Sheridan (Tavistock Publications, 1977) 263–5 and *passim*.
9. V. Nabokov, *Lectures on Russian Literature* (Pan, 1983) p. 11.
10. See *The Language of Music* (Oxford, 1959) by Deryck Cooke, who argues, however, that musical language is innate and not conventional.
11. A difficulty seems to be raised here by the kind of avant-garde art in which, for instance, a chair is put on exhibition, and entitled 'Chair'. The answer is, I think, that if the chair is truly considered as a chair, it does not leave over any surplus of desire and is therefore not a work of art at all, while if it is considered as a representation, symbol or idea of a chair, it does leave a surplus of desire and is therefore art. The fact that one is usually discouraged from sitting on furniture exhibited in a gallery allows a sufficient surplus of desire for the majority of such objects to be acknowledged as art.
12. B. S. Johnson, *The Unfortunates* (Secker & Warburg, 1969).
13. A. Storr, *The Dynamics of Creation* (Secker & Warburg, 1972) p. 27.
14. John Crowe Ransom, 'The Understanding of Fiction', *Kenyon Review*, XII (1950) p. 197.
15. Berkeley, *The Principles of Human Knowledge*, ed. G. J. Warnock (Collins/Fontana, 1962) p. 43.

2 OBJECTIONS FROM HISTORICAL REALISM

1. Kenneth Grahame, *The Wind in the Willows* (Methuen, 1961) p. 7.
2. Malcolm Lowry, *Under the Volcano* (Penguin, 1962) p. 9.
3. Tolstoy, *Anna Karenin*, tr. Rosemary Edmonds (Penguin, 1954) p. 13.
4. G. Lukács, *Solzhenitsyn*, tr. W. D. Graf (Merlin Press, 1970) p. 34.
5. G. Lukács, *Studies in European Realism*, tr. E. Bone (Merlin Press, 1972) p. 241.
6. See p. 77.
7. e.g. the *Athenaeum*, 25 December 1847; quoted in the casebook on *Wuthering Heights* ed. M. Allott (Macmillan, 1970) p. 39.
8. See S. J. Curtis, *History of Education in Great Britain* (London: University Tutorial Press, 1953) chapters V and VII.
9. I am counting jokes ('This two-headed man walks into a bar ...') as an informal sub-species of fiction for this purpose.
10. Cf. *Jokes and their Relation to the Unconscious*, tr. J. Strachey, *The Standard Edition of the Complete Psychological Works*, V (Hogarth Press) pp. 125–7 and *passim*.
11. Michael Scott, *Tom Cringle's Log* (1836). See Edmund Gosse, *Father and Son* (Penguin, 1949) p. 142.
12. F. R. and Q. D. Leavis, *Dickens the Novelist* (Chatto & Windus, 1970) p. 323.
13. 'Normally' because the reader's mind can, of course, translate a statement out of the context of its discourse conventions – as a reader of Beckett's *Molloy* with a taste for esoteric theology might pause to consider the orthodoxy or heresy of Moran's speculations about the posture of the serpent or the pains of the devils in hell. Some fictional passages (the symposia in Peacock, for example) may indeed encourage this tendency. But though the thoughts and speeches of some characters may be felt to be about, or to be appropriately testable against, the primary world, they remain secondary, imaginary thoughts and speeches, not propositions advanced by the novel.
14. R. Williams, *The Country and the City* (Chatto & Windus, 1973).
15. G. Ewart Evans, *The Pattern under the Plough* (Faber, 1966) p. 17; quoted in *The Country and the City* p. 258.
16. Williams, *The Country and the City*, p. 258.
17. This point is pursued further in the *Appendix*, especially pp. 224–8.
18. J. Gross, *The Rise and Fall of the Man of Letters* (Weidenfeld & Nicolson, 1969) pp. 295–6.
19. Angus Wilson, *No Laughing Matter* (Secker & Warburg, 1967) p. 11.
20. Shakespeare, *King John*, II, i, 1. Arden edn, ed. E. A. J. Honigmann (Methuen, 1954).
21. Discontent with this necessity perhaps accounts (in part) for Shaw's arrogation of novelistic licence in his droll, elaborately descriptive stage directions – which nevertheless cannot be read, though they can to some extent be realised, in the theatre.

22. Shakespeare, *Antony and Cleopatra*, I, i, 1–6, Arden edn, M. R. Ridley (Methuen, 1954).
23. Charlotte Brontë, *Jane Eyre*, ed. Q. D. Leavis (Penguin, 1966) p. 39.
24. D. Lodge, *The Language of Fiction* (Routledge & Kegan Paul, 1966) p. 69.
25. See p. 12.
26. An apparent complication would be presented here by a work in which true inconsistency (such that A = B at one point, and A ≠ B at another) were exploited for a comic or disturbing purpose; as distinct, that is, from works such as *Peter Pan* or the typical ghost story, in which the observed laws of the primary world are merely *supplemented* by other, suppositious laws or phenomena. The simple reply is that such a work would present a world in which radical unpredictability (or the possibility thereof) was among the laws; the affects induced by the representation of radical unpredictability would be characteristic of the zone of feeling addressed. Some of Kafka comes close to this kind of quality.
27. F. R. Leavis, *'Anna Karenina' and Other Essays* (Chatto & Windus, 1967) p. 24.
28. G. Lukács, *The Theory of the Novel*, tr. A. Bostock (Merlin Press, 1971).
29. G. Lukács, *The Historical Novel*, tr. H. and S. Mitchell (Merlin Press, 1962).
30. Lukács, *Studies in European Realism*, p. 147.
31. Ibid., p. 139.
32. Ibid., pp. 147–8.
33. Ibid., p. 148.
34. Lukács discusses this process most extensively in *The Meaning of Contemporary Realism*, tr. J. and N. Mander (Merlin Press, 1962).
35. Lukács, *Studies in European Realism*, pp. 141–2.
36. Lukács, *The Historical Novel*, p. 142.
37. Lukács, *Studies in European Realism*, p. 150.
38. Tolstoy, *Anna Karenin*, VII, 15, p. 748.
39. Lukács, *The Historical Novel*, p. 87.
40. Tolstoy, *War and Peace*, Book 1, Part 3, 19; tr. R. Edmonds (Penguin, 1957) pp. 338–40.
41. Ibid., 1, 3, 12; p. 306.
42. Lukács, *The Theory of the Novel*, pp. 145–6.
43. We know from E. J. Simmons (*Tolstoy*, Routledge & Kegan Paul, 1973, p. 93) that Tolstoy, not long after the completion of *War and Peace*, spoke of Schopenhauer as 'the greatest genius among men'. John Bayley (*Tolstoy and the Novel*, Chatto & Windus, 1966, pp. 82–132) points out that the captive Pierre's exclamation as he gazes at the night sky during the bivouac on the retreat from Moscow – 'And all that is me, all that is within me, and it is all I' – is borrowed from Schopenhauer, as is an important image in the passage describing the death of Prince Andrei.
44. Tolstoy, *Anna Karenin*, IV, 17; p. 438.
45. Tolstoy, *War and Peace*, 3, 3, 12; p. 1010.

46. Tolstoy, *Resurrection*, tr. R. Edmonds (Penguin, 1966) p. 335.
47. Tolstoy, 'The Death of Ivan Ilyich', *'The Cossacks' and other stories*, tr. R. Edmonds (Penguin, 1960) pp. 160–1.

3 OBJECTIONS FROM MORAL REALISM

1. See p. 10.
2. This ethical point is of some legal and political interest. If a public speaker by eloquent rhetoric (but without himself conspiring to perform any action) 'incites' a crowd to an act of violence, many will say that his responsibility for the act is equal to or even greater than that of those who actually commit it. At any rate, disapproval on these occasions often falls more heavily on the inciter than on the incited – understandably when, as is usually the case, the former is at a higher social and educational level than the latter; and it is not uncommon for the inciter to be prosecuted (e.g. the impeachment of Dr Sacheverell in 1710; the present legislation on incitement to racial hatred). This is certainly more practicable and cheaper than prosecuting a rioting crowd, but the underlying ethical principle is a rather questionable one. It implies that human beings are not to be considered fully responsible moral agents when they decide whether or not to submit to the will of a demagogue – indeed that in some sense they cannot be said to 'decide' at all, but are simply instruments manipulated by one who is a moral agent. (If this is true, the case for democracy is notably weakened, as there seems little to be hoped from a political system which invests notional ultimate sovereignty in the helpless puppets of demagogues.) But the moral obligation to act rightly might reasonably be thought to entail an obligation to disregard those who counsel us to act wrongly. If we abandon this view, in fact, we cannot logically expect to prosecute anybody, since it is open to the inciter to say that he himself was incited; and so backwards for ever, or until we encounter someone willing to be prosecuted. Moreover, a decision to punish the word as well as, or rather than, the deed (where the word is not itself in essence the deed, i.e. a conspiracy to act) is a repudiation of intellectual liberty, and opens the door to grosser forms of censorship; since in the last resort any utterance or publication implying rejection of the *status quo* may be imagined as influencing someone or other in the direction of anti-social acts, and a society which begins by prosecuting demagogues is in danger of arriving at this conclusion by slow degrees.
3. The truly decisive argument against censorship, however, seems to me to be a strictly political one: that it confers on the censor a power over the discourse of his fellow-citizens for which no kind of qualification can readily be imagined and which is almost certain ultimately to be abused.
4. F. R. Leavis, *The Great Tradition* (Penguin, 1972) p. 15.
5. Ibid., p. 12.

6. Ibid., p. 184.
7. This does not mean, of course, that all works of episodic design concerned with sex are pornographic, or compositionally facile – the *Canterbury Tales* of Chaucer, for example, are not. It is perhaps significant, though, that even the *Canterbury Tales* can easily (like the *Decameron* or the *Tales of the Arabian Nights*) be adapted into something very like pornography – Pasolini's film, perhaps unintentionally, conveyed something of this impression; and that Sade used the same facilitating device, the group of *raconteurs*, in his *Les 120 Journées de Sodome*.
8. F. R. and Q. D. Leavis, *Dickens the Novelist* (Chatto & Windus, 1970) p. 280.
9. Cf. F. R. Leavis in the space of four pages in *The Great Tradition* (pp. 35–8): 'Lawrence, in the English language, was the great genius of our time . . . as a novelist, the representative of vital and significant development . . . his genius . . . the genius . . . the significance of works of genius . . . astonishing works of genius . . . as indubitably successful works of genius as any the world has to show.'
10. Leavis, *The Great Tradition*, p. 41.
11. Ibid., pp. 42–3.
12. Leavis, *Dickens the Novelist*, p. 315.
13. Chapter VI of *Dickens the Novelist*; pp. 277–331.
14. See pp. 27–8.
15. Leavis, *Dickens the Novelist*, pp. 280–1.
16. Leavis, *The Great Tradition*, p. 10.
17. Leavis, *Dickens the Novelist*, p. 326.
18. Dickens, *Great Expectations*, ch. 57; ed. Angus Calder (Penguin, 1965) p. 478.
19. Leavis, *Dickens the Novelist*, p. 327.
20. Dickens, *Great Expectations*, ch. 5; p. 71.
21. Dickens, *Great Expectations*, ch. 2; p. 40.
22. Leavis, *Dickens the Novelist*, pp. 328–9.
23. Dickens, *Great Expectations*, ch. 58; p. 488.
24. Ibid., ch. 57; p. 481.
25. Leavis, *Dickens the Novelist*, p. 300.
26. Ibid., pp. 329–30.
27. Dickens, *Great Expectations*, ch. 59; p. 491.
28. Ibid., ch. 38; p. 319.
29. Ibid., ch. 59; pp. 492–3.
30. Leavis, *Dickens the Novelist*, p. 301.
31. Cf. Proust's narrator after first seeing Gilberte: 'I walked away, carrying with me, then and for ever afterwards, as the first illustration of a type of happiness rendered inaccessible to a little boy of my kind by certain laws of nature which it was impossible to transgress, the picture of a little girl with reddish hair, and a skin freckled with tiny pink marks, who held a trowel in her hand, and smiled as she directed towards me a long and subtle and inexpressive stare. And already the charm with which her name, like a cloud of incense, had filled that archway in the pink

hawthorn through which she and I had, together, heard its sound, was beginning to conquer, to cover, to embalm, to beautify everything with which it had any association.' (*Swann's Way*, tr. C. K. Scott Moncrieff, *Remembrance of Things Past* (Chatto & Windus, 1966) p. 195).

32. Leavis, *Dickens the Novelist*, p. 302.
33. See note 31.
34. Leavis, *Dickens the Novelist*, p. 302.
35. Dickens, *Great Expectations*, ch. 44; p. 378.
36. Ibid., ch. 44; p. 377.
37. Ibid., ch. 44; p. 375.
38. e. g. ' "And Joe and Biddy both, as you have been to church to-day, and are in charity and love with all mankind, receive my humble thanks for all you have done for me and all I have so ill repaid!" ' et seq. (Ibid., ch. 58; p. 488).

4 OBJECTIONS CONCERNING LANGUAGE

1. R. Fowler, *Linguistics and the Novel* (Methuen, 1977).
2. See pp. 13–15.
3. D. Lodge, *Language of Fiction* (Routledge & Kegan Paul, 1966).
4. Fowler, *Linguistics and the Novel*, p. 10.
5. Ibid., p. 11.
6. Ibid., p. 76.
7. My argument here runs parallel to that used by W. K. Wimsatt and M. C. Beardsley against a distinction between 'cognitive' and 'emotive' meaning in literary works: that the 'emotive' quality of a work is largely the product of its cognitive meanings. See p. 136.
8. George Eliot, *The Mill on the Floss*, chapter 4, first paragraph: ed. A. S. Byatt (Penguin, 1979) p. 78.
9. Fowler, *Linguistics and the Novel*, pp. 7–9.
10. This point has been well made by Peter Barry, in 'Linguistics and Literary Criticism: a Polytheism Without Gods', *English*, 29 (Summer 1980).
11. Lodge, *Language of Fiction*, p. 74.
12. Ibid., p. 80.
13. Ibid., pp. 80–1.
14. Ibid., p. 82.
15. V. Nabokov, *Invitation to a Beheading* (Weidenfield & Nicolson, 1960).
16. Samuel Beckett, *Murphy* (Routledge & Kegan Paul, 1938).
17. Kingsley Amis, *Lucky Jim* (Penguin, 1964) p. 61.
18. William Faulkner, *The Sound and the Fury* (Penguin, 1964) p. 11.
19. Lodge, *Language of Fiction*, pp. 147, 163.
20. Dickens, *Hard Times*, II, 6 (Penguin, 1969) p. 189.
21. Lodge, *Language of Fiction*, p. 75.
22. Lodge, *Language of Fiction*, pp. 154–5, 163.

23. Henry James, *The Turn of the Screw* (Penguin, 1969) pp. 26–8.
24. Proust, *Swann's Way*, tr. C. K. Scott Moncrieff, *Remembrance of Things Past* (Chatto & Windus, 1966) Part One, p. 62.
25. One can imagine a third-person narrative which questioned its *own* authority – indeed John Fowles's *The French Lieutenant's Woman* (Cape, 1969), with its ostentatious alternative ending, does so. But this makes no difference to the reader, who is now simply expected to have confidence in the narrative's non-confidence. The narrative in such a case remains authoritative in my sense: its alternativeness is 'inextricably associated with the novel's conceptional totality' and cannot be subverted by other conceptions – though a reader can, of course, take an aversion to the narrative *persona* (a quite different matter).

5 OBJECTIONS CONCERNING AFFECT

1. As proposed by Robert Crosman, 'Do Readers Make Meaning?', *The Reader in the Text*, ed. S. R. Sulieman & I. Crosman (Princeton, 1980) p. 160. Crosman repudiates even the notion of *probable* validity or invalidity in interpretation as 'unsuited to a modern democracy' (p. 160). But in envisaging a collaborative discussion in which 'minds are changed on a point here or there' (p. 159) even he commonsensically backslides towards an implicit acceptance of the possible persuasiveness of objective (i.e. collectively available) criteria.
2. W. K. Wimsatt & M. C. Beardsley, *The Verbal Icon* (University of Kentucky Press, 1954) p. 21.
3. Ibid., p. 34.
4. I. A. Richards, *Principles of Literary Criticism* (Routledge & Kegan Paul, second edn, 1926) pp. 267–8.
5. Ibid., chapter XXXII; pp. 239–53. Richards describes the aesthetic experience in many different ways without ever quite making it clear whether the equilibrium to which impulses are brought by art is an equilibrium which satisfies them, or brings them to some kind of quietus, or an equilibrium which *if it were possible to maintain it in ordinary living* would procure a high return in satisfaction or rewarding activity. Some passages suggest the former. 'Pity, the impulse to approach, and Terror, the impulse to retreat, are brought in Tragedy to a reconciliation which they find nowhere else .... This is the explanation of that sense of release, or repose in the midst of stress, of balance and composure, given by Tragedy, for there is no other way in which such impulses, once awakened, can be set at rest without suppression .... This balanced poise ... is a general characteristic of all the most valuable experiences of the arts' (pp. 245–6, 248). Note 'set at rest'. Other passages seem to represent the value of art as finally exhibited only in consequent transformations of life and personality. 'It is not the intensity of the conscious

experience, its thrill, its pleasure or its poignancy which gives it value, but the organisation of its impulses for freedom and fullness of life .... The after-effects, the permanent modifications in the structure of the mind, which works of art can produce, have been overlooked' (p. 132). On the whole, the balance seems to be with the view that the experiences offered by the arts are satisfying and self-sufficient; Richards insists that they are 'not incomplete' (p. 233).

6. Richards, *Principles of Literary Criticism*, pp. 279–80, 283.
7. See p. 136. The confusion is also parallel to that noted in an argument of Roger Fowler's on p. 100.
8. Richards's formulations vary from work to work: in *Poetries and Sciences* (Routledge & Kegan Paul, 1935, 1970), for example, he avoids the notion of emotive 'belief'. But the tenor of his argument is essentially the same.
9. See p. 33.
10. Shakespeare, *King Lear*, V, iii, 140.
11. E. V. Rieu, preface to his translation of the *Odyssey* (Penguin, 1946) p. 14.
12. Shakespeare, *Macbeth*, V, v, 19–28. Arden edn, ed. K. Muir (Methuen, 1961).
13. T. S. Eliot, *The Waste Land*, I, 1–7: *Complete Poems and Plays* (Faber, 1969) p. 61.

6 RECAPITULATION AND ANALYSIS

1. Unsigned review in *Britannia*, 15 January 1848.
2. Quotations from *Wuthering Heights* are identified in the text by chapter number; where necessary, brief quotations and highly specific allusions will be further identified by page references to the Penguin edition, ed. D. Daiches, 1965.
3. This distinction of 'types' is grossly simplified, of course, since novelists typically use a variety of structural methods to arrest and maintain the reader's attention and interest: in *Great Expectations*, for instance, detective-story mystification, the continuity of a single character's perspective, and the progressive interlocking of plot-components are all at work.
4. This has to be inferred from a series of scattered indications. See note 8 below.
5. Cf. Mary Shelley, *Frankenstein*, chapter 24. 'He paused, looking on me with wonder, and again turning towards the lifeless form of his creator, seemed to forget my presence, and every feature and gesture seemed instigated by the wildest rage of some uncontrollable passion.

"That is also my victim!" he exclaimed. "In his murder my crimes are consummated: the miserable series of my being is wound to its close! Oh, Frankenstein! Generous and self-devoted being! What

does it avail that I now ask thee to pardon me? I, who irretrievably destroyed thee by destroying all thou lovedst ... (etc)." '
(Everyman Library, Dent, 1963, pp. 237–8.)

6. It would be interesting to know whether this anti-honorific use of both Christian name and surname is, as I suspect, particularly characteristic (a) of Northern England and (b) of the speech of children. I have traced no research on the question. The formula may be borrowed from pedagogical address ('You – Sissy Jupe!' etc.) in which case my comment in the text is probably anachronistic.

7. On chronological, legal and sociological accuracy, see e.g. C. P. Sanger, *The Structure of 'Wuthering Heights'* (Hogarth Press, 1926); T. Winnifrith, *The Brontës and their Background* (Macmillan, 1973); and the appendices to the Clarendon edition of *Wuthering Heights*, ed. H. Marsden and I. Jack (Oxford, 1976). On psychological insight, see especially J. H. Hagan, 'The Control of Sympathy in *Wuthering Heights*', *Nineteenth Century Fiction*, 21, 4 (March 1967).

8. See *13*, 181, (' "the adjective *our* gave mortal offence" '), *14*, 187 (' "You'd hardly credit it, but the very morrow of the wedding, she was weeping to go home" '), 188, (' "I have avoided ... giving her the slightest right to claim a separation" '), *17*, 207 (' "put poor Catherine's baby away – I don't like to see it" '), 208 (' "he detests me to the point of its annoying him seriously to have me within earshot, or eye-sight" '), and 218 ('there she had a son born, a few months subsequent to her escape').

9. To the second edition, 1850; reprinted in the Penguin edition pp. 37–41, and the Clarendon edition (Oxford), pp. 441–5.

10. Outstanding examples are: A. Kettle, *An Introduction to the English Novel* (Hutchinson, 1951) pp. 139–155; Q. D. Leavis, 'A Fresh Approach to *Wuthering Heights*', *Lectures in America* (with F. R. Leavis) (Chatto & Windus, 1969); T. Winnifrith, *The Brontës and their Background* (Macmillan, 1973); and T. Eagleton, *Myths of Power* (Macmillan, 1976), chapter 6.

11. It would be fair to add that, though Dr Eagleton sees the young Heathcliff as 'in general an admirable character', and the novel's sympathies as lying 'on balance with the Heights rather than the Grange' (*Myths of Power*, pp. 111, 117), his chapter on the novel is not primarily devoted to exculpating Heathcliff, but to demonstrating in the work the refraction of sociological and ideological issues.

12. Winnifrith, *The Brontës and their Background*, pp. 190–1.

13. Eagleton, *Myths of Power*, p. 106.

14. Ibid.

15. Ibid., p. 107.

16. e.g. *Wuthering Heights, 17*, 223; *33*, 349–50.

17. Sanger, *The Structure of 'Wuthering Heights'*, p. 17.

18. Eagleton, *Myths of Power*, p. 112.

19. I do not, of course, suggest that Emily Brontë consciously constructed Heathcliff's character around a *concept* of 'wilfulness'; one guesses that an author's conception of a character, and

perception of the compositional disciplines necessary for its realisation, are at least in the first instance largely intuitive.

20. It *is* an inability, not a refusal; an expiration of will, not a negative decision. The text is very persistent in making this clear – e.g. 34, 357: 'He took his knife and fork, and was going to commence eating, when the inclination appeared to become suddenly extinct.'

21. We might, of course, equally say that a context is appropriate to its detail, i.e. that an individual character or situation falls within the expressive scope of an image or concept: 'Hindley Earnshaw' (particular) is a 'wild beast' (universal).

APPENDIX; THE JUSTIFICATION OF CRITICISM

1. See p. 38.
2. See p. 12.
3. This remark would no doubt strike a political theorist as question-begging. I am, in fact, intentionally sweeping aside theories which see the purpose of organised society in non-humanistic terms (as obedience to the will of God, for example), and theories which attribute to it no purpose at all. But I do not mean particularly to indicate agreement with utilitarian theories at the expense of others (such as the view that justice takes priority over utility) which nevertheless seem to me to ground their primary values upon human prospects of happiness, or to be trivialised if they do not.
4. R. Dworkin and B. Magee, 'Philosophy and Politics', in B. Magee (ed.), *Men of Ideas* (BBC Publications, 1978) p. 259.
5. Ibid., pp. 259–60.
6. See e.g. P. Widdowson (ed.), *Re-reading English* (Methuen, 1982); 'Professing Literature' (symposium), *Times Literary Supplement*, 10 December 1982, pp. 1355–63; 'Complete diversity – or disarray?' (symposium), *Times Higher Education Supplement*, 11 February 1983, pp. 12–13; L. Lerner (ed.), *Reconstructing Literature* (Oxford: Blackwell, 1983).
7. See e.g. 'Literary criticism and philosophy', Scrutiny, VI, 1 (June 1937), pp. 59–70; *New Bearings in English Poetry* (Penguin, 1972) p. 17.
8. C. Snee, 'Period Studies and the place of criticism', in P. Widdowson (ed.), *Re-reading English*, pp. 166–7.
9. See pp. 27–8, 77.
10. T. Eagleton, *Literary Theory* (Oxford: Blackwell, 1983), p. 60.
11. F. de Saussure, *Course in General Linguistics*, tr. C. Bally and A. Sechehaye (New York: McGraw Hill, 1966) pp. 111–13.
12. Wittgenstein, *Philosophical Investigations*, tr. G. E. M. Anscombe (Oxford: Blackwell, 1972) § 78.
13. Ibid., § 268.
14. Ibid., § 569.
15. Ibid., § 304.

16. Wittgenstein, *Tractatus Logico-philosophicus*, tr. D. F. Pears and B. F. McGuinness, second edn (Routledge & Kegan Paul, 1971) §5, 6.
17. See Chapter 2, I, especially pp. 32–3, for a more extended argument on this point.
18. See Chapter 4, II, pp. 95–105.
19. See pp. 147–8, 153–6.
20. See p. 152.
21. C. Hill, *Milton and the English Revolution* (Faber, 1977) pp. 49–52.
22. See p. 238.
23. J. Rawls, *A Theory of Justice*, (Oxford, 1972) p. 523.
24. See pp. 152–3.
25. The most plausible argument I know for asserting the pre-eminence of a literary culture (defined in broader terms, however, than the 'imaginative literature' with which this book has concerned itself) is that implicit in Thomas Mann's *Doctor Faustus*, but I do not wish to pursue it here.
26. See p. 228.
27. Rawls, *A Theory of Justice*, pp. 523–4.

Index

261